SCHOOL DEVELOPMENT SERIES

General Editors: David Hopkins and David Reynolds

IMPROVING EDUCATION

IMPROVING EDUCATION
Promoting quality in schools

Edited by
Peter Ribbins and Elizabeth Burridge

CASSELL

Cassell

Villiers House   387 Park Avenue South
41/47 Strand   New York
London WC2N 5JE   NY 10016-8810

First published 1994

British Library Cataloguing-in-Publication Data
A catalogue record for this book is available from the British Library.

ISBN 0-304-32743-3 (hardback)
       0-304-32735-2 (paperback)

Typeset by Colset Pte. Ltd., Singapore

Printed and bound in Great Britain by
Redwood Books, Trowbridge, Wiltshire

Contents

Contents

Series Editors' Foreword

Concern for the promotion of quality is not new in British schools but the way in which this highly topical book approaches the issue *is* new. It is based upon a series of seminars that took place in Birmingham towards the end of 1991 and represents a compendious, creative and purposive addition to the literature on the search for enhanced school quality.

Chapters and themes in the book cover the history of concern with quality in education, the 'market-oriented' mechanisms of quality assurance in recent legislation, the contribution of school effectiveness knowledge to quality enhancement, the contribution of school improvement knowledge to quality development and the precise mechanics of the quality monitoring systems that are on offer to measure the 'value added' and the 'system performance' of individual schools and educational systems. The book's final chapters report very usefully on the practice-related projects that are going on in various schools and local education authorities.

It is of course clear from the very range of contributors to the book that there is no 'recipe' that will generate enhanced educational quality in all settings in all contexts and in all times: the educational world is too complex for that. It is also clear that the knowledge base concerning the generation of quality is in its early stages of development; this is inevitable.

However, it is also clear from the contributions which Peter Ribbins and Elizabeth Burridge have assembled that we now know enough to intervene in the lives of schools and children with a very good chance of enhancing their academic and social progress and their later life chances. For the assembly of the knowledge base represented in this book, we should all be very grateful, whether we be practitioners, policy-makers or educational academics.

David Hopkins
David Reynolds

Series Editors

About the Contributors

Alison Bullock undertook her doctoral studies at the University of Aberystwyth and was then appointed as a Research Fellow at the School of Education, University of Birmingham. Since her appointment to the university, she has been working with Hywel Thomas on projects funded by Leverhulme and the NAHT, researching into aspects of the local management of schools in general and of formula funding in particular.

Elizabeth Burridge (formerly **Whale**) is Policy Adviser for Monitoring and Evaluation for the LEA in Birmingham. She has carried much of the day-to-day responsibility for the city's initiative in quality development in colleges and schools and has made a major contribution to the evolution of the ideas that underpin it. Before that she was Co-ordinator of Quality Development in the Continuing Education Division. She has taught in further education and in primary schools. She is an Honorary Lecturer at the University of Birmingham and has written and lectured extensively on a wide range of aspects of monitoring and evaluation in education.

Ian Cleland has had over twenty years' experience in schools, over eight of which were as a member of a senior management team, either as deputy headteacher or as headteacher. He moved to Dudley as Humanities Adviser in 1982 and following a period as Senior Secondary Adviser was appointed Chief Adviser in 1985. Currently, his main interests are in the application of BS 5750 in schools, total quality management strategies in education, the development of strategies to enhance pupil achievement through cross-curricular issues and the concept of management applied to the core processes of school effectiveness.

Carlton Duncan is headteacher of George Dixon Comprehensive (one of the largest schools in Birmingham). Before that he taught in the ILEA, Brent and Coventry and was for four years headteacher of Wyke Manor Upper School in Bradford. He was born in Kingston in Jamaica and moved to the United Kingdom in 1961. He was a member of the Rampton and Swann Inquiries and is a County Court Assessor under the Race Relations Act of 1976 and a former member of the NUT's Antiracist Education Sub-committee. He is the author of numerous articles, chapters and books, including *Pastoral Care — an Antiracist/Multicultural Perspective*.

Trevor Edinborough is headteacher of a secondary school within Birmingham, and has previously worked in a variety of schools and in a number of local education authorities. He has been closely associated with the management of Birmingham's quality development strategy. During 1991-92 he also worked at the School of Education of the University of Birmingham as an Honorary Fellow in Monitoring and Evaluation in Schools. Over the past few years he has contributed to a range of training and development programmes within and beyond the city.

Bob Findlay is a disability equality trainer/consultant who is presently employed as Director of the Birmingham Information Federation. He is the Birmingham Disability Rights Group's representative to the British Council of Organizations of Disabled People and sits on West Midlands and National Councils.

Carol Fitz-Gibbon is Professor of Education at the School of Education at the University of Newcastle upon Tyne. Before that she was Senior Lecturer in Research Methods at the same university. She has for several years directed the team working on the A Level Information System (ALIS) project and more recently has sought to apply the ideas developed within it to aspects of the measurement of performance in a wide range of educational contexts. In doing so she has contributed significantly to the literature on this and a variety of associated themes.

Harvey Goldstein is currently Professor of Statistical Methods at the Department of Mathematics, Statistics and Computing of the Institute of Education, University of London. He has for many years been interested in aspects of the measurement of school and pupil performance and is one of the most influential writers in this field, both within the United Kingdom and in many other countries.

David Hopkins is a Tutor at the University of Cambridge Institute of Education. He was Co-director of the School Development Plan project funded by the DES in 1989/90. The findings of the project are summarized in *The Empowered School: The Management and Practice of Development Planning*. His other recent books include *Evaluation for School Development, An Introduction to Teacher Appraisal* and *School Improvement in an ERA of Change*. He is co-editor of the series *School Development*.

Denis Lawton is Professor of Curriculum Studies at the Institute of Education of the University of London. Previously he was the Director of the Institute. He has long been particularly interested in aspects of the school curriculum and its control. He has lectured and written widely on these and associated themes and his publications include *The Politics of the School Curriculum* and *Education, Culture and the National Curriculum*.

David Reynolds is Professor of Education at the School of Education, University of Newcastle upon Tyne, and has published extensively within the areas of school effectiveness, school improvement and the sociology of the school. In this context, his most recent book is *School Effectiveness* (1992) and he is currently working in the International School Effectiveness Research Programme (ISERP) on the identification of factors that aid student learning in different cultures. He co-edits the series *School Development*.

Peter Ribbins is Professor of Educational Management and Deputy Dean at the Faculty of Education, University of Birmingham. He has worked in public sector higher education, as an LEA officer and as a secondary school teacher. For many years he has been Consultant to the Quality Development Initiative in Birmingham and led the team that evaluated its piloting. He was the main author of the report *Proving, Improving and Learning in Schools*. He has written over seventy books and articles on a wide variety of themes to do with education and its management and is currently editor for BEMAS of the journal *Educational Management and Administration*.

Pamela Sammons is a Research Fellow at the Institute of Education, University of London. She has been involved in educational research for over fifteen years and has worked in both the university sector and the ILEA. Her research interests include school effectiveness and improvement. She has had considerable experience of in-service work for headteachers and teachers in the UK and abroad. She has contributed to a variety of influential texts on school effectiveness, including, in particular, *School Matters: The Junior Years*.

Geoff Southworth is presently Tutor in Primary Education and Management at the University of Cambridge Institute of Education. Before joining the Institute staff he was headteacher of a junior school in Lancashire. He has been involved in two school-based research projects, evaluated pilot work in teacher appraisal and run numerous course and workshops on school leadership, school development, the management of change, and mentoring and curriculum development. He is particularly interested in the role of heads and deputies, as well as the weekly results of Cambridge United.

Jo Stephens is currently Chief Education Officer of Oxfordshire County Council. Her professional work began as a social worker for special school pupils and their families before she switched to teaching in primary and secondary schools. Later she spent ten years as an Inspector working in Surrey and for the Inner London Education Authority. All these experiences have contributed to her beliefs about the processes which improve the quality of education.

Nick Stuart was, in 1991 when his chapter was written, Deputy Secretary at the Department of Education and Science in charge of schools policy, a post he had held since 1987. Over that period he was responsible for overseeing the development and subsequent implementation of the Education Reform Act. He moved in August 1992 to become Director of Resources and Strategy at the Department of Employment.

Hywel Thomas is Professor of Economics of Education and Head of Research at the School of Education, University of Birmingham. He has been a teacher in comprehensive schools. In addition to applying economics in teaching educational management, he has been researching into economic aspects of upper secondary schools. In 1982 he began to act as consultant to the local management of schools initiative in Solihull and since then has been researching this theme in projects funded by Leverhulme and the NAHT. He has written extensively on this and related themes and is currently working on the concept of the market as applied to educational contexts.

Gaby Weiner is Professor of Educational Research in the School of Education and Health Studies at South Bank University. She has edited a number of collections, including *Just a Bunch of Girls*, *The Primary School and Equal Opportunities*, *Gender and the Politics of Schooling*, *Gender under Scrutiny* and *Women's Education in Europe*. She has written widely on equal opportunities in education, women's history and feminist theory and politics, and is currently director of a research project on equity and staffing in higher education funded by the ESRC. She is editor of the *British Educational Research Journal*.

Introduction

Elizabeth Burridge and Peter Ribbins

CONTEXT AND PURPOSE

Between June and December 1991, a series of seven seminars that focused on different aspects of quality in education in general and schooling in particular took place in Birmingham. The series was organized as a joint venture between the Education Department of the City Council in Birmingham and the School of Education of the University of Birmingham. It had seven main objectives:

1 To explore the issue of quality in education with some of those who have made a significant contribution to thinking and practice in this and associated fields.

2 To examine innovative quality initiatives with a selection of the many LEAs and schools known to be evolving interesting approaches.

3 To test, refine and develop the ideas that underpin Birmingham's quality initiative in the light of these theories and practices.

4 To establish the reputation of the city in partnership with the university as a leading national centre in the study and practice of all aspects of quality in educational contexts.

5 To generate a network of authorities interested in sharing ideas and experiences of planning for quality in education.

6 To enable and encourage staff in Birmingham engaged or about to be engaged in the city's quality development initiative to take part in the seminar series and to contribute to the achievement of its purposes.

7 To plan the series in such a way as to enable the production of a book derived from the seminar proceedings which will represent an authoritative and stimulating statement of contemporary thinking on quality development, quality assurance and quality control in schools and school systems.

To achieve the last purpose, contributors were informed that their papers might be included in a book derived from the seminar series, as well as being made available to seminar participants. It was hoped that this would enrich the discussions which took place and thus identify such revisions as might be required prior to publication. Most contributors subsequently made some revisions to their original texts but in only a minority of cases had these been designed to take substantial note of such more recent developments as the Schools Act of 1992, the White Paper on *Choice and Diversity* and the Education Act 1993. In this introduction to the text we shall discuss the main themes of the seminar programme and say something about each of the sixteen papers included in *Improving Education*.

THEMES AND TEXT

Each of the individual seminars that made up the series programme was of one day's duration. Each day focused on a particular theme, which took place in the following order: 'The meaning and context of quality', 'Schools and quality', 'Equality and quality', 'Planning for quality', 'Reporting on quality', 'Working for quality' and 'Cases of quality'. The papers as presented in the text roughly reflect this order but we found in practice that some rationalization was necessary. Thus, for example, the papers given under the headings of 'Schools and quality' and 'Planning for quality' were conflated into a single section, as were those dealing with 'Working for quality' and 'Cases of quality'.

The first two chapters deal respectively with aspects of the meaning and recent history of quality in schools. As Denis Lawton comments in the introduction to his chapter, mapping out the meaning that might be given to 'quality' is 'not an easy task'. In seeking to do so he draws upon the findings of an OECD project on quality with which he was involved in the 1980s. This eventually came up with a multi-dimensional account of quality structured around five key areas, which focused on: the curriculum; the role of teachers; school organization; assessment, appraisal and monitoring; and resources. His own account is based on views of quality in education as this might be seen from the perspectives of each of four ideological perspectives that have dominated thinking in recent times: the privatizers, the minimalists or segregators, the pluralists and the comprehensive planners. This model offers a useful preface to the account of the recent history of quality in education from the perspective of a senior civil servant most closely associated with the 1988 Education Reform Act. In his chapter, Nick Stuart, reflecting on his many years in educational administration, stresses how relatively recent has been the rise in concern for quality. He identifies three things that have brought this interest to the forefront: a set of economic arguments, a set of political arguments and a set of educational arguments. From the perspective of 1991 he stresses the extent to which the Education Reform Bill has 'created the framework and the context within which our pursuit of quality in education has begun to flourish'. In this context an interesting issue would be to examine how far the educational developments initiated in 1992 are, in quality terms, best seen as an evolution of the reforms set in train by the 1988 Act or as a major new direction. This is an issue discussed briefly in our own chapter.

The next five papers all consider aspects of school effectiveness, school improvement and planning in schools and beyond. In the first and second of these chapters, David Reynolds and Pamela Sammons consider various aspects of our contemporary understanding of the findings of research and practice in school effectiveness. In her chapter, Sammons, from the perspective of her involvement in one of the most influential contemporary studies of school effectiveness, the Inner London Education Authority's Junior School Project, comments upon both this and the literature in general. In the latter part of her discussion, Sammons considers aspects of the link between the literatures of school effectiveness and school improvement and also discusses the extent to which school effectiveness research methods offer a basis for judging the quality of schools. In this context, Reynolds identifies an important paradox. Just as the new 'paradigm' of school effectiveness as a means of explaining variations in the educational growth of children is gaining greater attention within the theory and practice of education, many of its established findings are being challenged by more recent research. At the same time the articulation between what we know about school effectiveness on the one hand and our understanding of the theory and practice of school improvement and development planning as its delivery mechanisms on the other, has become increasingly problematic.

The next couple of chapters suggest ways in which this paradox might be resolved. Geoff Southworth discusses an approach that has become increasingly fashionable in recent times. He stresses that while the idea of the learning school is no panacea it seems, nevertheless, to be an effective method of stimulating high levels of pupil learning. It does so by stressing the need for stimulating five levels of learning: children's learning, teacher learning, staff learning, organizational learning and leadership learning. Each of these levels of learning is discussed in some detail within the chapter. Following this, David Hopkins considers how the pressure for change can result in school improvement. In doing so he discusses the nature of knowledge on school improvement and reviews the various approaches canvassed in the literature. He draws upon the research he has been involved in, which has sought to examine how development planning, as a school improvement strategy, can assist schools to achieve their development priorities and, where necessary, to change aspects of their culture. In the final chapter in this section, Hywel Thomas and Alison Bullock consider money, monitoring and management and their implications for the curriculum experiences of children in the context of a study of resource planning at institutional, local and national levels. How these different facets of the processes of educational planning affect levels of efficiency and equity is a component of the discussion of each of these themes and of planning for quality as a whole.

The third section of the book examines aspects of quality and equality in education. In the first of three chapters, Carlton Duncan revisits some of the evidence that identifies the plight of black children in terms of underachievement in schools. He argues that a crucial factor contributing to such underachievement is the curricula of schools that are mainly white. In an important part of his argument, Duncan considers the extent to which the 1988 Education Reform Act, and other legislation, enables a purposeful antiracist and multicultural approach to the curriculum. Gaby Weiner, in the next chapter, considers the development of educational policy on gender in recent years. In doing so she considers the contribution of teachers in the gender policy-making processes and discusses the options for change currently available. The author's intention is to seek to put on record some of the important work that has been undertaken within this area and to explore some of the theoretical frameworks that have informed it. The aim of the final paper is to suggest that the education system will not offer people who experience disability equality of opportunities or an improved quality of educational standards until it breaks with the dominant ideologies and practices associated with disability. In this regard, Bob Findlay criticizes 'individual tragedy' or 'special needs' approaches on the grounds that they focus too much attention on the individual instead of addressing the disabling barriers encountered.

The fourth section includes two chapters that consider various aspects of the collection, analysis and interpretation of evidence that might be used to report on performance in schools. Carol Fitz-Gibbon asks why we should spend time and money doing this using performance indicators. Ostensibly to enable the system's performance to improve. But do performance indicators improve systems? Much of the chapter focuses upon the ways in which educational managers can and should approach the design of performance indicator systems and how they might do so in ways that represent relative effectiveness in terms of value-added measures. In the second of these chapters, Harvey Goldstein also explores ways in which student achievement could be used to say something about school quality. He argues that comparisons of schools should be done in a way that avoids the kinds of simple-minded judgements all too often canvassed in recent times. This is not to argue that schools should not be held accountable for the ways in which they educate their pupils. The real issue is how is this to be done and by whom.

The fifth and final section contains four chapters. The first, by Trevor Edinborough, the headteacher of Queensbridge School in Birmingham, seeks to chart the stages of development undertaken by his school in its pursuit of higher quality through supported self-evaluation strategies. It places development planning at the heart of its work and draws upon the experience gained through the Birmingham LEA's Quality Development Strategy. The chapter provides insights into the specific strategies being pursued by the school and concludes with a reassertion of the importance of supported self-evaluation for the 'learning community', while acknowledging that other forms have a significant role to play in promoting quality.

The final three chapters all report on LEA-led quality initiatives. We are aware of many such initiatives in other parts of the country. These include comprehensive approaches to quality in authorities as different as Bradford and Strathclyde and Bexley and Warwickshire. The purpose of Ian Cleland's chapter is to argue that the concept of quality is not static — not only does agreement about what is 'quality' change over time, it also often depends on the individual values of those who undertake the role of quality assessors. Quality in product derives more from the way in which people work than from static product definition. Quality comes from shared values, which are in turn the product of a climate that has grown from the interaction of people who are committed to improvement. During the 1980s Dudley LEA has created a structural framework based on networking, which has enabled the development of a culture of improvement that operates at every level from the individual to the institution and the whole authority.

In a similar vein, in the introduction to her chapter, Jo Stephens suggests that what we know about children's learning and teacher development have all too often not been properly taken into account in contemporary debates on quality. In her chapter she spells out the collaborative assumptions that underpin the Oxfordshire approach and describes its central assessment contexts (evaluation of school performance, assessment of student performance and appraisal of staff performance) and key processes (self-review of progress against stated criteria, external consultancy in that review and clear target setting in the next phase).

Similar ideas inform the holistic approach to the promotion of quality within its schools and colleges which the LEA in Birmingham has sought to develop since the early 1980s. This approach and the way in which it has evolved and been implemented is the subject of the final chapter by Elizabeth Burridge and Peter Ribbins. In this, they describe the key purposes, principles and working practices of an approach that is based on the notion of supported self-evaluation. To date some 170 schools are at various stages of the process of introducing and embedding the ideas of supported self-evaluation. In this context, much of the chapter takes the form of a detailed account of the way in which the LEA and its schools intend to collaborate together to implement the approach across the authority as a whole.

A NOTE ON THE CONTRIBUTORS

The eighteen contributors to this book are drawn from across the educational spectrum. The great majority have been school teachers (with both primary and secondary represented) at some stage in their careers and at least three have been (or are) headteachers. Most are parents. Many have been school governors and some have chaired such bodies. Several have carried major responsibilities for the administration of education at either a national or a local level. A number carry advisory responsibilities, many currently work in higher education and all have contributed significantly to the theory and practice of improving education. At a time when, as Jo Stephens points out, the quality of education is all too often being threatened by actions which are ironically presented as a means to improve it, what they have to say is, we hope, worth attending to.

Chapter 1

Defining Quality

Denis Lawton

INTRODUCTION

I have been asked to 'map out' the question of quality in education. This is not an easy task. And I have a feeling of *déjà vu*. I was involved in the OECD project on quality in the 1980s, which eventually resulted in *Schools and Quality: an International Report* (1989).

In the Introduction to that Report a number of important points were made, for example, that 'Education is not an assembly-line process of mechanically increasing inputs and raising productivity.' (In that sense the Government is right when it says that quality is not just a matter of increasing resources — but it is not right when it says that resources are not an issue.) The OECD Report goes on to say, 'How to improve its quality raises fundamental questions about societal aims, the nature of participation in decision-making at all levels, and the very purposes of the school as an institution' (p.9).

There were other problems in the search for the meaning of quality in education. Nevertheless, the OECD eventually came up with a multi-dimensional view of quality with five key areas:

1 The curriculum.
2 The role of teachers.
3 School organization.
4 Assessment, appraisal and monitoring.
5 Resources.

I do not intend going over that ground again. The book (OECD, 1989) should certainly be read by everyone attending this conference. But it was an international report and I would prefer to look more specifically at quality in the UK context.

THE DEVELOPING IMPORTANCE OF QUALITY

For that I think we must look briefly at the development of the importance of 'quality' as an issue, and perhaps a problem.

In 1944 the question of improving education was seen largely as a question of *quantity* — extending the benefits of education to a larger proportion of the population, and therefore extending the period of compulsory schooling for all. Improving education meant building more schools, training more teachers, providing more books and other resources.

Significantly, the content of education — the curriculum — was not seen as an issue and was not even mentioned in the 1944 Act. Widening access to educational opportunity was the goal, and it was not thought necessary, except by a few cranky educational theorists in documents like *The Content of Education* (Council for Curriculum Reform, 1945) to call into question what should be on offer to the new secondary pupils. This unquestioning attitude began to change in the late 1960s and early 1970s. Critical questions about quality of provision were asked by parents, employers and eventually by politicians.

By the 1970s, consensus was breaking down for a variety of reasons. Schools were not solving the nation's social and economic problems. By now the political right was generally critical of collectivist planning, and equally critical of progressive policies in education. In 1969 Cox and Dyson produced the first *Black Paper*, which was originally intended to attack the state of higher education but was extended at a late stage to cover progressive policies in primary and secondary education.

The oil crisis of 1973-4 precipitated cuts in public spending. Criticisms of the education service intensified. In 1976 Callaghan made a speech that was critical of education, particularly the lack of co-ordination between schools and industry. The Great Debate was launched and this encouraged a trend towards centralization, including greater control of the curriculum. This kind of centralism would probably have continued irrespective of what political party was in government. But a party political influence became significant after the 1979 general election.

The election of Margaret Thatcher as Leader of the Conservative Party in 1975 and as Prime Minister in 1979 marked a clear swing to the right in terms of economic, social and education policies. Andrew Gamble (1988) has summed up her social and economic policies as 'the free economy and the strong state'; in education the influence of the New Right was much more complex.

FOUR IDEOLOGIES

It is useful to think of views on education in terms of four ideologies:

1 The privatizers.
2 The minimalists or segregators.
3 The pluralists.
4 The comprehensive planners.

These positions do not correspond exactly with political parties.

The privatizers would advocate leaving everything to the market. The extreme version of this view would recommend privatizing all education from pre-school provision to university. *Our Schools* (Sexton, 1987) recommended privatizing schools; others have recommended the abolition of state subsidies for higher education. Local education authorities (LEAs) would be disbanded;

all schools would be run by boards of governors or private companies. Parents would have complete freedom to choose — moderated only by their ability to pay. The ideological background for this view is *laissez-faire* capitalism with reliance on market mechanisms to control the relation between supply and demand in education.

Minimalists believe in a mixed economy in education. The state should provide basic schooling (as cheaply as possible) and parents would have the right of buying additional extras or of opting out of the state system altogether. Minimalists believe in the market but the market must be moderated. A minimalist programme leads to what Tawney (1931) criticized as a system run by those who felt that it was not good enough for their own children. The Assisted Places Scheme is characteristic of the thinking behind minimalism (state schools are not really good enough for bright children). City Technology Colleges represent another example of this kind of thinking — as well as hostility towards LEAs. Minimalists also tend to be segregators; they want to separate children according to social class, or supposed intellectual ability, perhaps even sex.

The political background to minimalism lies in the history of Tory paternalism — the idea that those who have the good fortune to be born into a position of wealth or rank have a duty to provide for the less fortunate (the deserving poor). Education must be provided for all, partly to train them for useful work, but also to provide for their social and moral well-being. But the education provided should not be too good — not so good that it will give them ideas above their station — and not too expensive.

The pluralists would want to provide a state system so good that there would be little or no incentive to use independent schools. Their regard for individual freedom of choice would, however, not allow them to legislate private schools out of existence. Freedom to choose is more important than social justice or equality of opportunity. Socialists such as Tony Crosland came somewhat reluctantly to that point of view. The Conservative Minister David Eccles was also in this category, but further to the right along the continuum.

Pluralists have invented such terms as 'parity of esteem'. They tend to think that organizational factors in providing good educational opportunities for all are more important than curriculum. They also tend to meritocratic beliefs in education, favouring the metaphor of 'the ladder of opportunity' rather than 'the broad highway'.

'The comprehensive planners' is a useful generic title for those who recognize the need to change the secondary curriculum (and to a lesser extent the primary curriculum) to adjust to the needs of mass education. Comprehensive planners acknowledge that a watered-down version of pseudo-high culture curricula will not do for a society committed to genuine secondary education for all. They will also tend to criticize the grammar school curriculum for other reasons — epistemological, cultural and social as well as political.

Quality has a slightly different meaning for each of the four ideological groups. For the privatizers quality is something you pay for: individual parents should have the right to pay for whatever level of quality they want or can afford. Minimalists advocate two kinds of quality: one range of quality options

3

for those who pay; a lower level of quality for those who use the state system, where the principle of 'value for money' rather than quality must operate. Pluralists want to raise the quality of state schools to that of the best of private schools, but doubt whether it can be done. Within state schools they would envisage different kinds of quality for different kinds of pupil. Finally, comprehensive planners would want high quality for all, and would be suspicious of different kinds of provision lest they conceal differences in quality disguised as different routes.

Before 1979 the major debate within the Conservative Party was between minimalists and pluralists; after 1979 the influence of the privatizers became more and more significant — not least in the 1988 Education Reform Act (ERA). The 1988 Act is a mixture of ideologies, with some inevitable contradictions. The most immediate effect on schools has been the introduction of a National Curriculum. But perhaps more important in the long run are the clauses that deal with 'opting out' of LEA control (by means of grant-maintained school status) and the policy of 'open enrolment' for schools, which gives priority to parental choice at the expense of LEA planning.

LEAs were clearly intended to have diminished powers of control. The market was preferred to local planning. Apart from grant-maintained schools and the open enrolment referred to above, schools were given greater control over their own finances (Local Management of Schools or LMS). The creation of City Technology Colleges outside LEA control similarly diminished LEA powers to plan for a whole region. In 1990-1 the policy was continued with the announcement of the intention of removing FE colleges and, later, tertiary colleges and sixth-form colleges from LEA control.

QUALITY AND THE CURRICULUM

Since 1976 quality has been seen as partly a question of improving the quality of the curriculum. But as is often the case, questions of quality get mixed up with other issues. Her Majesty's Inspectorate (HMI), perceiving in the 1970s that the Schools Council was not tackling major questions of curriculum planning, embarked on some interesting work on an entitlement curriculum based on an areas of experience model. Soon there was a political urge for more central control, but when politicians talk of quality they often mean something else. As a result, the National Curriculum in the 1988 ERA is not completely compatible with the HMI quality model.

Nevertheless, there are positive features of the 1988 National Curriculum and, given other favourable factors, even this kind of National Curriculum could contribute to improvements in quality provided that the professionals are given enough scope to make the best of it. And all is not lost on National Curriculum assessment (NCA). The Task Group for Assessment and Training (TGAT) Report contained a number of important leads towards improving quality (e.g. the ten-level model emphasizing progression) but they must not be spoilt by the impatience of politicians and their desire to link NCA to market forces (there is more on this below).

SCHOOL ORGANIZATION

I would like to look now at another of the key areas identified by OECD: school organization. In particular I want to examine the variation in 'effectiveness' between different schools in providing good results, even with the same kind of student intake.

In the USA in the 1960s, there was a reaction against 'throwing money at problems', i.e. the notion that 'failure' or 'poor performance' could be overcome simply by increasing resources. The early studies of Coleman *et al.* (1966) and Jencks *et al.* (1972) seemed to be pessimistic in that they showed the school to be a much less significant factor than home background. Schools cannot compensate for society!

These studies stimulated groups of unbelieving researchers to look for key variables which would demonstrate that schooling could make a difference. They isolated such factors as time on task, the teacher-pupil ratio and money spent on books, in the hope that they could identify the magic ingredient. Hundreds of studies were done — with negative or contradictory results. Pessimism was confirmed. But a reworking of the data by Purkey and Smith (1983) gave rise to much more hopeful conclusions (and a later study by Coleman *et al.* (1982) was also more optimistic). The result of the reworked data was an abandonment of the search for single factors that made schools good or effective. The re-analysis study showed that it was much more a question of the ethos or culture of the school as a whole. But within an effective school culture there are certain prerequisites:

1 A commitment to clearly and commonly identified norms and goals.
2 Collaborative planning, shared decision-making and collegial work in a framework of experimentation and evaluation.
3 Positive leadership in initiating and maintaining improvement.
4 Staff stability.
5 A strategy for continuing staff development related to each school's pedagogical and organizational needs.
6 Working to a carefully planned and co-ordinated curriculum that ensures sufficient place for each student to acquire essential knowledge and skills.
7 A high level of parental involvement and support.
8 The pursuit and recognition of school-wide values rather than individual ones.
9 Maximum use of learning time.
10 The active and substantial support of the responsible education authority.

However, it must be stressed again and again that these ten characteristics are aspects of a culture: simply working to improve these ten features in isolation from the top or from the outside would not produce a better school. It is a much more complex question of school-based cultural change.

Similarly, the work done by Rutter *et al.* (1979) and Mortimore *et al.* (1988) is very important in a discussion of quality. Their lists of important features can be helpful, provided that we remember the OECD warning I mentioned at the beginning: 'Education is not an assembly-line process of mechanically increasing inputs and raising productivity.' And the same is true of the list of fifty performance indicators produced by the DES in 1989. I am quite convinced, for example, that truancy is a good indicator of school quality — but a high truancy rate is almost certainly a symptom rather than a cause of a poor school. Simply to attack truancy as the problem would do little to achieve greater quality.

It has to be said that indicators are no more than the word suggests, i.e. they indicate (but do not measure or explain) success or effectiveness of a limited kind. To achieve a more effective school culture is a much more complex process of cultural change involving the school as a whole.

CHOICE, THE MARKET AND CULTURE

Finally, I would like to mention another false god (perhaps two false gods): choice and market mechanisms in education. There are good private schools and very bad private schools — despite the operation of market mechanisms. There are good LEA schools and bad ones. Simply encouraging schools to opt out will not make them better.

Moreover, the market does not work well as a means of enhancing quality in education. There are a number of reasons to explain this:

1 The free market has probably been generally 'over-sold' as a means of encouraging quality. Very few markets anywhere are completely free. It is usually found necessary to plan restrictions on the market mechanisms of supply and demand. What is so marvellous about a 'hidden hand' anyway? There are occasions when conscious planning is superior, especially in education.

2 Markets only operate with efficiency when there is 'perfect knowledge' (or at least very good knowledge). To choose *rationally* between schools, parents must know everything about those schools. This is rarely possible, and even if it were, the information would need careful analysis and interpretation of a kind beyond the skills of most parents.

3 Parents often do not choose 'rationally'. They have prejudices or are misled by simplistic slogans. We know, for example, that parents often think that a good school is one where pupils wear uniform (a feature that is not listed in any of the studies quoted above).

4 Parents may also be more impressed by non-educational reasons, e.g. they choose a private school not for the quality of education but in the hope that their child will acquire middle-class speech and manners.

To encourage parents to choose schools on the basis of published examination or test results — as threatened by the 1988 ERA — is either extremely naive or blatantly dishonest.

Looked at in this way, much of the 1988 ERA is a distraction from the real task of improving quality. Moreover, one factor that has been almost completely ignored is given considerable emphasis by the OECD: the quality of the teachers. This means not only recruiting, training and retaining good teachers, but also using them to greater effect in the search for quality — working together co-operatively as members of the community, sharing certain experiences and being concerned to improve the quality of life in that community and not just to raise a few scores on a list of performance indicators.

REFERENCES

Coleman, J. S. *et al.* (1966) *Equality of Educational Opportunity.* Washington, DC: US Government Printing Office.

Coleman, J. S. *et al.* (1982) *High School Achievement.* New York: Basic Books.

Council for Curriculum Reform (1945) *The Content of Education.* London: University of London Press.

Gamble, A. (1988) *The Free Economy and the Strong State: The Politics of Thatcherism.* London: Macmillan.

Jencks, C. *et al.* (1972) *Inequality.* New York: Basic Books.

Kogan, M. (1988) 'Managerialism in higher education', in D. Lawton (ed.), *The Education Reform Act: Choice and Control.* London: Hodder.

Hillgate Group (1986) *Whose Schools?* London: Hillgate Group.

Hillgate Group (1987) *The Reform of British Education.* London: Hillgate Group.

Lawlor, S. (1988) *Away with LEAs.* London: Centre for Policy Studies.

Lawton, D. (1989) *Education, Culture and the National Curriculum.* London: Hodder.

Lawton, D. (1992) *Education and Politics in the 1990s.* London: Falmer.

Maclure, S. (1989) *Education Re-formed.* London: Hodder.

Mortimore, P. *et al.* (1988) *School Matters.* Wells: Open Books.

OECD (1989) *Schools and Quality: An International Report.* Paris: OECD.

O'Keeffe, D. (1990) *The Wayward Elite.* London: Adam Smith Institute.

Purkey, S. and Smith, M. (1983) 'Effective schools — a review', *Elementary School Journal*, 83, 427-52.

Rutter, M. *et al.* (1979) *Fifteen Thousand Hours.* Wells: Open Books.

Sexton, S. (1987) *Our Schools — a Radical Policy.* London: Institute of Economic Affairs.

Tawney, R. H. (1931) *Equality.* London: Allen and Unwin.

Chapter 2

Quality in Education

Nick Stuart

INTRODUCTION

It is fair to say that for most of my early years in education administration, a discussion of quality in education was not the priority. At both central and local government levels the emphasis in the 1960s and much of the 1970s was on structure, organization and resources. In many ways we were still building the post-war system: raising the school-leaving age to sixteen; expanding the further education system; restructuring secondary education; reducing oversize classes; paring down the number of LEAs. Success tended to be measured not by outputs — what we were getting for our money — but by the volume of inputs.

I believe that there were essentially three things that brought concern about quality to the forefront:

- there was clearly a set of *economic arguments*. One of these was growing disbelief that there was some kind of natural or automatic relationship between education investment and economic success. If there was such a connection, it needed to be demonstrated. What was the country getting for the volume of resources being put in? Another facet of the economic argument was one that had been around since at least the nineteenth century: our economic performance as a nation was poor not because we were spending too little on education but because the education system was not delivering the right human skills to compete with the rest of the world.

- There were *political arguments*. At a time when most people gave priority to controlling and in due course reducing public expenditure as a proportion of GDP, education as a public spending priority lost its edge. The Conservatives' priorities in 1979 were pensions, health and law and order, together with defence. At the same time demography was working against the service.

- There were *educational arguments*. From Callaghan's Ruskin speech onwards, there was an increasing questioning of performance. HMI inspection evidence confirmed the impressions of low expectations, limited curriculum planning and vague objectives. International comparisons began to show up our performance, particularly in relation to the average or below average performer. Parents were beginning to question more and more whether their children were being sufficiently stretched. Confidence in new approaches to teaching began to ebb.

I do not intend this as a kind of potted educational history but simply as a brief backcloth to where we stand in 1991, almost four years after the introduction of the Education Reform Bill. Do you remember GERBIL, which became ERA? It already seems half a lifetime away. But that Act in my view has created the framework and the context within which our pursuit of quality in education has begun to flourish. I want to trace how and why in my view that is so. In essence the remainder of what I have to say revolves around three words. They are: choice, objectives and management.

CHOICE

In introducing his Bill in 1987 Kenneth Baker said:

> We must give consumers of education a central part in decision-making. That means freeing schools and colleges to deliver the standards that parents and employers want. It means encouraging the consumer to expect and demand that all educational bodies do the best job possible. In a word, it means choice.

You see *there* a crucial and essential strand in the reforms of the past few years. It has as its starting-point the notion that schools will do better if they are able to have a greater responsibility for and direct control over their own destiny. They must have a life and soul of their own. Quality will not thrive in a local system forced into one uniform pattern with heads in a subordinate position and without access to any responsible body of governors. Put like that, this is an old idea: it is roughly how Sir Robert Morant, the first Permanent Secretary of the Board of Education, expressed it around the turn of this century. He tended to be rather virulent about the tendency, as he saw it, of chief education officers to make the emerging secondary school sector the creature of the local authority education committee.

So as the Government has seen it, an important starting-point for securing better quality has been to free up individual institutions so that:

- they are better able to express their own objectives and have the means and the scope to pursue them;
- they are better able to define their own ethos and character and respond to their parent bodies, local employers and the needs of their pupils.

The aim is to maximize the opportunities available for each individual part of the system to flourish, rather than to put the emphasis on the system itself. If individual schools are allowed to thrive that is to the benefit of the whole system. It is also the way to make the citizen feel that he or she has some measure of real choice.

The 1988 Education Reform Act provides a framework within which this basic objective of bringing a new vitality into our schools system can be given reality. In the years since 1988 we have been putting it into place. It has been a huge job and I am conscious of the enormous load on schools. I think that was inevitable and necessary. Let me quote from the black anti-slavery crusader, Frederick Douglass:

> If there is no struggle, there is no progress. Those who profess to favour freedom and yet deprecate agitation are men who want crops without ploughing up the ground; they want rain without thunder and lightening. They want the ocean without the awful roar of its many waters.

Yes, there has been a lot of ploughing up the ground in the last three years but there is also evidence of considerable progress. Let me identify some of the strands of that progress.

First, all local education authorities outside inner London now have schemes of local management approved and in place. From April 1991, 80 per cent of secondary schools and 30 per cent of primary schools have had delegated budgets. By 1994 all schools will have delegation extended to them. We have supported through specific grants a large and still continuing programme to help LEAs equip schools with the necessary financial management information systems, to train staff and to support governing bodies. Circular 7/91 further strengthens the principles of LMS by tightening the limits on the items of expenditure excluded from delegation. By April 1993 at least 85 per cent of the relevant education budget must be delegated to the school level and 80 per cent of that must be determined by the number of pupils at the school. For each percentage point delegated a further £100 million switches directly to the control of schools. There are some hopeful signs of better resource management using the new flexibilities available and of schools constructing school development plans in accordance with clear objectives. I shall want to return to that later.

The opportunities for individual schools to take what the Secretary of State has described as the logical step after LMS — grant-maintained (GM) status — are now being seized at a rapidly increasing rate. Over eighty schools had by 1991 been approved for GM status; there are a growing number in the pipeline; by April 1992 I anticipate a list almost 200 strong. In Birmingham we already have some of the first schools to go GM. GM schools do not form part of the independent school sector; they are part of the maintained school sector with the same duties and obligations. As with LMS, so with GMS: there is a lot of evidence to show that GM schools are making very effective use of their wider management flexibility; that they are responding with new vigour and indeed enthusiasm to new responsibilities. The impact is to be seen across the country in sharply increasing admissions. The climate and conditions exist for raising performance.

We have made substantial progress towards a much more open system, which offers both parents and the public better information about the schools that serve them. This both enhances choice and improves accountability. There is now clear information about what schools cost, how funds are allocated and distributed, and how those funds are deployed within schools. We are also building upon earlier legislation to ensure that aspects of performance, including examination performance, and most recently absentee rates, are made publicly available in a simple and readily understandable form. As we develop the assessment arrangements at each Key Stage in support of the National Curriculum, so more evidence about school performance will become available to be set against performance nationally and at LEA level.

All of this is part of a wider attempt to engage parents more actively in the education of their children: parents are, after all, potentially the main educators, certainly of young children. That is why we have been seeking to improve arrangements for reporting achievement to parents. The National Curriculum is common property — all parents can find out what their children should be learning and what they should have mastered at each stage. It is encouraging that SCI's Annual Report in 1991 indicated considerable improvement in the arrangements made by secondary schools to establish positive links with parents on a regular basis. The parents of about three out of every four children now attend meetings to discuss academic progress. Too often we tend to talk about quality solely in professional terms — about changing curricula and teaching methods — and we ignore the fact that education must be a shared process involving pupil, teacher and parent. Empowering parents is equally important on the road to better quality.

Finally, in the context of choice, implementation of the more open enrolment provisions of the Act combined with funding arrangements that firmly relate to the principle that the size of the budget is directly related to the recruitment of pupils further underpins schools' accountability. In particular, pupil-led funding offers all schools positive and powerful incentives to respond to parental wishes and pupils' needs, and where necessary to adapt. Under these arrangements management is given the incentive to manage in the best interests of the clients.

OBJECTIVES

Let me turn now to my second keyword: 'objectives'. The first thing to say is that our objectives are ambitious and far from easy. Let me quote from Machiavelli: 'There is nothing more difficult to take in hand, more perilous to conduct, more uncertain in its success than to take the lead in the introduction of a new order of things.' And that is indeed what we are doing. For England a National Curriculum supported by a national assessment system is a new order of things. It is a sharp break with the past in two important respects: for the first time we have a single set of expectations about what pupils should know and should be able to do and for the first time we have arrangements for national testing against those expectations at regular intervals through compulsory schooling. Moreover, we cannot look to international models. Linking assessment directly to the curriculum in the way we propose is new. Other countries have expressed enormous interest in what we are doing. In the USA, for example, President Bush announced in April 1991 his intention to establish nationwide achievement tests in five core subjects tied to national attainment targets and 'designed to foster good teaching and learning as well as to monitor student progress'.

I want, therefore, to look at the significance and impact of the National Curriculum. If LMS helps to create the climate and conditions within which schools can seek to improve quality, the National Curriculum creates the framework and agenda for such improvement. There is now a wide national agreement about the importance of the National Curriculum as a means to better quality.

It has enormous potential for helping to focus the attention of schools on bringing clarity and rigour to their definition of the objectives of teaching and learning. It is not, of course, that schools had lacked objectives or curriculum policies before the National Curriculum, but it is evident that in far too many cases those policies were vague, and badly co-ordinated and did not serve to infuse the whole school with a clear mission of the job to be done. Nor would I wish to argue that attainment targets and programmes of study are sufficient in themselves as a statement of a school's policy. Not only do they leave plenty of room for school and teacher to exercise professional imagination and judgement, but there are important aspects of education enshrined in Section 1 of the 1988 Act that lie outside the National Curriculum and that schools must build in to their overall curriculum.

It offers potential for translating clear objectives into practice through effective curriculum planning. HMI's evidence is that the effort of bringing in the National Curriculum is already beginning to pay off in greatly improved planning at class, department and school level. In primary schools, in particular, there are welcome signs of more rigorous attempts to plan the curriculum as a whole to ensure that there really is a balance. In the past we took that balance for granted without knowing whether it really existed. And yet HMI is telling us, for example, that history and geography in any worthwhile sense have only a vestigial presence in many primary schools. No doubt it will be some time yet before primary schools do full justice to all National Curriculum subjects while maintaining the attention that they now give to the core subjects. But the point is that we now have, for the first time, an agreed framework for improvement.

It offers potential for developing real curriculum continuity, not only within schools but between schools. I suspect that as a nation we have lost a large but unquantified amount of real education down through the cracks of our educational system, particularly at the ages of transfer between schools. Many have identified weaknesses in curriculum continuity in the past. Links between schools have been spasmodic and where they have existed they have largely been about pastoral arrangements, not about the curriculum. The National Curriculum has created a common curriculum framework for schools: it forces attention towards progression and continuity. It is encouraging that more schools are now forging curriculum links across the age of transfer and beginning to work together professionally. We now have a structure and common language for ensuring that there is such co-operation.

This potential for beneficial change is widely recognized. And we have come a long way since 1988 in establishing the detail of the National Curriculum, in identifying some of the inevitable teething troubles and in making a start upon necessary refinement.

In May 1991 the Final Orders for geography and history were approved by both Houses of Parliament. We have just received advice from the National Curriculum Council (NCC) on the basis for a draft order on modern foreign languages. Final reports from the Working Groups on music, art and PE are due shortly. The plan was to have the full National Curriculum of ten subjects specified and in place by 1992, although implementation across all key stages will take until the second half of the decade.

The Secretary of State in 1991 published new proposals for the structure of attainment targets and programmes of study for maths and science. He proposes a revision of existing materials, which reduces the number of attainment targets to five for each subject and at the same time more than halves the number of statements of attainment. The objective of these proposals, which result from a thorough review, is to simplify and improve manageability of assessment. The load on teachers in assessment, recording and reporting on their pupils will be substantially reduced. The curriculum requirements as expressed through the programmes of study remain unchanged. The NCC was consulting on these proposals until July 1991. I believe that they will prove welcome simplification that brings assessment requirements more into line with other subjects, like English and technology, which also have five attainment targets apiece.

We are making proposals as a basis for consultation designed to carry forward the Secretary of State's intentions to create greater flexibility for schools at Key Stage 4. These cover making history and geography alternatives within the National Curriculum (a proposal recently published), music and art as optional choices, and enabling classes of pupils as well as individuals to complete Key Stage 4 in individual subjects early. The flexibility thus afforded is at the disposal of schools. It will be for them to respond to the needs of their pupils and to exercise their judgement. No school has to offer every conceivable option available. The choices are there for you to make; the responsibility within the framework of the National Curriculum is for you to exercise. What this flexibility should increasingly permit is the development of well-structured courses with a vocational content both within and outside the National Curriculum. All such qualifications will have to meet criteria every bit as rigorous as those for GCSE, and where they embrace National Curriculum subjects, the Attainment Targets (ATs) and programmes of study requirements. Work is underway with the vocational examining bodies to ensure that appropriate qualifications to meet the needs of schools are developed.

That brings me to assessment and testing, about which there is much topical sound and fury. Let me try briefly to put events into context. It seems to me that there is now widespread agreement that there *is* value in seeking to integrate effectively into the teaching and learning process the systematic assessment of pupils' progress. Assessment is not something new. It is part and parcel of the teaching process. What is new is the attempt for the first time to organize the amount of external assessment that has always gone on into a national system which is supportive of good teaching and helpful to pupils' learning.

Against this background, where have we got to? I do not want to add significantly to the hundreds of thousands of words already pronounced about the SATs for 7-year-olds. The essential issue is how to find the right balance between tests which are reliable in the sense that they do help to measure performance against the ATs and tests which are also manageable by the teacher in the classroom. Some nationally prescribed tests are essential to establish national standards and to provide the benchmarks against which teachers can develop their teacher assessment techniques. The issue is not, therefore, about whether we should have tests at all. The arrangements were of course significantly simplified as a result of 1990's pilot, and I believe that there is room for further simplification. The Secretary of State made it clear that he would be looking closely at all the evidence of 1991's national testing. The new proposals for streamlining the maths and science curriculum structure will undoubtedly help.

At Key Stage 3 the Secretary of State announced that summer 1992 would be an extended voluntary trial of the test arrangements. He deferred the introduction of statutory requirements. The changes proposed for maths and science made that necessary but in any case there is advantage in making certain that the tests do serve their purpose in a manageable way. He intended that the examining boards should have a pivotal role in assuring the quality of the testing arrangements. The School Examinations and Assessment Council (SEAC) was working in 1991, in the light of the pilot work that was being carried out, to design SATs which, wherever possible, were close to short external examinations. These exams should not represent a significant additional burden in schools: they should supersede schools' own traditional internal end-of-year exams for 14-year-olds.

The examining groups and SEAC were also working together to ensure that new GCSE syllabuses calibrated to the National Curriculum were in place in the core subjects from September 1991 — leading to examinations in the summer of 1994. The new maths and science structure is designed to facilitate that. Both the Joint Board and the SEAC were confident of achieving the timescale.

I have talked about the National Curriculum and assessment under the banner of objectives. As I have said, a lack of clear objectives at every level — national, local and school — has in my view been a fundamental weakness in our school system. It accounts for historically low expectations of what children can achieve; for the difficulties that we have had in generalizing recognized good practice across the system; for the discontinuities and incoherence that exists from 5 to 16; and for the weaknesses of planning that have led to lack of balance, breadth and proper differentiation within the curriculum. Now, reaching a national agreement on objectives does not immediately put all that right but it can create a climate and provide the structure within which we can secure improvement. The key to securing that improvement then lies in better management.

MANAGEMENT

I want to talk briefly about management at school level. You can have the best curriculum in the world but if there are no effective systems within each school for translating that curriculum into effective teaching and learning, not a great deal will be achieved. What is good on paper must also be good in practice. I think that is better realized than ever before. There used to be a time when the very notion of a teacher as manager was somehow deemed to be demeaning of the profession. Asked to describe their role, headteachers were anything but managers: they were curriculum innovators, they set objectives, they established the ethos of the school, they were the principal link with the governors, the parents and the community, they monitored quality; but they were not managers. Yet their own description of the attributes required for and the tasks of headship was always all about management.

I believe that the combination of bringing real responsibility to school level and of establishing a national framework of objectives creates the basis for improving management at all levels. First, at the whole school level, it is now common to find staff working together on the articulation of a school development plan relating objectives to available resources and seeking to develop means of establishing how well the objectives set are actually being achieved. Such plans can reinforce a school's sense of purpose, give it a greater sense of coherence and help to motivate all concerned. It is also the means of pulling together all the different aspects of the planning process — curriculum planning can be linked to an INSET policy, both can be related to a careful scrutiny of resources. Above all, the school has a route towards deciding upon its own priorities. And with LMS those decisions are real. That means that the choices that a school makes have really got to count: if you forgo one desirable use of resources to concentrate on another — and the choice is yours — there is a powerful incentive to see that the way resources are deployed does work to the maximum benefit. Quality will flow from the use of resources in committed and effective ways.

Second, management of the curriculum within this overall process has assumed a much greater profile. What is happening already is very encouraging. If primary school teachers now worry — and they do — about how they will fit in the requirements of the new Orders for history and geography, I sympathize but I also rejoice. It is not in practice a question that would have been addressed only a short time ago. Some content in some important areas of the curriculum tended to go by default because there were implicit priorities at work with serious unplanned consequences. History and geography were both becoming quite glaring areas of neglect in many schools. Managing the curriculum in the classroom to achieve balance and continuity is a central issue and I think that there is real evidence that it is now getting the degree of attention that it deserves. And the outcome is already the beginnings of real improvement in the balance and quality of work for pupils of all abilities.

Third, better management also requires, in my view, two further steps. The first is a realization that if you manage to define more clearly where you want to get to, there is an equal obligation to try to identify whether you got there. Schools must set up systems that aim to measure their performance. I see this as an internal management function, an internal process to help the organization achieve its own objectives. In that sense, performance indicators are a supportive and necessary part of a school's own management system. Devising such systems in education is not easy. Often they will be partial and incomplete. But indicators are indicators; they focus the attention on an issue that may require further investigation. But management also requires some external support offering quality assurance. There must be effective quality assurance systems by LEAs through their inspection and advisory services in support of the management of schools. Self-evaluation is necessary but it is not enough. Management needs the external stimulus of a check on how its systems are working, with advice about how they might be improved and the steps necessary to accomplish that improvement. By enhancing accountability in this way, we can also help to enhance performance.

In this respect, GM schools are also turning their attention to self-evaluation strategies and to the role of external monitoring and evaluation. GM heads and governors met on several occasions in 1991 to discuss these topics. We have encouraged them to produce school development plans and performance indicators. Many of them are buying inspection and advisory services, either from former maintaining or neighbouring LEAs or from higher education. Although GM schools are directly accountable to parents, there is a growing recognition by the schools that more needs to be done on quality monitoring. The GM schools themselves, with the help of the Grant Maintained Centre, are considering a code of practice on monitoring and evaluation. This would commit schools both to rigorous self-evaluation strategies and to external quality audit on a rolling programme. This development is a further sign of the emphasis on the issue of quality, which is such a feature of contemporary discussion on education.

Better management is also about getting the best out of staff. There are therefore two further essentials:

- A system of appraisal that will help all teachers in their professional development and career planning and will help the managers of teachers in the decisions they have to take about appointment, assignment and promotion. The Secretary of State intends to introduce a national appraisal system over the next four years and will shortly be laying regulations before Parliament to achieve that.

- A pay system that is capable of rewarding achievement and responsibility. Managers need the support of a flexible pay system which can be used in this way in accordance with the particular needs and circumstances of each school. The Government is taking steps to build on the achievements of the IAC over the past few years in introducing greater differentiation and discretion into the pay system by establishing a pay review body for school teachers. It is also the next essential step in raising the status of the profession and ensuring that the achievements receive proper public recognition.

CONCLUSION

I have ranged widely. Let me end by saying that the analysis I offer implies no lack of respect or lack of pride in the real achievements of schools now or in the past. I have been, on and off, in education administration for twenty-seven years. In that time, I have seen and been involved in a great deal of successful development. All of it has depended on a thoroughly professional teaching force. It is because we have such a teaching force at the heart and foundation of our system that we have made so much progress in so short a time in carrying through the reforms of the 1988 Act. It is that above anything else which makes me optimistic that schools can and will take forward and use the new opportunities now presented to improve quality.

Chapter 3

School Effectiveness and Quality in Education

David Reynolds

The entry on to the educational stage of research and practice in the area of school effectiveness has been one of the major changes in educational thinking of the past decade. A decade ago, the predominant 'paradigm' by which researchers explained variation in children's educational growth over time involved relating achievement to features of children's home background, community characteristics and individual intellectual and personal attributes. Now, the findings of school effectiveness research are increasingly used in educational debate and are increasingly being accessed by practitioners wanting a knowledge base to inform their improvement programmes in schools (see Reynolds and Cuttance, 1992, for a survey).

Yet, paradoxically, just as the new 'paradigm' is receiving greater and greater support and attention within educational practice and indeed within educational policy-making, many of the simplistic certainties that appeared to emanate from the earlier work in the field in Britain and internationally have been challenged by the emergence of recent research. In addition, the 'delivery mechanisms' of school improvement and school development programmes, which have been the accepted mechanisms of generating change in schools in Britain, have appeared increasingly unable to cope either intellectually or practically with the incorporation of the school effectiveness knowledge base. Indeed, the school improvement paradigm has historically been a very different paradigmatic creature. The increasing complexity of the knowledge base and the implications of that for any concern to improve 'quality' in educational outcomes, and the problem of actually getting school effectiveness to 'root' in schools if school development programmes have different disciplinary and practical orientations, form the subjects of this chapter.

THE SCHOOL EFFECTIVENESS KNOWLEDGE BASE

The development of this field over time has been extensively described by myself and others elsewhere (Creemers and Scheerens, 1989; Reynolds *et al.*, 1989a; Reynolds, 1991) and is increasingly well known, so only an outline seems necessary here. In both the United States and in Britain, studies such as that by Coleman *et al.* (1966), the work of Jencks *et al.* (1971) and the British Plowden

Report of the Central Advisory Council for Education (1967) all concluded that schools bring little independent influence to bear upon the development of their pupils. This period has been gradually followed in both societies by the emergence of a wide range of 'effective schools', 'school effectiveness' or 'school effects' studies, which argue for the importance of school influence, beginning in the United States with various qualitative case studies and moving on to a wide range of quantitative studies, and beginning in Britain with work by Power *et al.* (1967), Gath (1977), Reynolds (1976, 1982; Reynolds *et al.*, 1987), Rutter *et al.* (1979), Galloway (1985) and Gray *et al.* (1990). Subsequent studies have been made by Mortimore and his colleagues (1988) in primary schools and by Smith and Tomlinson (1989) in multicultural secondary schools. Work in these two societies has been recently joined by that from the Netherlands, Australia and Canada, and by a recent resurgence of studies done in and about Third World societies.

From all this work it is clear that schools *do* have substantial effects upon pupils and that there are processes that 'work' across schools to maximize their outcomes. In the important British secondary school study of Rutter *et al.* (1979), the factors that were linked with effectiveness could be grouped under the following broad headings:

- *the pupil control system*, with effective schools using rewards, praise, encouragement and appreciation more than punishments;

- *the school environment provided for pupils*, with effective schools providing good working conditions for pupils and for their teachers, being responsive to pupil needs and also providing buildings that were well cared for and well decorated;

- *the involvement of pupils*, with effective schools giving ample opportunities for pupils to take positions of responsibility and to participate in the running of the school and in the educational activities within the classrooms;

- *the academic development of pupils*, with effective schools making positive use of homework, setting clear and explicit academic goals, and with the teachers in these effective schools having high expectations of, and positive views of, the capabilities of their pupils;

- *the behaviour of teachers*, with effective schools providing good models of behaviour through teachers exhibiting good time-keeping and a clearly apparent willingness to deal with pupils' personal and social problems;

- *management in the classroom*, with effective schools possessing teachers who prepared lessons in advance, who kept the attention of the whole class, who managed to maintain discipline in an unobtrusive way, who focused upon the rewarding of good behaviour and who were able to take swift action to deal with any disruption by pupils;

- *the management structure*, with effective schools combining firm leadership by the headteacher with a decision-making process in which all teachers felt that their views were represented.

Our own work in Wales (see references above) is parallel in many of its findings to those of the Rutter *et al.* study, although our limited data on the intakes into our sample of schools made us less able than the Rutter team to prove conclusively that the large differences between our schools were in fact due to the effects of what was going on within the schools themselves.

The detailed observations on our schools over a decade showed a number of features that were associated with being an effective school. These were:

- *high levels of pupil involvement*, as shown by the co-option of a large proportion of pupils into a prefect system, for example, and as shown by the use of pupil monitors in lesson time that helped with the distribution of books and equipment;
- *low levels of certain institutional controls*, as shown by a tolerant attitude towards the enforcement of certain key rules covering pupil dress and the like;
- *a low concentration upon punishment* (particularly physical punishment) and the use of more informal, verbal sanctions;
- *high expectations of what pupils could achieve*, both academically and in terms of their behaviour, linked to a positive view of the pupils' home backgrounds and communities.

Many of the British findings about the characteristics of effective secondary and primary schools are also paralleled by the large volume of international studies into school effectiveness. In the United States, Lezotte (1989) and others have popularized the 'five-factor' theory of school effectiveness, which sees schools that are academically highly performing as possessing the following characteristics:

- strong principal leadership and attention to the quality of instruction;
- a pervasive and broadly understood instructional focus;
- an orderly, safe climate conducive to teaching and learning;
- teacher behaviours that convey the expectation that all students are expected to obtain at least a basic mastery of simple skills;
- the use of measures of pupil achievement as the basis for programme evaluation.

Although the original development of the five-factor theory was from research in the elementary school sector, very similar theories have been utilized to describe and explain the highly effective high school (or secondary school) in North America, and such research as there has been into the secondary sector again confirms the general applicability of the theory above (for a comprehensive summary of research see Levine and Lezotte, 1990). Corcoran and Wilson's (1989) study of exceptionally successful secondary schools generated a list of common elements in their effective schools that has distinct similarities with findings from the British secondary school studies. Their common elements were:

- a positive attitude towards the students by teachers and the principal;
- strong and competent leadership;
- highly committed teaching staff;
- high expectations and standards;
- an emphasis upon high achievement in academic subjects;
- intensive and personal support services for at-risk students;
- stable leadership and public support in the catchment area of the school for a period of years sufficient to implement new policies.

The certainties that are reflected in the above international account of 'what works' are now, however, increasingly being replaced by uncertainty, controversy and disagreements as to what the 'core' beliefs of the school effectiveness paradigm are.

First, on the size of school effects, it seems that early beliefs that school influence might be as large as family or community influences were misplaced, since a very large number of studies in the past five years show only 8 to 15 per cent of the variation in pupil outcomes as due to between-school differences (Bosker and Scheerens, 1989; Cuttance, 1992).

Second, on the causes of school effects, it seems that early beliefs that school influences were distinct from teacher or classroom influences were misplaced, since a large number of studies utilizing multi-level modelling show that the great majority of variation between schools is in fact due to classroom variation and that the unique variance due to the influence of the school, and not the classroom, shrinks to very small levels (Scheerens et al., 1989).

Indeed, some re-analyses of international studies show that in certain societies, such as Sweden, the amount of variation in achievement due to the influence of the school is virtually zero, a consequence perhaps of educational policies at 'macro' state or 'meso' local state level to ensure that all schools had equal resources, balanced intakes and equally competent teacher/headteacher management across geographical areas (see results in Scheerens et al., 1989).

Third, on the consistency of school effects, it seems that early beliefs that 'effective', or 'ineffective', schools stayed so over quite considerable time periods of five to seven years were invalid, since it now appears that school performance can vary quite rapidly over two or three years (Nuttall et al., 1989). (The recent publication of the academic outcomes of schooling, such as the results of pupils' examinations, involves utilizing only one year's figures and is clearly a worrying policy if school performance is unstable.)

At A Level, indeed, there is new evidence that suggests rather surprising variability in the effectiveness or ineffectiveness 'status' of schools over time. On a single three-category scale for raw, unadjusted results at A Level, 30 per cent of schools changed category between 1991 and 1992. Use of a 'value-added' approach to calculate 'true' effectiveness levels increased the percentage of schools changing category to approximately 45 per cent (Nuttall, 1992).

Fourth, on the relative consistency of the performance of schools across a range of outcome measures, it used to be thought that the 'effective school' was so across a range of both academic and social outcomes, yet now we have much evidence that schools need not be effective or ineffective 'across the board'. The Junior School Project of Mortimore *et al.* (1988) showed, for example, a virtually complete independence of schools on different outcome measures, suggesting strongly that academic effectiveness is not necessarily associated with social or 'affective' effectiveness.

Our own research on system-wide differences in educational effectiveness between selective and comprehensive systems (Reynolds *et al.*, 1987) also showed large differences in system effects upon affective or social outcomes, such as pupils' attendance rates, self-conceptions and delinquency rates, but very small differences in system effects upon academic outcomes. Indeed, recent evidence from the 'ALIS' project of Fitz-Gibbon and colleagues (1989) suggests that it is unwise even to talk about a school's academic effectiveness only, since there is a substantial range of effectiveness across subject departments. Even 'ineffective' schools overall may have effective subjects or effective departments within them. The same variation in effectiveness by subjects is shown in the Smith and Tomlinson (1989) study of multiracial comprehensive schools.

Fifth, on the question of effectiveness across different groups of pupils, the traditional belief that schools are effective or ineffective for all sub-groups of pupils within them is no longer tenable in view of the evidence that there can be different school effects for children of different ethnic groups, ability ranges and socio-economic status within the *same* school (Aitken and Longford, 1986; Nuttall *et al.*, 1989).

The evidence from Scotland on the effects of comprehensive school reorganization, where it was particularly working-class pupils who benefited from the policy change (McPherson and Willms, 1987), again tells us that different groups may be differently affected by their educational experience.

Sixth, on the question of what factors make schools more or less effective, the traditional belief (Edmonds, 1979) that there was a blueprint or 'recipe' independent of school history, context or personnel is no longer tenable, since what is effective may vary in accordance with the context of the social environment of the school's catchment area (Hallinger and Murphy, 1986), with the stage of development of the school itself (Stringfield and Teddlie, 1990), and with the particular outcome measure being considered (Mortimore *et al.*, 1988). Even if the characteristics of effective schools are found to be similar across contexts, the actual *generation* of these characteristics at the level of day-to-day school management may be different, as shown in the American work of Brookover *et al.* (1979) and in a neglected study by Galloway (1983) in New Zealand, where four schools exhibiting low rates of disruptive behaviour exhibited similar 'effective school' characteristics but also contained two autocratic principals, one democratic and one of 'mixed style'. The principals all generated 'collegiality' among their staff groups and all generated 'effective' school outputs, but they did so in *different* ways appropriate to their own personalities, the dynamics of their local contexts and the stage of development of their school.

The variation in what makes schools effective also, of course, extends to differences in the outcome measures utilized. The Rutter *et al.* (1979) study and that of Mortimore and his associates (1988) show different patterns of school process factors associated with different outcomes. However, it is clear that we have thus far been able to explain more of the variation in the academic outcomes than we have in the social outcomes of schooling, as exemplified in the Rutter *et al.* (1979) study, where only seven process factors were linked with a school's delinquency rate, by comparison with over twenty linked with a school's academic achievement rate.

Seventh, on the last issue of what makes schools effective, it is abundantly clear that there is no cross-cultural agreement on this matter. Assertive instructional leadership from the principal recurs repeatedly in North American five-, six- or seven-factor theories of school effectiveness research (Levine and Lezotte, 1990), yet is not an important factor determining school effectiveness in the great majority of the Dutch research on effective school practices (Creemers and Scheerens, 1989). Frequent monitoring of pupil performance is again a characteristic of some American effective school studies (Levine and Lezotte, 1990), yet this is not found in British primary schools, where in the Junior School Project frequent monitoring of school performance was a characteristic of *ineffective* schools (Mortimore *et al.*, 1988).

Resolving these areas of controversy is not the only problem within school effectiveness research. In Britain and internationally, there is a sense in which the entire enterprise of school effectiveness appears in a 'time warp'. The studies that have been conducted are all ageing rapidly and are of less and less use in the educational world of the 1990s. This world has new needs at the level of pupil outcomes from schools — the skills to access information and to work collaboratively in groups, and the social outcomes of being able to cope in a highly complex world are just three new educational goals which are never used as outcomes in the school effectiveness literature. Will the schools that generated high test score performance in the 1970s and 1980s be the schools that also generate these new social and academic achievements? It seems rather unlikely.

The picture of effective school management that appears in the research may also be very dated. The effective headteacher of the 1980s got his or her school moving in the absence of any external pressure for change; the effective headteacher of the 1990s has somehow to broker the external change agenda to his or her staff, a very different and much more complex task. The 1990s headteacher has to relate to parents, be a public relations person, cope with uncertainty, motivate staff in the absence of substantial instrumental rewards to offer them, be a financial manager, have a robust psychology, be entrepreneurial and be able to cope with rapid changes. The sorts of headteacher that stand out in the old school effectiveness literature are unlikely to be those that really 'work' in the 1990s (see Reynolds, 1992, for further speculations).

For all the doubts and uncertainties in the field, it is important to remember that school effectiveness research has enduring usefulness for schools and teachers. First, the movement has destroyed forever the alibi of teachers and others that it was home background or social disadvantage which was the reason why children failed at school, and that consequently little could be done to change things. Nowadays, it is the school which is held more accountable for whether its children can perform academically and socially, since it is the school which is seen as responsible for pupil success and failure.

Second, although the British government continues to insist on the publication of 'raw' SAT scores for 7-year-olds and on publication of 'raw' school examination results, the contribution of school effectiveness research and methodology has been to argue for the 'value-added' approach to measuring school performance. Schools must be seen in context, the effectiveness movement argues, and therefore it is the increment to each child's performance and not the absolute level that should be studied and reacted to within the educational system. This is an important message for hard-pressed teachers in schools in difficult social circumstances.

Third, the great contribution of school effectiveness research is its concern for pupils and their academic and social outcomes from education. All manner of fads and fantasies have been paraded over the past few decades in terms of what are argued to be effectiveness-producing school processes. School effectiveness researchers 'back map' from the outcomes of education to the processes and only count as effective those processes where there is definitive proof that the processes actually worked.

Fourth, although it may be difficult to see what works across countries and although we need more up-to-date research appropriate to the new educational processes and outcomes of the 1990s, it is likely that there are some enduring truths in the processes that have been found to be effective within countries. The notion that high expectations of pupils, in terms of their perceived capabilities to achieve, will actually generate that achievement has major implications for teachers, as does the well-established finding that high levels of pupil involvement in lessons, clubs, societies and leadership positions are also effectiveness-generating.

In looking at pupil discipline, the research tells us that it is better to reward good behaviour rather than punish bad behaviour, a lesson that many punishment-orientated British schools would do well to heed. For the organization to evoke the commitment of pupils, the research tells us that the effective school has the big C's — cohesion, consistency and constancy — which in the end will generate control. High staff turnover, the use of supply teachers not versed in the school's ways and the inconsistency of rules and expectations that may exist when a school staff does not 'own' a school and share in its governance are areas of contemporary education that the research base should make us wary of permitting in schools.

APPLYING THE SCHOOL EFFECTIVENESS KNOWLEDGE BASE

It is clear that although we have now made some progress in our understanding of what makes effective schools, it is perhaps in the *application* of school effectiveness knowledge that we have encountered most problems. There is no doubt that the character of the research described above has not helped its rapid translation into practice in schools. There are high levels of abstraction and use of jargon in some of the effective schools' process factors mentioned. The administrative implications for teachers of the research are often unclear, and the school effectiveness knowledge base is weak on the management and the 'technology' of schooling. The focal concerns of most practitioners — the curriculum and their instructional practices within classrooms — are not areas that school effectiveness researchers have been much interested in.

It is understandable, then, that getting the effective schools knowledge base to 'take root' in schools has been a difficult process, judged by the experience of those researchers and practitioners in Britain who have tried it. Rutter and his colleagues (Maughan *et al.*, 1990; Ouston and Maughan, 1991) attempted major and lengthy intervention work with three of the schools that had formed the basis of their earlier school effectiveness research, using the findings of this earlier work in a direct attempt to improve school practice. Of the three schools involved, only two showed some improvement and even these were in what the researchers called 'restricted areas'. By comparison with some schools that changed rapidly because of the appointment of a new headteacher, 'change at these schools was less wide ranging, affecting either only one or other of our main outcome measures or being focussed primarily on particular segments of the pupil intakes' (Maughan *et al.*, 1990, p.207).

Other somewhat disappointing results have occurred when 'consultancy' methods have been used to bring the school effectiveness knowledge into ineffective schools, since the knowledge base is often threatening to established ways of thinking within schools. It is also likely that the school effectiveness knowledge may be *personally* threatening to staff groups in ineffective schools and that the arrival of new knowledge in these schools may create disturbance, both individually and collectively among the whole staff group (Murgatroyd and Reynolds, 1985; Reynolds, 1987).

LINKING SCHOOL EFFECTIVENESS AND SCHOOL IMPROVEMENT

If, as the evidence above suggests, the application of school effectiveness knowledge in schools to improve their educational practice has been difficult in the past, then the conclusion must be that the school effectiveness and school improvement communities need to be linked together on this same task. However, the school effectiveness research paradigm has, of course, a very different intellectual history and has exhibited a very different set of core beliefs concerning operationalization, conceptualization and measurement by comparison with the approaches of most school improvers. It has been strongly quantitative in orientation, with researchers arguing that the dominant, psychologically orientated beliefs in the importance of outside school factors (e.g. Coleman *et al.*, 1966; Jencks *et al.*, 1971) had to be destroyed by utilization of the same paradigm as that used by those researchers, not by utilization of a different, more qualitatively orientated one. Linked to this position on the importance of quantitative measurement has also been a view that sees the elite knowledge produced by research as potentially highly valid accounts of school life, which are of considerable use to practitioners within schools.

Adherents to the school effectiveness paradigm are primarily concerned with pupil outcomes, which is not surprising given the political history of school effectiveness research in the United States, where it has grown on and built on the beliefs of Ron Edmonds and his associates that 'all children can learn'. Processes within schools that so interest school improvers only have an importance within the school effectiveness paradigm to the extent that they affect outcomes — indeed, one 'back maps' within the paradigm *from* outcomes *to* processes. Furthermore, the school effectiveness paradigm regards pupil and school outcomes as fundamentally unproblematic and as given; indeed, in the great majority of the North American effectiveness research, the outcomes used are derived from only the very limited, official educational definitions of the school as a purely academic institution. School effectiveness researchers often talk of a 'good' or 'excellent' school as if the definition of 'good' or 'excellent' is unproblematic, in ways unusual for school improvers. Lastly, the school effectiveness paradigm is organizationally rather than process based in terms of its analytic and descriptive orientation, preferring to restrict itself to the more easily quantifiable or measurable. As an example, Fullan's (1985) process factors, such as a 'feel for the process of leadership', 'a guiding value system' or 'intense interaction and communication', are largely eschewed in favour of organizationally and behaviourally orientated process variables such as 'clear goals and high expectations' or 'parental involvement and support'. Additionally, the focus within school improvement on the attitudinal, and on personal and group inner states, is replaced within school effectiveness research by a focus on the more easily measured behaviour of persons.

The school improvement paradigm, by contrast, has clearly believed in 'bottom up' school improvement, in which improvement attempts are 'owned' by those at school level, although outside school researchers, consultants or experts are allowed to put their knowledge forward for possible utilization. It celebrates the importance of the 'lore' or practical knowledge of practitioners rather than of the knowledge base of those who conduct research. It wishes to change educational processes, rather than the school management or the organizational features, which it sees as reified constructs. It wants the outcomes or goals of school improvement programmes to be debated and discussed, rather than accepted as given. Indeed, the process of school development is often seen by school improvers as a process of making value choices explicit rather than implicit, in which the resultant values debate aids the improvement process. The paradigm also wishes to operate at the level of practitioners rather than at school level, with a qualitative and naturalistically orientated evaluation of the enterprise being preferred to a quantitative evaluation (these ideas are further developed in Reynolds, 1988).

The 'core' beliefs of the school improvement paradigm are nicely captured in the writings of another contributor to this book, David Hopkins (1990, pp.185-91) in his description of the fourteen country International School Improvement Project (ISIP), in which he notes that 'ISIP . . . sees the process of setting goals as part of the improvement process', that 'quality is defined in terms of the teaching and learning process' and that the following list 'captures the spirit that pervades the working methods of ISIP':

- a concern to generate an understanding of phenomena;
- a concern to focus upon the meaning human actors give to their actions;

- a concern to avoid use of numerical data and to substitute verbal accounts wherever possible;
- a concern to make educational accounts available to participants in the educational process.

FROM CONFLICT TO COHESION?

There is little doubt, then, that the two paradigms of school effectiveness and school improvement have been 'coming from' (to use the American term!) different directions. The knowledge base of the school effectiveness researchers outlined above has not easily been translated into improved practice within schools, and the school improvement enterprise, and with it the bodies of knowledge in related fields like school self-evaluation and school review, has not been close enough to school effectiveness in its concerns to provide an effective 'delivery mechanism'. Indeed, we have seen that many within what I loosely called 'the school improvement paradigm' stand opposed to virtually all the philosophical, methodological and practical beliefs of those within what is internationally called 'the school effectiveness movement'.

The urgent need to improve the standards of educational practice within schools, however, and the need for the educational systems of most societies to change their schools to avoid the likely imposition of potentially destructive changes from the political system outside schools (as analysed in Hargreaves and Reynolds, 1989) necessitates the growth of links between the two, now 'rival', paradigms. School effectiveness has the potential to inform us about what makes 'good' schools (allowing for variation between and within countries as to what that 'good' is) and the school improvement movement has the power to make schools 'good' as they begin to grow and develop and as they incorporate, and yet still critique, school effectiveness knowledge (see Reynolds, 1993, for further development of this theme).

Where such links *are* being made between the two formerly rather separate traditions, there is the beginning of evidence that there may be a fruitful 'synergy' between them, leading to the development of a knowledge base about practice, policy and research that is not either 'effectiveness' or 'improvement' orientated but that is both at the same time. Three examples seem to be particularly illustrative of this (further details are in Reynolds *et al.*, 1993).

First, the 'Improving the Quality of Education' project at the Cambridge Institute of Education, outlined by Hopkins in this volume, represents a useful blend of approaches and methods that have until now only been used exclusively in either effectiveness or improvement initiatives. It is pupil outcome orientated and involves measurement of programme success or failure at outcome level, but is also concerned with the within-school study of school processes from a qualitative orientation. In the school improvement knowledge base that is to generate and inform practice and professional development, there is space for the 'elite', research-determined knowledge concerning school effectiveness and instructional effectiveness, and in addition there is space for the results of professional collaboration, reflection and education to influence the chosen improvement strategies, in a blend of research and practitioner knowledge.

27

A second example is a series of school improvement programmes run by the Halton Board of Education in Canada (Stoll and Fink, 1989). These began as an inspired attempt to bring the results of school effectiveness work done within one culture (Mortimore *et al.*, 1988) into the schooling practices of another, but it soon became clear to the programme operators that there were major problems involved in the implementation of the effectiveness programmes that had to be resolved by the adoption at school level of organizational and planning arrangements taken from the school improvement literature. The result was a blend of the effectiveness knowledge base, about effective practices, and the improvement-generated knowledge base, about successful school based planning and change. There was simply a major paradigmatic shift that happened within the Halton Board enterprise, and a commitment to make the Halton schools more effective for all students through the *blended* application of school effectiveness and school improvement insights.

The third and final example of a fruitful blending or synthesis of perspectives from what have hitherto been labelled as school 'effectiveness' and school 'improvement' approaches is perhaps our own school improvement attempts at Cardiff (Reynolds *et al.*, 1989b). Our school effectiveness knowledge base, derived from British work on the topic, was blended with grassroots practitioner 'lore' as to what made for effectiveness at school level, and the knowledge base was applied within schools by utilizing the improvement methodology characteristic of the 'OD' or 'change agent' variety. Our focus was upon changing schools' pupil outcomes but we also attempted a full appreciation of the importance of studying school processes as they were changing. The emergent improvement programme was a blend of quantitative *and* qualitative methodologies, of elite *and* professional knowledge, of effectiveness *and* improvement scholarship, and of behavioural, school outcome based approaches *together* with appreciation of the attitudinal and 'deep structural' components of schools' and teachers' individual and institutional dynamics.

CONCLUSIONS

It is clear from the review of our knowledge in this chapter that much has been achieved in the separate disciplines or 'specialities' of school effectiveness and school improvement. From school effectiveness we have an emerging sense of the factors associated with effective schooling, and from school improvement we have a set of delivery mechanisms that may be useful in implanting the knowledge into school programmes.

Yet it is also clear from this chapter how great are the knowledge needs that must be satisfied if we are truly to generate higher quality in our schools. School effectiveness researchers need to develop new contemporary outcome measures and to focus upon new areas of school functioning that may have been brought into prominence by the educational reforms and changing educational climate of the past decade. School improvement practitioners and researchers also need to change, perhaps by adopting an 'outcomes' perspective and testing the actual effects of educational improvement strategies for whether they generate improved student learning.

In spite of the importance of both effectiveness and improvement persons generating a linked, coherent and practitioner-friendly enterprise concerned with improving the quality of schooling, one has major doubts as to whether this 'synergistic' enterprise that is much needed will happen in reality. Disciplinary boundaries, friendship groups, specialist languages and the professional rivalries that are an inevitable part of disciplinary debate in the social sciences may prove to be relatively impermeable and hard to change, even though the prospects for research and practice of a linked intellectual enterprise might appear to be so exciting. If these links do not flourish, though, one can only be very concerned at what may happen. The absence of a valid knowledge base on effectiveness and improvement plays into the hands of those who have already highly developed, but unfortunately non-rational, policy schemes for further market-based reforms of education practice. One hopes that persons involved in the continued disciplinary problems at the 'cutting edge' where effectiveness and improvement interact will remember this.

REFERENCES

Aitken, M. and Longford, N. (1986) 'Statistical modelling issues in school effectiveness studies', *Journal of the Royal Statistical Society, Series A*, 149(1), 1-43.

Bosker, R. J. and Scheerens, J. (1989) 'Issues in the interpretation of the results of school effectiveness research', *International Journal of Educational Research*, 13(7), 741-51.

Brookover, W. B., Beady, C., Flood, P., Schweitzer, J. and Wisenbaker, J. (1979) *School Social Systems and Student Achievement*. New York: Praeger.

Central Advisory Council for Education (1967) *Children and Their Primary Schools (The Plowden Report)*. London: HMSO.

Coleman, J. *et al.* (1966) *Equality of Educational Opportunity*. Washington, DC: US Government Printing Office.

Corcoran, T. and Wilson, B. (1989) *Successful Secondary Schools*. Lewes: Falmer Press.

Creemers, B. and Scheerens, J. (eds) (1989) 'Developments in school effectiveness research', a special issue of *International Journal of Educational Research*, 13(7), 685-825.

Cuttance, P. (1992) 'Assessing the effectiveness of schools', in D. Reynolds and P. Cuttance (eds), *School Effectiveness*. London: Cassell.

Edmonds, R. R. (1979) 'Effective schools for the urban poor', *Educational Leadership*, 37(15-18), 20-24.

Fitz-Gibbon, C., Tymms, P. B. and Hazelwood, R. D. (1989) 'Performance indicators and information systems', in D. Reynolds, B. P. M. Creemers and T. Peters (eds), *School Effectiveness and Improvement*. Groningen: RION.

Fullan, M. (1985) 'Change processes and strategies at the local level', *Elementary School Journal*, 85(13), 391-421.

Galloway, D. (1983) 'Disruptive pupils and effective pastoral care', *School Organisation*, 13, 245-54.

Galloway, D. (1985) *Schools and Persistent Absentees*. Oxford: Pergamon Press.

Gath, D. (1977) *Child Guidance and Delinquency in a London Borough*. London: Oxford University Press.

Gray, J., Jesson, D. and Sime, N. (1990) 'Estimating differences in the examination performance of secondary schools in six LEAS — a multi-level approach to school effectiveness', *Oxford Review of Education*, 16(2), 137-58.

Hallinger, P. and Murphy, J. (1986) 'The social context of effective schools', *American Journal of Education*, 94, 328-55.

Hargreaves, A. and Reynolds, D. (eds) (1989) *Education Policy: Controversies and Critiques*. Lewes: Falmer Press.

Hopkins, D. (1990) 'The International School Improvement Project (ISIP) and effective schooling: towards a synthesis', *School Organisation*, 10(3), 179-94.

Jencks, C. *et al.* (1971) *Inequality*. London: Allen Lane.

Levine, D. and Lezotte, L. (1990) *Unusually Effective Schools: a Review and Analysis of Research and Practice*. Madison, WI: NCESRD Publications.

Lezotte, L. (1989) 'School improvement based on the effective schools research', *International Journal of Educational Research*, 13(7), 815-25.

McPherson, A. and Willms, D. (1987) 'Equalisation and improvement: some effects of comprehensive re-organisation in Scotland', *Sociology*, 21(4), 509-40.

Maughan, B., Ouston, J., Pickles, A. and Rutter, M. (1990) 'Can schools change 1 — outcomes at six London secondary schools', *School Effectiveness and Improvement*, 1(3), 188-210.

Mortimore, P., Sammons, P., Ecob, R. and Stoll, L. (1988) *School Matters: The Junior Years*. Salisbury: Open Books.

Murgatroyd, S. J. and Reynolds, D. (1985) 'The creative consultant', *School Organisation*, 4(3), 321-35.

Nuttall, D. (1992) Letter, *The Independent*, 21 November 1992.

Nuttall, D., Goldstein, H., Prosser, R. and Rasbash, J. (1989) 'Differential school effectiveness', *International Journal of Educational Research*, 13(7), 769-76.

Ouston, J. and Maughan, B. (1991) 'Can schools change 2', *School Effectiveness and School Improvement*, 2(1), 3-13.

Power, M. J. *et al.* (1967) 'Delinquent schools', *New Society*, 10, 542-43.

Reynolds, D. (1976) 'The delinquent school', in P. Woods (ed.), *The Process of Schooling*. London: Routledge and Kegan Paul.

Reynolds, D. (1982) 'The search for effective schools', *School Organisation*, 2(3), 215-37.

Reynolds, D. (1987) 'The consultant sociologist: a method for linking sociology of education and teachers', in P. Woods and A. Pollard (eds), *Sociology and Teaching*. London: Croom Helm.

Reynolds, D. (1988) 'British school improvement research: the contribution of qualitative studies', *International Journal of Qualitative Studies in Education*, 1(2), 143-54.

Reynolds, D. (1991) 'School effectiveness in secondary schools: research and its policy implications', in S. Riddell and S. Brown (eds), *School Effectiveness Research*. Edinburgh: HMSO.

Reynolds, D. (1992) 'School effectiveness and school improvement: an updated review of the British literature', in D. Reynolds and P. Cuttance (eds), *School Effectiveness*. London: Cassell.

Reynolds, D. (1993) 'Linking school effectiveness knowledge and school improvement practice', in C. Dimmock (ed.) *Leadership, School Based Decision Making and School Effectiveness*. London: Routledge and Kegan Paul.

Reynolds, D. and Cuttance, P. (eds) (1992) *School Effectiveness: Research, Policy and Practice*. London: Cassell.

Reynolds, D., Creemers, B. and Peters, T. (1989a) *School Effectiveness and Improvement: Proceedings of the First International Congress, London, 1988*. Groningen: University of Groningen, RION.

Reynolds, D., Davie, R. and Phillips, D. (1989b) 'The Cardiff programme — an effective school improvement programme based on school effectiveness research', *International Journal of Educational Research*, 13(7), 800-14.

Reynolds, D., Hopkins, D. and Stoll, L. (1993) 'Linking school effectiveness knowledge and school improvement practice: towards a synergy', *School Effectiveness and School Improvement*, 4(1), 37-58.

Reynolds, D., Sullivan, M. and Murgatroyd, S. J. (1987) *The Comprehensive Experiment*. Lewes: Falmer Press.

Rutter, M., Maughan, B., Mortimore, P. and Ouston, J. (1979) *Fifteen Thousand Hours: Secondary Schools and Their Effects on Children*. Wells: Open Books.

Scheerens, J., Vermeulen, C. J. and Pelgrum, W. J. (1989) 'Generalizability of school and instructional effectiveness indicators across nations', *International Journal of Educational Research*, 13(7), 789-99.

Smith, D. and Tomlinson, S. (1989) *The School Effect: A Study of Multi-Racial Comprehensives*. London: Policy Studies Institute.

Stoll, L. and Fink, D. (1989) 'An effective schools project: the Halton approach', in D. Reynolds, B. Creemers and T. Peters (eds), *School Effectiveness and Improvement*. Groningen: University of Groningen Press.

Stringfield, S. and Teddlie, C. (1990) 'School improvement efforts: qualitative and quantitative data from four naturally occurring experiments in Phases 3 and 4 of the Louisiana School Effectiveness Study', *School Effectiveness and School Improvement*, 1(2), 139-61.

Chapter 4

Findings from School Effectiveness Research: Some Implications for Improving the Quality of Schools

Pamela Sammons

INTRODUCTION

This chapter examines the methods and some of the main findings from a recent research study into school effectiveness and their implications for improving the quality of schools. The first section provides some background context, focusing on the increasing interest in measuring quality in education, evident among policy-makers and practitioners alike. Recent changes in legislation are noted and various definitions of quality are outlined. The second section describes some of the findings from studies of school effectiveness, and the way such findings can assist those concerned with developing systems to measure quality and monitor the performance of schools.

BACKGROUND

In the UK, schools have been subjected to a period of rapid and radical change as a result of the implementation of the provisions of the 1988 Education Reform Act (ERA). The introduction of a National Curriculum and associated teacher assessments (TAs) and externally monitored standard assessment tasks (SATS) for pupils at four Key Stages (at age 7, 11, 14 and 16 years) are beginning to have a major impact upon the content and processes of teaching and learning (what is taught, how it is taught and how it is assessed).

In addition, as with other public services, local education authorities (LEAs) and schools have been increasingly affected by public and government demands for greater accountability and freedom of information during the past decade (Tomlinson *et al.*, 1988). For example, the 1982 Local Government Finance Act requires the auditors appointed by the Audit Commission to satisfy themselves that authorities have made proper arrangements to secure 'the three Es, economy, efficiency and effectiveness in the use of resources'. However, in commenting on these 'three Es', Young (1990, p.7) has noted that their interpretation, particularly in education, is not always easy.

Desirable, and indeed simple as the criteria may appear to be, their meanings are complex and their use for auditing or managerial purposes is often problematic, indefinite and capable of different and conflicting interpretations ... in the provision of services like education, the last of the 'three Es', effectiveness, can be far more difficult to judge, since one cannot measure effectiveness with any precision against some sort of numerical scale.

More recently, Local Management of Schools (LMS) has been introduced in an attempt to ensure greater financial independence and accountability for individual schools. As with the other changes resulting from the ERA, such as the National Curriculum and national assessment, the government's stated aim is to improve the quality of education in schools. It is intended that LMS should be evaluated nationally and locally in order to assess 'the success of LEAs in implementing schemes' and of 'local management in raising the quality of education in schools' (DES, 1988, para.226).

Levacic (1990) has commented that, in evaluating the impact of LMS, predetermined goals can be investigated because the Government has made explicit its aims for this initiative:

To improve the quality of teaching and learning in schools....
Effective schemes of local management will enable governing bodies and headteachers to plan their use of resources ... to maximum effect in accordance with their own needs and priorities, and to make schools more responsive to their clients, parents, pupils, and the local community and employers. (DES, 1988, paras.9 and 10)

Recent legislation has given LEAs some specific responsibilities for the monitoring of the education service, particularly of schools (DES, 1988). The favoured term to describe the measures to be used to evaluate the performance of schools is performance indicators (PIs). 'A PI can be defined as an item of information collected at regular intervals to track the performance of a system' (Fitz-Gibbon, 1990, p.1). Much discussion has occurred among policy-makers, researchers and educational practitioners alike concerning the choice of PIs, their benefits, limitations and possible abuses or negative side-effects.

The collection and use of performance indicator information is intended to promote accountability, and to help to identify areas where improvement is required at a variety of levels: LEA, individual school or classroom. In order to be useful for planning and policy-making purposes indicators will need to be collected on a regular basis to allow the monitoring of changes over time. In addition, a consistent approach to PIs would need to be adopted by LEAs and individual schools if valid comparisons are to be made between different authorities or institutions.

Uncertainty over the future of LEAs arising out of proposals in the recent White Paper *Choice and Diversity* (DfE, 1992) will limit a coherent approach to the monitoring of school quality at the local level.

QUALITY AND SCHOOLS

The stated intention of the recent legislative changes is to improve the quality of schools. Although this aim may receive broad support, there is no consensus as to how the quality of schooling should be defined, and whether or how it can be measured. Even more controversy abounds as to how the quality of schooling may be improved. As Mortimore and Stone (1990, p. 69) commented, the question of how to measure educational quality is not new and is 'intimately bound up with more fundamental questions about the nature of education itself'. The concept of education as 'an essentially instrumental activity designed to bring about the achievement of specifiable and uncontroversial goals' was contrasted with a more 'Aristotelian' view of education practice 'as an essentially ethical activity guided by values which are open to continual debate and refinement by practitioners and others'.

Mortimore and Stone drew attention to the normative or comparative element implied by the term quality, noting that the term has been used as: an attribute or defining essence; a degree of relative worth; a description of something good or excellent; and a non-quantified trait. While recognizing the need to employ caution, Mortimore and Stone nevertheless argued that it is possible to discuss the educational quality of different components of the education system and that such discussion is necessary to ensure the important goal of accountability of the education service.

An OECD report entitled *Schools and Quality* (1989) discussed some of the issues involved in attempts to measure and improve quality. It concluded that

> The assessment of quality is thus complex and value laden. There is
> no simple uni-dimensional measure of quality. In the same way as
> the definition of what constitutes high quality in education is
> multi-dimensional, so there is no simple prescription of the
> ingredients necessary to achieve high quality education; many factors
> interact — students and their backgrounds; staff and their skills;
> schools and their structure and ethos; curricular; and societal
> expectations. (OECD, 1989, p.27)

School effectiveness research can help to disentangle and clarify such interactions, and because of this it has an important role to play in analysing the constituents of quality in education.

Likewise, Lagerweij and Voogt (1990) have stated that the concept of quality of education cannot be easily defined in a clear and exact manner. They noted that 'any definition of quality should be expected to change over time, because it necessarily reflects a society's interpretation of educational needs and the intensity of its moral and financial commitment to fulfilling them' (p.100). In addition, they commented that 'Judgements about quality can refer to different, but closely related aspects, for example: the goals or functions, the contents, the processes, the effect and the conditions or means' (p.100), and discussed some of the ways educational improvement may be directed to one or more of these aspects.

INCREASED VARIABILITY IN SCHOOL QUALITY

Reynolds (1991) predicted that the 1990s will see an increase in the influence that schools have over the development of young people. He suggested that a variety of factors would be responsible for this phenomenon (e.g. the integration of children with special educational needs, concern to keep troublesome, delinquent or disturbed children in ordinary schools and the policy of decentralization of power within the education system down to the level of the individual school). Reynolds argued that the result of such changes, in the short term at least, is likely to be

> a substantial increase in the variation in their quality between individual schools. . . . the huge additional range of powers, roles and responsibilities that will fall upon schools and particularly upon their principals or headteachers, will also increase school variability substantially. Schools will also differ markedly in their ability to cope with rapid externally induced change. (Reynolds, 1991, p.5)

He pointed out that the Government's intention in Britain is that the major mechanism of quality control will be locally determined market mechanisms of parental choice: 'schools judged by parents to be ineffective will rapidly lose pupil numbers and will eventually shut' (p.5). He argued that in the long term this may reduce the variation between schools in their quality. Such a view may well prove to be unduly optimistic, however, since the extent to which parents in reality are able to exercise choice will vary much in different geographical localities (e.g. depending upon the existence of alternative schools and their accessibility) and in the availability of appropriate information upon which to make informed choices.

There is growing evidence from research into choice of secondary schools that parents vary in the way they choose schools, and in the extent of the child's involvement in the decision. For example, in a survey of parents West and Varlaam (1991) found that the four factors most frequently mentioned as important (without prompting) when choosing a secondary school were: the child wanting to go there, good discipline, emphasis on good examination results and ease of access. Three-quarters of parents said there were particular schools to which they did not want their child to go — the predominant reason given was 'its bad reputation'.

The extent to which parents' knowledge and judgements of quality and effectiveness are based on up-to-date and accurate information is open to question. School reputations may rest upon past circumstances and bear little relation to the current situation, for example. Particular difficulties surround the use of information about pupils' academic achievement (as demonstrated through examination or test results) as a measure of the quality of schools. Unless information about schools' examination or test results is presented in context and takes account of the 'value added' by the school (by taking account of differences between schools in the pupils taught, in terms of background factors and prior attainment at intake) it is likely to be misleading (see Mortimore et al., 1988a, c; Gray, 1990; Nuttall, 1990; Sammons et al., 1993). In the absence of a strong commitment to provision of *useful and usable* information for parents (Tomlinson, Mortimore and Sammons, 1988), it seems unlikely that reliance on the market mechanism of parental choice will lead to improvements in the quality of schools.

Secondary schools have been required to publish their 'raw' (i.e. not adjusted for intake and prior attainment) public examination results since 1981. Under the ERA, LEAs are required to publish National Curriculum assessment results. There is no requirement to take account of intake, although schools may provide details about their intakes as contextual information.

In commenting on parental choice of schools and possible problems arising from the intention to publish National Curriculum assessment results, Nuttall (1990, p. 25) argued that

> insofar as the initiative is to increase the accountability of schools, natural justice demands that schools are held accountable only for those things that they can influence (for good or ill), and not for all the pre-existing differences between their intakes. The investigation of differential school effectiveness, concentrating on the progress students make while at that school, therefore has a major role to play in future.

SCHOOL EFFECTIVENESS RESEARCH

During the past two decades much research was conducted into the field of school effects or school effectiveness in the search for ways of creating effective schools (see reviews by Gray, 1981; Purkey and Smith, 1983; US Department of Education, 1986; Reynolds, 1989; Mortimore, 1991a). The terms school effects and school effectiveness are sometimes used interchangeably. However, most commonly school effects refers to the impact particular schools have on their pupils' educational outcomes, taking account of differences in intake, whereas school effectiveness refers to studies of the factors and processes related to positive or negative effects on such outcomes. An effective school is one that has a positive effect upon its pupils' educational outcomes, when account is taken of intake.

Research into ways of measuring the quality of schools has a number of advantages, as Mortimore and Stone (1991) have argued. As a way of identifying components of educational quality, research is superior to other methods. This is because its methods should be public and can be examined for bias, and its scope is very broad. While the idea of perfectly value-free research is now recognized as something of a myth, there are well-tried methods of limiting bias and of guarding against systematic distortion of evidence-gathering techniques. Perhaps the most potent aspect of research, as opposed to other ways of gathering information, is that its methods are stated publicly and are open to critical scrutiny.

Although the cost of research and the time needed to conduct the necessary longitudinal surveys of pupil progress mean that it is not a practical way to assess individual schools on a regular basis, the results of research, its techniques and instruments have much to offer those concerned with school improvement, school self-evaluation and the development of performance indicators for schools.

Educational goals for students — criteria for measuring quality

Ron Edmonds (Edmonds 1979a, b, 1982) has been much concerned with school effectiveness research and improving the quality of schooling in the USA. He has stated that the major aim of schools should be *educational excellence*, which he defined as meaning that students become independent, creative thinkers and learn to work co-operatively. Edmonds (1982, p.14) made a particular point of emphasizing student mastery of basic skills. John Goodlad (1984) has also proposed a variety of different goals for education. These are much broader than a narrow focus on basic skills, and include:

- academic development;
- intellectual development;
- vocational goals;
- social, civic and cultural goals;
- personal goals.

If the need to strive for educational excellence and the importance of the different goals noted above are accepted, then the findings of research that attempts to increase our understanding of how schools influence their students, and what promotes their progress and development, need careful consideration.

As noted earlier, several extensive reviews of school effectiveness literature exist. In this chapter the main focus of attention is on the findings of the Inner London Education Authority's Junior School Project (JSP) (Mortimore *et al.*, 1986, 1988b). There are several reasons for looking at this study in some depth:

- it is the largest piece of school effectiveness research undertaken to date either in the UK or in North America;
- it examined a much broader range of pupils' educational outcomes than previous studies, avoiding a narrow focus on basic skills alone;
- the results support and confirm many earlier findings about school effectiveness;
- the results also extend our knowledge of what contributes to effectiveness in several important ways;
- in contrast to most previous studies, it examined both factors to do with the school as a whole and those to do with the teachers' classroom practices, and shows how these relate to student outcomes;
- the study demonstrates the methodology of school effectiveness research clearly, utilizing data about individual pupils, their teachers, classes and schools at the appropriate level;
- it makes clear the need to ensure that judgements of effectiveness of schools are based on appropriate comparisons of 'like with like', by taking full account of intake.

Similarities between the JSP findings and those produced by other research are discussed later in this chapter.

THE ILEA JUNIOR SCHOOL PROJECT

The Project begin in September 1980 when an age cohort of nearly 2000 seven-year-olds entered their junior classes, and concluded four years later when the students transferred to secondary school. The students attended a random sample of fifty schools in inner London.

Aims

The Project was designed to produce a detailed description of the students, teachers, curriculum and organization of schools in an inner city area. It attempted to answer three major questions.

1 Are some schools more effective than others in promoting students' learning and development, when account is taken of variations in the students' backgrounds?

2 Are some schools more effective than others for particular groups of children (for girls or boys, for those of different social class origins, or different racial backgrounds)?

3 If some schools are more effective than others, what factors contribute to such positive effects?

Information about students, schools and teachers

In order to answer the above questions information was collected on three major topics: students' background characteristics; students' learning and development; and school characteristics. These provided measures of the student *intakes* to schools; measures of students' *educational outcomes*; and measures of school and classroom *processes*.

Intakes Considerable evidence exists, from a strong tradition of educational research, of the importance of socio-economic and family background factors as influences upon pupils' educational achievements at all stages of their school careers (see, for example, Douglas, 1964; Davie *et al.*, 1972; Rutter and Madge, 1976; Hutchison *et al.*, 1979; Essen and Wedge, 1982; Mortimore and Blackstone, 1982; Sammons *et al.*, 1983). Detailed information was obtained for each child about: sex, age, social, ethnic, language and family background; pre-school and infant school experiences; and initial attainments at entry to junior school. These data were needed so that the study could: establish the impact of such background factors on students' attainments, progress and development; take into account differences between schools in intakes; quantify the relative importance of school compared with background as influences upon students; and explore the effectiveness of schooling for different groups.

Outcomes The second set of information is related to students' learning and development. Reynolds and Creemers (1990, p.2) have noted that 'In certain countries the school effectiveness movement has already become associated with a narrow, back-to-basics orientation for the teaching of basic skills'. Such a narrow focus is inappropriate because the goals of education, teachers' aims and objectives for pupils' learning and the curriculum are much broader than a concern with the 'three Rs' alone.

The JSP study focused on more than attainment in 'basic skill' areas, important though these are. To take account of the diversity of aims and curricula of primary education a wide range of outcomes was examined. In addition to reading and written maths, practical maths skills and visuo-spatial skills were assessed. Creative writing was assessed using measures that included the quality of language and ideas, as well as more technical aspects. To broaden the assessments of language, students' speaking skills were also studied. Oracy assessments focused on the ability to communicate effectively, and children were not penalized for using non-standard English.

Of equal interest to those concerned with the quality of education are non-cognitive or social outcomes of education, which have tended to be neglected in previous studies of school differences and effects. Information was obtained about students' attendance, their behaviour in school, their attitudes to school and to different types of school activities, and their self-concepts (including their perceptions of themselves as learners) in school.

Processes The third set of information is related to the characteristics of the schools, their organization and numerous aspects of the learning environment experienced by students. A wide variety of information was collected and the areas covered included the following: aims and philosophy of schools, aims and philosophy of class teacher, organization of school and policies, rewards and punishments (school), organization of classrooms, curriculum, structure of teaching, rewards and punishment (class), teacher-student communication, support services, books and resources, school appearance and classroom appearance.

Interviews (with headteachers and their deputies, class teachers, special needs teachers and parents), observations (of classrooms over a three-year period, and of the school environment) and questionnaires (with headteachers, deputy headteachers, teachers and students) were used to collect these data. Field officers also made detailed observations and kept extensive field notes of teachers and students in the classroom setting.

Measuring school effects

The analysis of all these data was complex, and various statistical techniques, particularly multi-level modelling (see Goldstein, 1987) were employed. The intention was to find out what impact schools had on their students' progress and development, once account was taken of their attainment at entry to junior school, and of the influences of age, sex and other background factors. It was possible to analyse student progress because the Project was longitudinal. By studying the progress of individual students account could be taken of the very

Table 4.1 *Differences between schools in students' attainment at entry (n = 50)*

	Reading skills	Maths skills	Visuo-spatial skills
Average score all schools	45.5	24.1	24.4
School with highest average score at entry	62.6	29.3	31.1
School with lowest average score at entry	17.3	18.3	19.4
Maximum possible score	91	42	40

different levels of skill possessed by children at entry to junior school. For each student, therefore, her or his initial attainment at entry was the baseline against which progress during later years was measured (Sammons, 1989).

The influence of background factors and school differences in intake

Strong relationships between background factors (especially age, social class and low income, sex and ethnic background) and students' attainments and development and, to a lesser extent, their progress during the junior years were found (Mortimore *et al.*, 1986, Part A). These differences were already marked at age 7 at entry to junior school. Full account, therefore, had to be taken of these relationships before schools' effects on their students could be examined.

Children's attainment in any particular basic skill area (e.g. reading, maths, writing) at entry to junior school was found to be a good predictor of their attainment in that area several years later. This is as might be expected, since those who are good readers at entry tend to remain good readers as they grow older (though it was also found that some children made more or less progress than might be predicted, given their attainment at entry).

Even at entry to junior school at age 7, there were very marked differences between individual students in their attainment in basic skills (well over a two year gap in reading ages among the year group, for example). Moreover, some schools received intakes that contained students who had a much higher average attainment than other schools (see Table 4.1). These figures on differences in intake demonstrate why in studying school effectiveness it is essential to focus on the concept of 'value added' by looking at student progress individually (for further details of this argument see Mortimore *et al.*, 1988a; McPherson, 1992). Unfortunately, the importance of the 'value added' concept has not been recognized in the legislation concerning the publication of National Curriculum assessment results for individual schools and classes. Without recognition of the impact of intake (especially prior attainment of pupils) the publication of 'raw' results will not provide a useful guide to the quality of schools. In fact, such results are likely to prove highly *misleading* because schools with advantaged intakes will appear to be successful, irrespective of their actual contribution to pupil progress.

In contrast, focusing on value added means that schools can be classified as effective whatever the absolute level of advantage/disadvantage of their pupil intake. Schools serving very *disadvantaged* populations can be highly effective. Similarly, schools serving very advantaged populations can fail to be effective and can foster underachievement amongst their pupils (Mortimore, 1991a).

School effects

Even after controlling for students' initial attainment at entry and for background factors, the JSP data show that the school made an important contribution to students' progress and development. In terms of the first question asked, it was found that schools *did* make a substantial difference to their students' progress and development. In fact, for many of the educational outcomes — especially progress in cognitive areas — the school was very much more important than background factors in accounting for variations between individuals. Analyses of students' oracy (speaking skills) and of the social outcomes (attendance, attitudes, behaviour etc.) confirmed the overriding importance of school.

The size of the effects of each of the sample schools on each of the measures of their pupils' educational outcomes was calculated. The differences were striking. For example, for reading the most effective school improved a student's attainment by an average of 15 points above that predicted by that child's attainment when he or she started junior school, taking into account her or his background. But in the least effective school, each child's attainment was, on average, 10 points lower than predicted. This compares with an overall average reading score for all students of 54 points, and a maximum possible of 100.

It was also important to establish whether some schools were *generally more effective* in promoting a broad range of educational outcomes than others. The results showed that a sizeable number of schools (fourteen in all) had positive effects on students' progress and development in most of the cognitive and most of the non-cognitive outcomes. These can be seen as the generally effective schools. In contrast, five schools were rather ineffective in most areas. Many schools were effective in a few, but not all, areas. However, there were very few schools that only had positive impacts on cognitive areas, but were unsuccessful at fostering non-cognitive development, or vice versa.

The findings demonstrate that schools often vary in their effectiveness in promoting different educational outcomes and this needs to be taken into account in any attempts to measure or improve the quality of schools. It is not appropriate, therefore, to divide institutions into simple categories of 'good' or 'bad'.

School effects on different groups

It was also possible to compare the effects of schools on the progress of different groups of students. Generally, for any particular outcome, schools that were effective in promoting the progress of one group of students were also effective for other groups, and those that were less effective for one group were also less effective for others. Thus, a school that was effective for boys was also effective for girls, one that was effective for a child from a non-manual worker's family was also effective for one from a working-class family. An effective school tended to 'jack up' the performance of all its students irrespective of their sex, social class origins or race. A recent re-analysis of the JSP data confirmed the original findings, although some evidence of differential effectiveness for pupils with different levels of prior attainment (an area not covered in the original study) was found; see Sammons et al., 1993. Moreover, the evidence indicates that although overall differences in attainment were not removed, on average a student from a working-class family attending one of the more effective schools ended up attaining more highly than one from a non-manual family attending one of the least effective schools.

Other more recent studies have suggested that there may be some differences within secondary schools in their effects on the examination results of particular groups (see Aitkin and Longford, 1986; Nuttall et al., 1989). The question of *differential effectiveness* is clearly of importance to those concerned with promoting equal opportunities and improving the quality of schooling for *all* pupils.

Understanding school effectiveness

The results of the JSP indicate that the particular school attended can make a substantial difference to the future educational prospects of individual students. Given this, the third question addressed by the Project is crucially important. What makes some schools more effective than others? In order to answer the third question it was necessary to establish what *factors* and *processes* were related to positive school effects. In other words, the aim was to identify the ways in which the more effective schools differed from those that were less effective.

A wide variety of process variables about the school as a whole, and ones specifically concerning individual classrooms, were investigated. These were divided into 'givens' and 'policies'. The 'givens' are aspects not directly under the control of the school (e.g. the size of its student roll, intake, stability of staff, pupil mobility). The policies, in contrast, are aspects that can be altered by the school (e.g. the headteacher's style of leadership, curriculum, the rewards and punishment system, organization, staff involvement and conditions). At the level of the individual classroom there are also a variety of 'givens' not under the direct control of the teacher (e.g. the size of the class, the composition of students in terms of balance of age, sex or ability, the resources available etc.). But many policy factors are under the class teacher's direct control (e.g. record-keeping, the system of rewards and punishments, the use of praise, the amount and type of communication with students, preparation and planning etc.).

Analyses indicated that much of the variation between schools in their effects on students' progress and development was accounted for by differences between schools in their policies and practices. Furthermore, a number of the significant variables were themselves associated. By a detailed examination of the ways in which classroom and school processes were interrelated, it was possible to gain a greater understanding of some of the important *mechanisms* by which effective education may be promoted.

Key factors for effective junior schooling

The JSP analyses identified a number of key factors that are important in accounting for the differential effectiveness of schools. These factors are not purely statistical constructs. They were not obtained solely by means of quantitative analysis but from a combination of careful examination and discussion of the statistical findings, and the use of educational and research judgement. They represent the interpretation of the research results by an interdisciplinary team of researchers and teachers.

Some schools were more advantaged in terms of their size, status, environment and stability of teaching staff. There was evidence that smaller schools tended to be more effective than larger ones. Class size is particularly relevant; smaller classes with less than 24 students (the average in the sample was 25, with a range of 16 to 34), had a positive association with student progress in maths, attainment in speaking skills, student behaviour, attitudes to school and self-concept, especially for progress in the earlier years (ages 7 to 9).

A good physical environment creates a positive location in which progress and development can be fostered. The stability of the school's teaching force is also important. Changes of headteacher and deputy headteacher, though inevitable in all schools at some stage, have an unsettling effect. Similarly, changes of class teacher *during* the school year had an adverse impact on students' progress and development. Gray (1990, p.213) has also drawn attention to the importance of adequate resources and the absence of staffing difficulties: 'Adequate levels of resourcing, then, seem to be a necessary but not a sufficient condition for a school to be effective . . . in twenty years of reading research on the characteristics of effective schools I have only once come across a record of an "excellent" school where the physical environment left something to be desired.'

None the less, although these favourable 'given' characteristics contribute to effectiveness, it appears that they do not, by themselves, ensure it. They provide a supporting framework within which the headteacher and teachers can work to promote student progress and development. The research suggests that it is the policies and processes within the control of the headteacher and teachers that are crucial. These are the factors that can be changed and improved.

Twelve key factors of effectiveness were identified (see Mortimore *et al.*, 1988a, for details):

1 Purposeful leadership of the staff by the headteacher.

2 The involvement of the deputy headteacher.

3 The involvement of teachers.

4 Consistency among teachers.

5 Structured sessions.

6 Intellectually challenging teaching.

7 Work-centred environment.

8 Limited focus within sessions.

9 Maximum communication between teachers and students.

10 Record-keeping.

11 Parental involvement.

12 Positive climate.

The first three factors concern the organization of the school and, in particular, relate to the quality of leadership of the headteacher and his or her management style. They point to the value of staff involvement in decisions. The fourth factor concerns the value of a 'whole-school' approach to the curriculum, with consistency among staff in the use of guidelines.

Factors 5 to 9 relate to the teacher's classroom behaviour, including the organization of pupils' work, the nature and level of communication with pupils, and the value of creating a work-centred environment and a limited focus within sessions. Recent work by Alexander (1992), conducted as part of the evaluation of the Leeds Primary Needs Programme, has provided confirmation of some of the JSP findings. Alexander (1992) has drawn attention to the advantages of maximizing communication with pupils, and to difficulties in managing a work-centred environment in classrooms where work in more than one curriculum area is organized in the same session.

The importance of the teacher's record-keeping was highlighted by the research (factor 10), as was the value of parental involvement in children's learning at home, in the school and as classroom helpers. The last factor drew attention to the benefits of a positive climate or ethos in the classroom and around the school. A positive climate appeared to be reflected in effective schools by happy, well-behaved students who were friendly towards each other and outsiders, and by the absence of graffiti.

From a detailed examination of the factors and processes that were related to schools' effects on their students, a picture evolves of what contributed towards effective education. In particular, twelve 'key factors' have been identified. The twelve factors identified by the research do not constitute a 'recipe' for effective schooling and should not be applied in a mechanistic way. It is important to remember that schools are not static institutions and that the JSP research took place prior to the changes surrounding the introduction of the National Curriculum. None the less, the findings do provide a framework within which the various partners in the life of the school — headteacher and staff, parents and students, and the community — can operate and on which they can build towards improvement.

LINKS WITH OTHER STUDIES OF SCHOOL EFFECTIVENESS

A detailed review of the links between the JSP findings and those of other studies of school effectiveness appears in Mortimore et al. (1986, 1988c). This section draws particular attention to similarities with an earlier major study of secondary schooling.

The Fifteen Thousand Hours study examined the educational outcomes of students attending twelve inner London secondary schools. The research design was similar to that used in the later JSP. Four measures of student outcome were studied: behaviour in school; attendance; examination success; and delinquency. The results revealed that there were marked differences between schools in all these outcomes, even when account was taken of differences in the pupil intakes. A number of specific aspects of school process were found to be especially important. These included the academic emphasis, leadership of the headteacher, teacher actions in lessons, the use of rewards and punishments, student conditions, student responsibility and participation, staff organization, and the skills of teachers.

The items found to contribute to an 'academic emphasis' in the Fifteen Thousand Hours study included the setting of homework by teachers (and checks by senior staff that this occurred), high teacher expectations for students, displays of students' work in classrooms and around the school, more teacher time devoted to teaching, group planning of courses by teachers and regular use of the library by students. The JSP also highlighted the importance of high teacher expectations of students and the value of intellectually challenging teaching, a work-centred classroom environment with more teacher and student time on task, the involvement of teachers in developing curriculum guidelines and consistency in their use throughout the school.

There was agreement between the two studies on the importance of teacher actions in lessons. Both found that more teacher time spent communicating about work and less time on administration was beneficial. Good time-keeping (starting lessons on time and not finishing them early), planning and organization by the teacher were also found to be important. Another similarity was the positive impact of teacher time spent communicating with the whole class. The Fifteen Thousand Hours team concluded that if teachers spent too much time focusing on individuals, they tended to lose the attention of the class as a whole. The JSP also found that teachers who spent too high a proportion of time communicating with individuals spent more time on supervising and management comments and less time on work matters. It went further by pointing out that the use of a balance of whole class and individual communication maximized the *overall level of teacher-student communication* that occurred during lessons. Findings on the value of a greater emphasis on rewards and the use of praise in class for good work and behaviour by the Fifteen Thousand Hours team were also confirmed by the JSP. It can be concluded that students benefit from teacher actions that focus on *positive* rather than negative aspects of their work and behaviour.

Links between measures of the quality of the school's physical environment and student outcomes are also noteworthy. Both studies found that a pleasant, well-cared-for environment had a positive impact. In addition, the two studies point to the value of organizing extra-curricular activities for students (educational visits and trips, lunch-time and after-school clubs etc.).

The key role of the headteacher in providing purposeful leadership and in fostering school effectiveness was identified in the JSP. The importance of the quality of leadership given to the school by the headteacher, and his or her actions in developing the school's climate and goals, had also been demonstrated by Fifteen Thousand Hours. Both studies indicate that the school's climate or ethos has a significant role in creating effective education (see also Sammons, 1987).

CONCLUSIONS

The findings of school effectiveness research consistently demonstrate that schools can make a difference to their students' educational outcomes, and that the difference can be substantial. The JSP finding of the existence of substantial differences between schools in their effects upon student progress has been supported by later studies of infant and secondary schools (Tizard *et al.*, 1988; Smith and Tomlinson, 1989). They also provide a guide to what factors about schools and about classroom practice help to make that difference. In other words, it is possible to begin to explain *why* some schools are more effective than others.

An examination of the links between two major studies of school effectiveness reveals many areas of agreement. The findings of the JSP support many of those of the Fifteen Thousand Hours study, suggesting that the mechanisms and processes which lead to greater effectiveness are of general applicability. The consistency in the findings gives greater confidence in using them to develop programmes for school improvement and self-evaluation (see Stoll and Fink, 1989). It is stressed, however, that they should not be used as a way of holding individual schools to account.

In a recent contribution to the debate about appropriate frameworks for judging the quality of schooling, Gray (1990, p.214) commented on current research on school effectiveness and factors that make a difference:

> In general terms it provides a relatively good introductory guide to the factors that make a difference. As a rule, schools which do the kinds of things the research suggests make a difference, tend to get better results (however these are measured or assessed). The problem is that these are tendencies not certainties. In betting terms the research would be right about seven out of ten times, especially if it could be supported by professional assessments.

Because of this he also cautioned that school effectiveness research should not be treated as a blueprint for success (in line with the views of Mortimore *et al.*, 1988c, and Reynolds and Creemers, 1990).

The findings of school effectiveness research have sometimes been criticized for being just a matter of 'common-sense'. There is a grain of truth in this argument. Because school effectiveness research by its very nature sets out to identify the components of good practice that is already occurring in many schools, it is inevitable that some of the findings are unsurprising to practitioners. Renihan *et al.* (1986, p.17) noted that 'The effective schools literature did not tell us anything startlingly revolutionary about organizing the school environment. Its major impact lay in highlighting factors vital to school success'. Similarly, Rutter *et al.* (1979, p.204) concluded that 'Research into practical issues, such as schooling, rarely comes up with findings which are totally unexpected. On the other hand, it is helpful in showing which of the abundance of good ideas available are related to successful outcomes.'

Recently it has been suggested that the many changes schools are currently experiencing (particularly through LMS and the National Curriculum) mean that findings from school effectiveness research conducted in the 1970s and 1980s will be less relevant for improving practice and the quality of education during the 1990s (Reynolds, 1990). This conclusion is, however, open to question. The findings from studies such as the JSP and Fifteen Thousand Hours have demonstrated the importance of factors relating to overall school policy and individual teachers' classroom organization and practice rather than particular features of the curriculum.

Although it is likely that headteachers' roles may change following LMS, it is unlikely that their importance in fostering a common sense of purpose (a school mission), staff involvement and a positive school climate will diminish. As Gray (1990) commented, the importance of the head's leadership role is one of the clearest of the messages from school effectiveness research. Similarly, although there are changes to curriculum and assessment, factors such as a work-centred environment, intellectually challenging teaching, maximum communication with pupils and good record-keeping are likely to continue to be important in promoting pupils' progress and development.

School improvement has been described as 'a systematic, sustained effort aimed at changing learning conditions and other related internal conditions in one or more schools, with the ultimate aim of accomplishing educational goals more effectively' (Van Velzen et al., 1985, p.48). I believe that the methodology developed for school effectiveness research, particularly the focus on progress or 'value added' and the recognition of the importance of school intake, has an important contribution to make to the development of appropriate and valid performance indicators for schools. If such methodology is ignored there is a real danger that simplistic indicators will be used, which will result in unfair and misleading comparisons of the quality of institutions (McPherson, 1992). In particular, I believe that school effectiveness research clearly demonstrates that the policy of publishing schools' 'raw' examination and National Curriculum assessment results will do nothing to improve the quality of schooling. On the contrary, it is likely to damage the reputations of institutions in disadvantaged communities in particular.

School effectiveness research methods offer a more appropriate basis for judging the quality of schools. The findings of such research should not be regarded as prescriptive, however. Rather they are a useful background for school self-evaluation and the development of school improvement programmes, which should be tailored to the needs of specific institutions.

Few programmes of school improvement have, as yet, been based directly on school effectiveness research (for an exception see Toews and Barker, 1985). However, an interesting example of the way the JSP and Fifteen Thousand Hours findings have been used to develop a practical school improvement programme in Ontario, Canada, has been described by Stoll and Fink (1989, 1991). Mortimore (1991b) has also proposed a number of postulates concerning ways of improving schools based on the results of school effectiveness research.

Many factors influence the extent to which schools can be successful in implementing change (see Fullan, 1988). The extent to which schools are able to set their own goals and priorities for improvement is important as are the extent of external changes and pressures affecting schools. The introduction of the

National Curriculum and assessment, LMS and other educational reforms may well absorb much of the energy and commitment of schools and their staff, which are required for the successful development and implementation of improvement programmes. A whole school approach to improvement and the active involvement of staff in the development of an improvement plan and its implementation are essential if the goal of improving the quality of schooling is to be achieved.

REFERENCES

Aitkin, M. and Longford, N. (1986) 'Statistical modelling issues in school effectiveness studies', *Journal of the Royal Statistical Society, Series A*, 149, 1-43.

Alexander, R. (1992) *Policy and Practice in Primary Education*. London: Routledge.

Davie, R., Butler, N. and Goldstein, H. (1972) *From Birth to Seven*. London: Longman.

DES (1988) *Circular 7/88 Education Reform Act: Local Management of Schools*. London: HMSO.

DfE (1992) *Choice and Diversity: A New Framework for Schools*. London: DfE.

Douglas, J. W. B. (1964) *The Home and the School*. London: MacGibbon & Kee.

Edmonds, R. R. (1979a) 'Effective schools for the urban poor', *Educational Leadership*, 37(1), 15-27.

Edmonds, R. R. (1979b) 'Some schools work and more can', *Social Policy*, 12(2), 56-60.

Edmonds, R. R. (1982) 'Programs of school improvement, an overview', *Educational Leadership*, 40(3), 4-11 (and interview, p. 14).

Essen, J. and Wedge, P. (1982) *Continuities in Childhood Disadvantage*. London: Heinemann.

Fitz-Gibbon, C. T. (ed.) (1990) 'Performance indicators', in *BERA Dialogues No. 2*. Clevedon: Multilingual Matters.

Fullan, M. (1988) *Change Processes in Secondary Schools: Towards a More Fundamental Agenda*. The University of Toronto (mimeo).

Goldstein, H. (1987) *Multilevel Models in Educational and Social Research*. London: Griffin; New York: Oxford University Press.

Goodlad, J. I. (1984) *A Place Called School*. New York: McGraw-Hill.

Gray, J. (1981) 'A competitive edge, examination results and the probable limits of secondary school effectiveness', *Educational Review*, 33(1) 25-35.

Gray, J. (1990) 'The quality of schooling: frameworks for judgement', *British Journal of Educational Studies*, 38(3), 204-23.

Gray, J and Hannon, V. (1986) 'HMI's interpretation of school examination results', *Journal of Education Policy*, 1(1), 23-33.

Hutchison, D., Prosser, H. and Wedge, P. (1979) 'The prediction of educational failure', *Educational Studies*, 5(1), 73-82.

Jencks, C. S. et al. (1972) *Inequality. A Reassessment of the Effect of Family and Schooling in America*. New York: Basic Books.

Lagerweij, N. A. J. and Voogt, J. C. (1990) 'Policy at school level', *School Effectiveness and School Improvement*, 1(2), 98-120.

Levacic, R. (1990) 'Evaluating local management of schools: establishing a methodological framework', in R. Saran and V. Trafford (eds), *Research in Education Management and Policy: Retrospect and Prospect*. Lewes: Falmer Press.

McPherson, A. (1992) 'Measuring added value in schools', *National Commission on Education Briefing No. 1*. February.

Miles, M. B. and Ekholm, M. (1985) 'School improvement at the school level', in *Making School Improvement Work*. Leuven: ACCO.

Mortimore, P. (1991a) 'The nature and findings of school effectiveness in the primary sector', in S. Riddell and S. Brown (eds), *School Effectiveness Research: Its Messages for School Improvement*. London: HMSO.

Mortimore, P. (1991b) 'School effectiveness research: which way at the crossroads?', paper presented at the Fourth International Congress for School Effectiveness and Improvement, Cardiff.

Mortimore, J. and Blackstone, T. (1982) *Disadvantage in Education*. London: Heinemann.

Mortimore, P., Sammons, P., Stoll, L., Lewis, D. and Ecob, R., (1986) *The ILEA Junior School Projects Parts A, B, C and Technical Appendices*. London: Research and Statistics Branch, ILEA.

Mortimore, P., Sammons, P. and Ecob, R. (1988a) 'Expressing the magnitude of school effects — a reply to Peter Preece', *Research Papers in Education*, 3(2), 99-101.

Mortimore, P., Sammons, P., Stoll, L., Ecob, R. and Lewis, D. (1988b) 'The effects of school membership on pupils' educational outcomes', *Research Papers in Education*, 3(1), 3-26.

Mortimore, P., Sammons, P., Stoll, L., Lewis, D. and Ecob, R. (1988c) *A School Matters: The Junior Years*. Wells: Open Books.

Mortimore, P. and Stone, C. (1990) 'Measuring educational quality', *British Journal of Educational Studies*, 39(1), 69-82.

Nuttall, D., Goldstein, H., Prosser, R. and Rasbash, J. (1989) 'Differential school effectiveness', *International Journal of Educational Research*, 13, 769-76.

Nuttall, D. L. (1990) *Differences in Examination Performance RS 1277/90*. London: ILEA.

OECD (1989) *Schools and Quality. An International Report*. Paris: OECD.

Purkey, S. C. and Smith, M. S. (1983) 'Effective schools, a review', *Elementary School Journal*, 83(4), 427-52.

Renihan, P. J. *et al.* (1986) 'The common ingredients of successful school effectiveness projects', *Education Canada*, Fall, 16-21.

Reynolds, D. (1982) 'The search for effective schools', *School Organization*, 2(3), 215-37.

Reynolds, D. (ed.) (1985) *Studying School Effectiveness*. Basingstoke: Falmer Press.

Reynolds, D. (1989) 'School effectiveness and school improvement: a review of the British literature', in D. Reynolds, B. P. M. Creemers and T. Peters (eds), *School Effectiveness and Improvement. Proceedings of First International Congress*. Gronigen: RION Institute of Educational Research.

Reynolds, D. (1991) 'School effectiveness and school improvement in the 1990s', *Association for Child Psychology and Psychiatry Newsletter*, 13(2), 5-9.

Reynolds, D. and Creemers, B. (1990) 'School effectiveness and school improvement: a mission statement', *School Effectiveness and School Improvement*, 1(1), 1-3.

Rutter, M., Maughan, B., Mortimore, P. and Ouston, J. (1979) *Fifteen Thousand Hours*. London: Open Books.

Rutter, M. and Madge, N. (1976) *Cycles of Disadvantage*. London: Heinemann.

Sammons, P. (1987) 'School climate, the key to fostering student progress and development?', paper presented to the Annual Convention of the Prince Edward Island Teachers' Federation on 'School Atmosphere, the Barometer of Success', 29-30 October, Charlottetown, Prince Edward Island, Canada.

Sammons, P. (1989) 'Measuring school effectiveness', in D. Reynolds, B. P. M. Creemers and T. Peters (eds), *School Effectiveness and Improvement*. Cardiff: School of Education, University of Wales College of Cardiff; Gronigen: RION Institute of Educational Research.

Sammons, P., Kysel, F. and Mortimore, P. (1983) 'Educational policy indices: a new perspective', *British Educational Research Journal*, 9(1), 27-40.

Sammons, P., Nuttall, D. and Cuttance, P. (1993) 'Differential school effectiveness: results from a reanalysis of the ILEA's Junior School Project data', *British Educational Research Journal* (forthcoming).

Smith, D. and Tomlinson, S. (1989) *The School Effect: A Study of Multi-racial Comprehensives*. London: Policy Studies Institute.

Stoll, L. and Fink, D. (1989) 'Implementing an effective schools project: the Halton approach', paper presented at the International Congress for School Effectiveness, Rotterdam.

Stoll, L. and Fink, D. (1991) 'Effecting school change: the Halton approach', paper presented at the Fourth Annual Conference of the International Congress of School Effectiveness and School Improvement, Cardiff.

Tizard, B., Blatchford, P., Burke, J., Farquhar, C. and Plewis, I. (1988) *Young Children at School in the Inner City*. Hove: Lawrence Erlbaum Associates.

Toews, J. and Barker, D. M. (1985) *The Baz Attack. A School Improvement Experience Utilizing Effective Schools Research 1981-1985*. Alberta: Ian Bazalgette Junior High School.

Tomlinson, J., Mortimore, P. and Sammons, P. (1988) 'Freedom and education: ways of increasing openness and accountability', Sheffield Papers in Education Management 76, Sheffield City Polytechnic.

United States Department of Education (1986) *What Works. Research about Teaching and Learning*. Washington, DC: United States Department of Education.

Van Velzen, W. G., Miles, M. B., Ekholm, M. *et al.* (1985) *Making School Improvement Work.* Leuven: ACCO.

West, A. and Varlaam, A. (1991) 'Choosing a secondary school: parents of junior school children', *Educational Research*, 33(1), 22-30.

Young, P. (1990) 'The Audit Commission and accountability', in R. Saran and V. Trafford (eds), *Research in Education Management and Policy: Retrospect and Prospect.* Lewes: Falmer Press.

Chapter 5

The Learning School

Geoff Southworth

Schools can be called many things. Some speak of the excellent school (Beare *et al.*, 1989), others write about the effective school (Mortimore *et al.*, 1988; Reynolds and Cuttance, 1992), the self-managing school (Caldwell and Spinks, 1992) or the empowered school (Hargreaves and Hopkins, 1991). It seems there is no shortage of titles for schools to adopt. At the risk of adding to these school types I want to suggest that staff in all schools should strive to make theirs a learning school.

CHARACTERISTICS OF A LEARNING SCHOOL

The idea of the learning school has been promoted by several writers (Holly and Southworth, 1989; Jenkins, 1991). Peter Holly and I adopted this term because our work with teachers told us that just as there can be no curriculum development without teacher development (Stenhouse, 1975), so schools will not develop unless their staff groups develop, and staff development meant, for us, teachers learning. In short, a learning school is a developing school.

Such a view is all-embracing. The equation that school development means staff development sounds simple but, in fact, it involves a number of processes and issues. For example, when, some years ago, HM Inspectors wrote about ten 'good' secondary schools they emphasized four things: a focus upon learning, effective leadership, shared aims and purposes, and a positive school climate (DES, 1977). Ten years later HM Inspectors wrote about the characteristics of 'good' primary schools and drew attention to very similar issues, although their emphasis upon effective leadership by the head was more muted (DES, 1987). Subsequent work (e.g. Ball, 1987; Nias *et al.*, 1989, 1992) has drawn attention to the complex nature of establishing shared educational values. As others have noted, staff development often relies upon teamwork, professional dialogue and a school culture that sustains teacher collaboration (Nias *et al.*, 1989; Lieberman, 1990) and these are far from easy to create and sustain in some schools. In other words, I wish to make it clear that the development of a learning school relies upon establishing a set of processes and conditions that are neither simple nor straightforward to put in place.

A learning school has five interrelated characteristics. In the learning school:

- the focus is on the pupils and their learning;
- individual teachers are encouraged to be continuing learners themselves;
- teachers (and sometimes others) who constitute the 'staff' are encouraged to collaborate by learning with and from each other;
- the school (all those people who constitute the school) learns its way forward, i.e. the school as an organization is a 'learning system' (Schon, 1971);
- the headteacher is the leading learner (Holly and Southworth, 1989).

These characteristics of learning amount to five 'levels of learning' which can be summarized as:

Level 1, children's learning

Level 2, teacher learning

Level 3, staff learning

Level 4, organizational learning

Level 5, leadership learning

I shall briefly comment upon each of these levels before offering some general observations, which will act as both a conclusion to this section and an introduction to the next. In that section I will draw upon some recent empirical evidence to illustrate these characteristics and levels. In the final section of this chapter I shall discuss the empirical data and further refine the characteristics.

Level 1: Children's learning

Notions of school effectiveness and quality teaching rest upon staff in school paying close and constant attention to the pupils' learning. Staff need to be constantly thinking about how the individuals in their classes are learning and developing, and how their teaching is, or is not, enabling the pupils to learn. In essence the teacher needs to learn from the learner how to teach and to teach the learner how to learn (Holly and Southworth, 1989).

Keeping a focus on the pupils' learning is now a strong tradition among classroom action researchers (e.g. Armstrong, 1980; Nixon, 1981; Holly and Whitehead, 1984; Rowlands, 1984; Hustler et al., 1986). Equally, there has been a continuing interest in classrooms and teaching throughout the 1980s, which has generated a considerable amount of material and ideas (e.g. Galton and Simon, 1980; Bennett et al., 1984; Pollard, 1985; Desforge and Cockburn, 1987; Mortimore et al., 1988; Galton, 1989). Hence there is no shortage either of techniques for teachers to use to help them focus upon aspects of teaching and learning (e.g. Hopkins, 1985; Conner, 1991) or of texts and ideas to stimulate thought and reflection. However, while analysis and deliberation are necessary, they are not sufficient. Teachers must be willing to adapt their practices and try out new approaches in a quest for improvement. The learning school becomes the developing school when the teachers accept that the underlying purpose is to improve the teaching and learning process in their classrooms and across the school (Holly and Southworth, 1989, p.8).

Level 2: Teacher learning

Aside from their personal and career needs, teachers as professionals need to keep abreast of new developments in the curriculum, extend their expertise and acquire new competences. As Joyce and Showers (1980) say, teachers have to fine-tune skills that they already possess and also add entirely new ones to their repertoires of teaching strategies. Together these form the substance of professional growth:

> Teaching is a performing art; therefore it is developed — like all other performing arts — through prolonged and intelligent practice. . . . Gifted teachers rarely come ready-made. They possess a finely tuned intuition, a capacity to develop understanding out of ordinary experience, and an ability to provoke genuine thinking in their students. They are problem-solvers rather than rule-followers . . . real rather than pretentious; and demanding rather than easily-satisfied. Above all, they are driven not only by ideals but by a corresponding passion for engineering their realization. (Rubin, 1978)

In addition, teachers learn by reflecting upon their practice (Dewey, 1933; Schon, 1983). Reflective action is composed of four essential characteristics:

1 Reflective teaching implies an active concern with aims and consequences, as well as with means and technical efficiency.

2 Reflective teaching combines enquiry and implementation skills with attitudes of open-mindedness, responsibility and wholeheartedness.

3 Reflective teaching is applied in a cyclical or spiralling process, in which teachers continually monitor, evaluate, and revise their own practice.

4 Reflective teaching is based on teacher judgement, informed partly by self-reflection and partly by insights from educational disciplines.

'A reflective teacher, therefore, is one who constantly questions his or her own aims and actions, monitors practice and outcomes, and considers the short-term and long-term effects upon each child' (Pollard and Tann, 1987).

There are two other points to make. First, all teachers can reflect upon their own and their pupils' actions. They are always in 'possession' of the essential materials for the exercise: their teaching and their perceptions of the pupils' actions. Second, although teachers can engage upon the exercise in isolation, it is often supported and nourished by off-site course work and on-site collaboration with colleagues.

Level 3: Staff learning

Teachers have always learned from one another, although sometimes learning has taken place in an *ad hoc* way, with an emphasis placed upon teaching tips and techniques, especially in the early years of teaching and when the novitiate teacher is preoccupied with classroom survival. However, in recent times emphasis has been placed upon the need for teachers to collaborate and work as members of a team (Rosenholtz, 1989; Fullan and Hargreaves, 1991). In part this emerging emphasis upon collaboration arises from a recognition that teaching can be an isolating and private activity (e.g. Little, 1985, 1990; Nias, 1989; Hargreaves, 1990). It also stems from school effectiveness and improvement studies. Generally these studies show that while effective schools obviously contain within them effective teachers, the work of individual teachers is enhanced by across-school policies, structures and processes (e.g. consistency among teachers, healthy teacher communications, clear guidelines, positive school climate). As a result there has been a call for whole-school policy-making (NCC, 1989, 1990), since it is now believed that 'schools cannot be improved without people working together' (Lieberman, 1986).

Undoubtedly, where staff have the capacity to collaborate professionally they increase their opportunities to learn from one another both informally and formally (e.g. staffroom conversations, staff meetings, working parties, committees). In fact, whenever staff work together they learn from one another. However, the challenge is for staff to organize themselves so that their professional growth is a central and explicit concern rather than a serendipitous process. Fortunately, the recent introduction of school-based in-service days on a national scale has added to the number of occasions when staff might meet together and explicitly learn with and from colleagues. Furthermore, the devolution of INSET funds to schools has stimulated teachers' thinking in respect of their individual and collective development. One major task for schools in the 1990s, therefore, is to co-ordinate their staff and school development plans so that teachers can learn collaboratively and grow as a group.

Level 4: Organizational learning

If teachers are to learn individually and collectively they need to do so in an organizational context which enables, rather than disables, both kinds of growth. The school as an organization needs to be innovative and flexible: 'a good organization is flexible, uses integrated structures, monitors itself [and its] organizational culture, develops strategic planning techniques and empowers its people' (Patterson et al., 1986). In a sense, the school needs to be responsive to the needs of its members (e.g. pupils, teachers, other staff) without becoming so 'inside-focused' that it fails to take account of other stakeholders (e.g. parents, governors) and the community in which it is located.

Interest in school management and organizational development, and school development planning, demonstrates that organizational learning has been an area of interest for some time. However, although these have helped to raise senior staff's awareness of organizational theories and structures they have not always created the circumstances for healthy communications or sustained a focus on learning.

Both these criticisms stem from the observations of Shipman (1990), who says that schools are typical of traditional organizations in having top-down information flows, whereas they actually need to circulate information:

> The 1988 Education Act demands more information, not only on the assessment of pupils, but on the performance of the school as a whole. Much of that has to be provided by teachers. It has to be made available to governors and parents as well as LEAs ... Not only assessment data and performance indicators but records of achievement will give more information to the public. (Shipman, 1990)

For Shipman all of this means that management information (e.g. budgets, resources, use of time) and curriculum information (e.g. assessment data, plans) need to be much more firmly synchronized than ever before. Information needs to flow up and down and all around the organization:

> The 1988 Education Act demands information at three levels: on pupils, on school classes or year groups and on the school as a whole. The information on pupil attainment is to be provided for parents at four reporting ages and records of achievement will extend the scope 'across and beyond' the national curriculum. (Shipman, 1990)

All of this means that staff will, potentially, have available to them a great deal of information upon which to reflect. It is hoped that these data will be used to stimulate discussion among staff and so nourish collaborative discourse and development. Importantly, since much of this information is concerned with learning, it should be used to sustain the focus upon learning. Then, whatever organizational changes and developments are made in the light of this information, they can be made with learning in mind. Then, and only then, will we have schools that are managing learning.

Level 5: Leadership for learning

There appears to be widespread agreement that the quality of leadership exercised by the head is crucial to the effectiveness of the school (Southworth, 1990) and to the creation of the learning school (Holly and Southworth, 1989). The head sets the tone for learning (by pupils and adults alike) by the educational beliefs and values she or he holds. A head's educational philosophy determines, in large measure, and especially in primary and middle schools, the nature of teaching and learning in the school she or he leads. Moreover, heads act as models for teacher and staff development. Where they talk openly about their growth and undertake further professional development they demonstrate to others the importance of professional learning. Where heads and other senior staff retain a strong and consistent interest in the pupils' learning they help to focus staff's attention on to these matters. And when they concern themselves with teachers' development and staff development activities they show how central they regard these processes to be to the school's development.

Heads do not simply lead by stating the direction in which they hope the school will go, they exemplify what they believe in through what they say and do. Leadership is a blend of ideals and, crucially, actions consistent with those ideals. It is not enough for heads to say learning is important: they must actively demonstrate the importance of learning by looking at what the pupils and staff are doing and by being learners themselves.

When these five levels of learning are taken together they create two other points. First, everyone in the school is a learner. Second, learning is not overlooked or left out of the school's management and development. In the learning school the quality of everyone's learning is important.

A LEARNING SCHOOL IN ACTION

Although it is relatively easy to make a case for the learning school, it is more difficult to find examples of them in practice; or, rather, it was until quite recently. Between 1988 and 1990 I, along with Jennifer Nias and Penny Campbell, undertook a research project, funded by the ESRC (ref. no. R000231069) to investigate whole school curriculum development in five primary schools. The project sought, in the first instance, to produce case studies of the curriculum developments undertaken in each school. We worked as part-time teachers in one or more of the project schools to undertake participant observation of the means by which staff developed the curriculum and of the ways they worked together to create a sense of 'whole school'. At the end of the year's fieldwork we constructed from our fieldnotes and interviews with the teachers five case studies (one per school). These were cleared with the schools' staffs and then analysed to identify a set of common themes (Nias *et al.*, 1992). Of the many issues that emerged from our analysis one is especially pertinent to the theme of the learning school: the ways and means by which teachers learned with and from one another (see Nias *et al.*, 1992, pp. 71-107).

From our detailed accounts, as well as interviews with staff, it emerged that what the teachers meant by curriculum development was their individual and collective professional learning. Often, though not always, their learning was focused upon what the children were doing or needed to be learning. Hence, in one school, when a racist remark was made by one child to another, the class teacher's reporting of the episode to colleagues prompted them all to begin to develop some school policies to deal with the issue. In short, some of the project schools were learning schools.

To illustrate some of the characteristics of learning schools discussed above and to provide empirical data for highlighting some additional points, I now include an extract from one of the case studies from the Whole School Curriculum Development research project.

The extract covers the developments undertaken in one primary school, which we called Fenton, in its craft, design and technology curriculum. The deputy head, Rob, played a leading part in introducing the initiative to colleagues and in sustaining their interest in it. However, the spread of CDT across the school was only assured when Barbara was asked to be head of science in the lower school. Her support for the work meant that staff working with the infant-aged children became more committed and fully involved. Throughout the whole sequence of events the headteacher, Simon, played a supporting role by being interested in the development.

The author of this case example, Penny Campbell, likened the development to a 'story', seeing it as an unfolding event. The story has been pieced together from interview transcripts and fieldnotes that Penny made while working in the school. The account is an edited version of what happened. It is a tidied-up version so that the developments which took place can be seen more clearly. In truth, reality was considerably more complicated and dynamic than this account suggests. Much of the story is described by the teachers in their own words. In this way, despite the version being strongly focused on this single development, the events are presented and explained by those who experienced the process.

At the end of the extract I will offer some personal observations. Perhaps as you now read the story of developing CDT at Fenton School you might try to identify some of the ways the staff learned, both individually and collectively, about CDT and how to teach it.

THE STORY OF CRAFT, DESIGN AND TECHNOLOGY AT FENTON PRIMARY SCHOOL

Craft, design and technology allied, as it was, to science became, first of all, the concern of an individual: Rob. Several things contributed to his growing awareness that it was an area of the curriculum that needed to be developed within the school.

> I became aware of it because of the National Curriculum thing that suddenly started appearing everywhere about CDT. There was a lot of talk about it. I'd always been interested in that side of things anyway and it gave me a push to actually do something and start thinking through some ideas and then Simon came back with one or two ideas he had seen in other schools that he talked to me about, for example, methods of joining wood, and then I started to read more literature about it. I joined the Science Association and they send a Primary Journal through every month and I got a lot of ideas out of that. (Rob)

He began to put these ideas into practice in his own classroom. 'I started putting that into my class and testing it out and seeing how it was going.' His interest was encouraged by Simon.

> Generally [Simon] would come to me with quite clearly formed ideas about what he wanted. For example, he said to me, 'We are going to pursue CDT, aren't we, because it's important,' and I agreed that it was important. (Rob)

> Rob and the science/CDT side of things. That's an issue he thinks is one we ought to be addressing and is working hard to establish that as good working practice with his own children before it starts filtering through the rest of the school, so there are lots of initiatives which actually start with an individual teacher within the school taking on board a particular notion and working it out from there. Again my role is that it's important that people are given their head to do these things. Not entirely off their own bat without any consultation. After

consultation and after we've all had a chance to think about it and talk about it. I think if you don't give people the opportunities to develop things you stagnate. (Simon, interview, 4 October 1988)

They made the decision together to raise awareness among the staff through the provision of some in-service training.

Then Simon and I made a conscious decision to push what was happening in CDT, to push it amongst the juniors to start with, so I did one or two in-service things. I did an in-service morning for the whole staff and also the afternoon was taken up with a Lego Technic thing. That gave the staff a bit of a push. Now, not a lot happened from that initial day. I forget how long ago it was now — a couple of years perhaps — and not much happened from that because people were still mulling it over in their minds. It was something that was bubbling up a bit but they'd got other things to do. (Rob)

This was followed by further in-service work, which began to capture the interest of other members of staff.

I had probably about 1 per cent knowledge of CDT in the past. . . . One of the courses we had at a staff meeting on one of the Baker days . . . we did Technical Lego, pulleys and systems like that. Well, that didn't inspire me at all. That was a complete switch off. I thought, 'I hate this. I'm not going to get into this CDT.' Then the next one that ran, which was a night course, was on axles and wheels and cutting and sawing and all that sort of thing. That actually appealed to me. From then I've been on lots of different courses with different people from the authority who have run marvellous courses. Super ideas. (Teacher)

Then, for the start of the academic year 1988-9 Rob prepared a document on CDT to present to the staff. It was discussed, among the other documents he and Simon had prepared, at a preliminary in-service training day.

At 12 o'clock the discussion went on to the document on CDT. Once again, Rob talked about this. He said it was based on a staff meeting held last year when the staff had talked together, plus a DES document, plus LEA documents, in particular one called 'Designing and making in the primary school'. He also referred to Science 5-13 books in the staffroom. Simon mentioned Rob's decision to set aside a time each week for his class to do CDT and invited Rob to talk about why. Rebecca referred to a stated intention last year to link the infants and the juniors so that there was the opportunity for skills to be passed on from one to the other. This was met by general approval signified by nodding and so on. Simon picked up on her suggestion and made it clear that he approved of the idea as well. The Baker day the Friday before half-term is obviously being spent on CDT and the hope was expressed that this would give the impetus for developing CDT in terms of the skills that ought to be encouraged. Rob admitted that he had some difficulties with the idea of CDT for infants, but Simon said that it was really a matter of building on things that already happen. For example, when children are making boxes, that could be extended to problem-solving about wheels and axles and so on. Clearly the school has new materials, several of which were listed in the document. One in particular was emphasized, called 'Starting technology', and there were sheets that could be worked through. Simon suggested that these should actually be worked through consistently because they are in a developmental sequence and they could then be reviewed at the end of the year. Tamsin told the group about a construction kit called 'Play school' that was available in the county and that could be borrowed. There was some discussion, particularly on the part of Simon and Rob, about structured, task-oriented play. Rob talked about the use of Plasticene, Blu-tak and rubber bands rather than glue in the lower part of the school, but Simon advocated avoiding Plasticene and Blu-tak because they weren't realistically used in real technological problem-solving. Susan raised the problem of getting the trolley containing the tools into the mobile classrooms and Simon suggested that these classrooms should have a basic kit of their own. He also referred to the design folder being used as a record as suggested on page 2 of the document and Rob emphasized that this was not merely a record of achievement, but a record that the children should refer back to themselves in the same way that designers did, rejecting and then picking up on designs. He also emphasized that the proper names of tools should be used consistently from the start and that their correct names were contained in a section in the LEA document. There was some discussion about children's reluctance to lose what they had constructed. Simon said that the school camera was kept in his room and that photographs could be kept as a record of the children's constructions. (Fieldnotes, 3 September 1988)

Rob put into practice in his own classroom the CDT he wanted to see developed throughout the school. He shared the results in assembly and through display, provided resources and encouraged staff to get involved in in-service training courses (providing them himself on occasion). Further discussions took place in staff meetings during the year. Gradually other staff began to implement some of the ideas themselves. A significant step was taken when Barbara was asked to take on the responsibility for lower school science. She began to work with her infant colleagues and Rob to develop a systematic progression through the school. The following extracts from fieldnotes illustrate the ways in which these initiatives were planned and implemented.

I suggested to Rob right at the beginning that it would be a good idea if he started at the top and worked down rather than start from the bottom and work up, so what he's done is work with his own children, which has demonstrated that they can do quite exciting things, and then done practical workshops for the staff, which has demonstrated that there are possibilities there for younger children, and has then made it perfectly clear to them by getting them to do things with their own children. For instance, Barbara's class are doing things that he started doing with his children and they're managing perfectly well at measuring, cutting and sticking wood and what we were saying to them right from the beginning was, 'What we're going to be doing with children at ten and eleven we really ought to be doing with children at five and six', and they've taken that on board, at least Barbara certainly, and Rebecca and Verity, have taken that on board and are getting it going. Verity's class are making their own chassis and so on. Great. So what he's done really is said, 'Look, all these things are really quite simple. Let's get started. Let's not do anything complicated', deliberately avoided getting too much in the way of pre-packed stuff, and said, 'Let's stick to the simple', and he's got most people interested and involved in doing things and it's worked really well. And again, it's being done in a way which is co-operative, everybody involved, everybody committed to the idea that if we do this at our level then it's going to enable children to do far more later on. (Simon, interview 4 October 1988)

So then I set up a trolley and I ordered a lot of things in and shortly after that I did quite a big thing with my class of making cars and bodyworks and everything and testing. I made a big thing of sharing that in assembly and made a big display and we talked about it a lot, and I made a point of talking about it a lot to staff, without pushing it down their throats and without saying, 'Look how great I am'. Just showing them what the children had done and people started saying things like, 'That's very good. How did you do this? How did you do that?' and I spread it down into the junior classes from that and got Kathryn and Susan doing it a little bit. Then Simon and I made another conscious decision to involve Barbara on that side of things and as soon as she got involved in it her enthusiasm took the rest on then because they could see where it fitted in the infant curriculum because she was coming back with infant ideas, because they obviously couldn't do lots of things we were doing at junior level. Then I saw my job as contributing lots of ideas for how we could get free materials and putting out pleas for all sorts. Once that starts coming in then people feel duty bound to use it and so it snowballed on from there. We had a science day that we joined in with in October where a bloke called Ken Giles did a day. . . . He was brilliant because he was very inspirational about it all. It was all very down to earth stuff, even though it was flying helicopters and things! It was extremely accessible and that gave the staff another buzz and another push on because it was somebody else and I think they'd had enough of me by then. It gave them some more ideas. It gave them a bit of enthusiasm for the whole thing. . . . [The in-service work] was essential because the trouble is you don't get enough time in school to spread these ideas and make sure that people feel happy about them. You can talk about them in an odd ten or five minutes to people but you're not actually taking them on any further. All you are doing is having a conversation with them about it. That's not in-service. What you need to do is set the thing up and give them something they can then take away and they can do it even for a short spell. Then, of course, there's the problem of resourcing it. It had to be things we could do, that I knew we had resources for, because otherwise it's pointless doing it, which is why I set up the trolley and did an in-service day and although it didn't spark people off straightaway it got people thinking about it. It started the ball rolling. Now I keep getting pressurized about not enough tools and not enough of this, that and everything else! That's all because people have had enough time to start feeling really happy about it, and about it as a process. It's still nowhere near perfect and we need more time, in-service time, to sit down and talk it over as a staff now. There are certain things that have happened this year that I would love to see repeated so that children go through a like experience, perhaps on a two-yearly cycle, but there's certain key things that we have to teach. . . . It doesn't matter if you're making a boat or a car or an aeroplane, there are certain key things that young children need to be taught, how to use a saw and techniques like that. . . . We need to make time as a staff to sit down and talk through steps that children could go through, hammering nails into pieces of wood, all this sort of thing. That's where I would see the in-service being vital. It gives us time when there's no pressure of children, there's no pressure of telephones ringing. You can sit down and you can talk on a professional level. But the big thing about it is that it's going to be better now because everybody, to some extent, has had experience of working it with their classes, so everybody's got a contribution they can make, so we've got past the point of somebody giving a whole input like Ken did in October. We've got past that point now. We are at the point where we can talk about our own experiences and where we get our own ideas from and make it our thing, our science and CDT progressions. (Rob, interview)

In the hall today there was a display of vehicles made of paper and cardboard. They were accompanied by statements by the children about what kind of modifications needed to be made in order to make them work more effectively. (Fieldnotes, 2 November 1988)

The major part of the evening was given over to talking about science and CDT. Rob led the discussion. He mentioned a book called *Springboards*, which is an Australian publication, saying that this provided a framework for science and CDT teaching in school, that it provided sequence and continuity that was linked with cognitive development. It had a similar approach to that agreed in the school's curriculum statement on science and CDT. Simon said, 'It's all to do with integrated learning, which is what we've said we want.' He also said that the philosophy behind it was not only similar to that within the school, but also to Science 5-13. There was an awareness in the discussion of the need for accountability and therefore the need to develop a means of record-keeping. . . . There was general agreement that they would wait for the National Curriculum document on science to arrive and then write their own curriculum guidelines based on Science 5-13 and *Springboards*. Rob and Barbara agreed to meet to discuss this further, Barbara now being in charge of science for the lower school. There were references to the value of the in-service training day on CDT that we all went to, and to the fact that there is now a workbench in the reception area so that even the youngest children can be taught how to use tools properly. There was quite a lot of discussion on the various construction kits in the school — Technic Lego, Constructs, Fisher Price — and a commitment to buying some more, particularly for Susan's classroom. The Constructs was particularly admired since some of Barbara's class had shown models made of this in assembly this morning. Simon emphasized that in construction the children should be encouraged not simply to use the kits but also to use other materials that needed adapting. (Fieldnotes, 10 January 1989)

[I got involved in the lower school science] by pure chance. Simon asked us to decide what we'd be responsible for. I'd actually decided I'd like to do the needlework and some of the art, but seeing that post had already been filled when I got my interview, together we came up with the lower school science, because Rob was doing the upper school science and I think, with being slightly inspired by the CDT courses, I thought, 'That sounds like a good area to be in. I can cope with that.' He encouraged me anyway and before I knew it I was doing lower school science. By chance really . . . I just think it's the challenge, a keenness to absorb more information and to share it with other members of staff. . . . I think that's the best part because you don't know where you want to start and it's a challenge. You want to go and find out. It's that. The new learning process. I want to know what comes next. Now I'm thinking what I can do with the top infants next year. I've taken the middles right through. Now I'm already scheming the next stages up. It's exciting. It's to get the progress right and then have a school policy to get it right for the future children coming through, because Verity and I have worked through the junk models with the receptions and then we always get together to see what the next stage is and we've got the next stage being just the stick-on wheels, then we've got the moving wheels, then we've got the inside-out cardboard boxes for the tops for them, then we're doing the frames, the cubes . . . we've got some nice books . . . with ideas . . . how to make 'T' joints and all that sort of thing, the next stages up, and 'After you've done this, do this', so just working through really and adjusting as we need. . . . Anything I need to know I just go trotting up to [Rob] or nagging him for more equipment or nagging him for more tubing or whatever.

'Where can I get this?' and so on. He probably runs a mile when he sees me coming. It's always, 'Rob!' (Barbara)

Yes, we do work together. If it wasn't for him running the courses initially I probably wouldn't have got started, nor would the others. It would have just been, 'I'll fit a bit in if I've got to because of the National Curriculum next year' and that would have been it. As it is it's really taken off. . . . Verity and I are producing a sort of infant booklet and we have taken photographs and whatever so we're going to have a photographic record of the sort of areas we've covered. We will probably make a list of the skills we've covered as well, if they've made a certain type of frame or whatever. (Barbara)

I suppose the biggest change would be the CDT input. Everybody's very aware that this is part of our curriculum, that we have to deliver it, and we have been on courses collectively and individually. . . . Everybody's trying hard to gain some expertise themselves and to work with the children to see what works and what doesn't and sharing ideas and sharing knowledge to make CDT important because most of us have never done any, especially the women staff. . . . The impetus for that has come from Rob in the first place, from Baker days which originally Rob set up one for us, and so I suppose from there and obviously from National Curriculum documents, and before that it was plain that this would be a part of teaching, and also obviously from reading your own articles and the educational press. . . . We have parents that are more skilled at CDT than we are. . . . Eric Coombe is the obvious example, which unfortunately is a man (I should be able to think of a woman but I can't), who comes in and he likes doing that sort of thing. We agreed that there were certain skills that they were going to learn in the reception year, one of which is how to use a hammer properly, how to use a saw properly, so when it came to the sawing he was around so I explained what we wanted to do and he's taken the children through that. They've all done some sawing and he's taught them how to use the tools and advised them how to hold the saw. (Barbara)

A boy showed a birdhouse that he'd made out of one of the construction kits in the classroom. . . . Verity said, 'Don't tell them what it is! Let them guess.' When the children had guessed Verity said to him, 'It's bigger than the one you made before, isn't it?' Then she asked him where he would put the food and suggested that perhaps he might find some way of making a platform where the birds could eat their food before going inside to sleep. The boy nodded enthusiastically and looked quite excited at this suggestion. (Fieldnotes, 1 December 1988)

Barbara and Marguerite both showed me with pride the musical instruments they'd been making this morning. . . . It was clear that Barbara was really pleased with the ingenuity that the children had demonstrated in making their instruments. . . . They'd developed the ideas. Some of them had made shakers with straws and bottle tops, which was an idea entirely their own. Others had modified the ideas that they were given by punching holes in things to find out how they could make different sounds and so on. (Fieldnotes, 19 June 1989)

Other children were instructed to join Barbara round a table where they were going to make things that were pneumatically propelled.... I think she mentioned the word 'aerodynamic' too, but I may be wrong.... Later, when the infants were out for afternoon play, some of them came to the doorway of the little room where I was sitting with a group of juniors. They wanted to show me what they'd made. They'd all designed little figures and, as part of the figures, were syringes. Some had put them in the chest of their figures, some in their eyes, some in their nose, and from the back of the syringe were long plastic tubes leading to the plunger, and a little plastic dart in the end of the syringe. What the children did was to push the plunger down and the dart came flying out of the creature's nose or eye or chest or tummy. The designs were intricate and beautifully crafted and the children were proud of their work. One little girl said to me, 'Would you like a go?' I said, 'Oh, I was dying to have a go!' So several of the others let me have a go with theirs as well. On the back of each figure was written, in an adult's hand, the words 'pneumatic power'. One of the children, seeing me look at this, said 'It's spelt with a "p". It's a silent "p"!' (Fieldnotes, 30 June 1989)

I took myself down to the reception area and asked Celia whether she could do with an extra pair of hands. She looked really pleased to see me and said she would appreciate an adult on 'that table there'. 'That table there' was piled high with all sorts of bits and pieces, different coloured sticky paper, egg boxes, cotton reels, glue, bits of plastic sacking and so on. Celia explained that all this week the children have been decorating the boats that she showed me so proudly last week. These boats were basically made out of two bottles, most of them plastic lemonade bottles, lashed together with string. Four pieces of wood are lashed in a square on top, and on top of that a structure made of various cardboard containers. Quite a number of children had clearly been busy all week decorating their boats and those that were finished were displayed on the top of the cupboard.... When they are all completed they will be launched on the school swimming pool.... Celia said the children knew exactly what they wanted to do but they needed an adult on hand to help them with the tricky bits, the cutting out that they couldn't do, for example. (Fieldnotes, 23 June 1989)

At the end of assembly ... Kathryn was talking to the juniors about a boat competition. Last week some of the infants had shown their boats in assembly and Kathryn had proposed that they have a school competition. One junior boy had gone home and made a boat out of various waterproof materials, polystyrene, tape, plastic and so on, and had brought it in to show her. She now showed it to the rest of the children and praised him for his enthusiasm. That the whole suggestion was a spur-of-the-moment idea was apparent from the fact that it hadn't been thought out in detail. Not that that mattered! 'We might make it the whole length of the swimming pool or the width of the swimming pool. It depends how it goes', said Kathryn. 'We'll see. We'll decide later.' Susan asked what the deadline was for the completion of the boats. 'Well, sometime in the last week of term I would think', replied Kathryn. (Fieldnotes, 30 June 1989)

I find the story of the development of CDT in the school an exciting one because it illustrates, better perhaps than any other part of this case study, the 'sparkiness' of what went on in the school. It highlights the importance in the process of development of the head's influence and encouragement; the concern, interest and enthusiasm of individuals; the sharing of responsibility; the provision of in-service training; the provision of appropriate resources; implementation in classrooms leading to the sharing of ideas through display and assembly; and, through it all, talk — formal discussion in staff meetings and informal chat day by day.

There are many points that might be made from this extract. First, let me address the question I posed at the start of the piece: in what ways did these teachers learn about CDT and how to teach it? I can identify nine ways:

1 By using books and materials supplied by the Science Association.
2 From INSET activities in school and workshops arranged by staff.
3 From INSET courses outside the school.
4 Formal staff meetings.
5 Informal conversations among members of staff.
6 Displays of children's work.
7 'Showing' assemblies.
8 Working together on joint projects and tasks.
9 Teachers sharing ideas, and successes.

These ways of learning from and with others are hardly original or revolutionary. We found them occurring in all the project schools. They are also familiar to me from my own experience of teaching in primary schools and from visiting other schools. Moreover, from sharing these ideas with teachers on in-service courses it is apparent that many others are familiar with them. However, while they are well known this should not mask their effectiveness in enabling staff in this and other schools to learn from each other and thus to develop the curriculum and their school. For sure, these are not spectacular findings but because they are commonplace and, seemingly, ordinary they are also taken for granted, perceived as merely practical ways of developing the curriculum. Yet such an outlook underestimates their power.

I and my project colleagues believe them to be powerful for three sets of reasons. First, they helped teachers to learn from one another and to do so in ways that, generally speaking, sustained attention upon the children's learning. At the same time, the process of learning together was sufficiently valuable to each member of staff that it encouraged them to continue to work together. Moreover, the process of learning was psychologically supportive in that no one appeared to face alone the introduction of CDT: there were always colleagues to turn to for help. The process was also practical: staff learned how to teach CDT in their classrooms. Yet attention to the practical was not at the expense of understanding the philosophy of teaching CDT and how it related to the school's educational principles, and this is the second set of reasons.

Learning was not a purely technical exercise, it was also concerned with sustaining and developing the beliefs the head and the majority of staff held about how children learn (e.g. first-hand experience) and what is the best way of teaching them (e.g. structured activities). Consequently, learning together helped to develop a sense of team, which, in turn, nurtured a sense of 'whole school'. Staff learned to share ideas and skills and developed and sustained a shared set of educational goals and values. Indeed, although the extract looks to be a relatively familiar example of teachers learning the skills and competences to be able to teach CDT, it also involved teachers in modifying their educational beliefs and values. What for some teachers was originally of little value to them and their teaching became, over time, something they saw as worthwhile, and so was incorporated into their teaching. Therefore, while this example looks on the surface to be simply concerned with practical matters it is, in fact, also concerned with educational beliefs and purposes. The case example shows that the two are inseparable. Moreover, curriculum development can require teachers to modify or change their beliefs about what is and is not relevant to themselves, their teaching and the children's learning. Such changes occurred here and suggest that their professional learning is the key to them altering or modifying their beliefs.

Third, all these ways of learning are practicable. They do not demand that staff take on new ways of learning and working together. Nor do they require new technologies or massive investment programmes. They are already happening and teachers are very familiar with them. As Fullan and Hargreaves (1991) say, these are not as glitzy and high status as other forms of staff development but they can be highly effective.

However, as the introduction to this chapter makes clear, teacher learning, while at the heart of the learning school, is not the only characteristic that needs to be present. To develop learning schools there are at least four other characteristics that need to be established in the school. These are: leadership, a culture of collaboration, learning and structure. Traces of all of them can be seen in the case example and are explored more fully in the two research projects with which I have been associated (Nias *et al.*, 1989, 1992) as well as in the recent writings of Fullan (Fullan *et al.*, 1990; Fullan and Hargreaves, 1991). I shall now briefly look at each of these characteristics in turn.

LEADERSHIP

Here I want to focus purely upon the role of the head. A number of studies point to the centrality of the headteacher in school improvement. Moreover, leadership needs to be stressed because in all five project schools the heads were leading learners. They played such an active part in the schools that we called them 'player managers'; by which we mean they were both leaders and participants (Nias *et al.*, 1992). Each head had also undertaken some form of further professional study (one had an MA and another was studying for one; two had Advanced Diplomas and strong records of INSET attendance; one was involved in providing INSET in art education for his LEA). In the case example, the head, Simon, influenced what was happening in the school by watching what was occurring in classrooms and linking this to resource needs. The head's knowledge informed the purchase of resources to encourage the development of CDT and the allocation of responsibilities to certain members of staff.

Throughout the Whole School Curriculum Development project schools we noted that the heads were watchful and attentive to what was occurring in classrooms. Their interest was not solely confined to resource needs but spread to many other aspects of teaching and learning. The heads monitored the extent to which school policies were implemented; they took an active interest in the teachers' work and lives; they promoted curriculum initiatives by encouraging experimentation; they attended to teachers' individual and collective needs and interests; they established ways in which staff could share and talk about their work in their classrooms (e.g. showing assemblies, staff meetings, informal visits by the head to teachers in their classrooms after school). In much of this the heads were seeking to establish and sustain an organizational culture that facilitated openness and sharing.

The most important point to highlight here, however, is that these heads demonstrate that while leadership is important it is, in fact, a particular kind of leadership that matters. As Fullan and Hargreaves (1991, p.51) say: 'It is not a charismatic, innovative high flier that moves school cultures forward. Rather, it is a more subtle kind of leadership which makes activity meaningful for others.' The prevailing view that heads and other leaders should be strong and purposeful needs to be set alongside the more recent view that they also need to be subtle; not in a manipulative sense, but in terms of being able to influence colleagues by asking questions, modelling a strong interest in teaching and learning and encouraging teacher reflection.

A CULTURE OF COLLABORATION

As the previous characteristic has already suggested, learning schools need an organizational culture that supports collaboration. A collaborative culture is built on four interacting beliefs. The first two specify ends: individuals should be valued but, because they are inseparable from the groups of which they are a part, groups too should be fostered and valued. The second two relate to means: the most effective ways of promoting these values are through openness and a sense of mutual security (Nias *et al.*, 1989). Such a culture in a school means that the individual and the group are inherently and simultaneously valued (Fullan and Hargreaves, 1991) and it becomes possible for staff to experience a sense of unity without feeling stifled by a narrow conformity (Nias *et al.*, 1992).

Yet, as others acknowledge and as the Whole School Curriculum Development project demonstrates, collaboration is too general and broad a notion.

While a culture of collaboration is a necessary condition for school improvement, it is not a sufficient condition. Rather, it is a particular *form* of collaboration that matters. As Little (1990) says, there is nothing particularly virtuous about collaboration *per se*, it could create 'groupthink' or a sense of 'cosiness' and complacency that hinders or blocks change. For collaboration to be effective it:

> must be linked to norms of continuous improvement and experimentation in which teachers are constantly seeking and assessing potentially better practices inside and outside their own schools (and contributing to other people's practice through dissemination). (Fullan *et al.*, 1990).

In other words, collaboration must include and enhance teacher learning.

Developing schools are ones where the power of the culture of collaboration is focused most strongly on learning. As Rosenholtz (1989) says, these are 'learning-enriched' schools where teacher development goes on in a natural and taken-for-granted way. Indeed, so powerful is this culture that merely by being a teacher working within it one's practice is positively affected and developed: 'Imagine that teachers can become better teachers just by virtue of being on the staff of a particular school — just from that one fact alone' (Little, 1990; cited in Fullan and Hargreaves, 1991, p. 46). In 'learning-enriched' schools 'joint work' is the most effective form of collaboration (e.g. paired teaching, planning, observation, action research, mentoring, peer coaching). Joint work creates stronger interdependence, shared responsibility and collective commitment (Little, 1990). Similar findings emerge from the Whole School Curriculum Development project (Nias *et al.*, 1992).

In advocating a culture of collaboration within which teacher learning takes place we need to be mindful that some other forms of collaboration are not propitious to growth. Fullan and Hargreaves (1991) cite Balkanization, comfortable collaboration and contrived collegiality as three forms which are best avoided.

The evidence concerning a culture of collaboration in which learning occurs points to collaborative cultures being highly sophisticated ones. They cannot be created overnight (Fullan and Hargreaves, 1991; Nias *et al.*, 1992). They are full of tension since the needs and interests of individuals need to reconciled with those of the group. Individualism needs to be reduced but not at the expense of individuality (Fullan and Hargreaves, 1991). Furthermore, the members of these cultures need to be able to participate in micropolitics. Here I use micropolitics not in a sinister sense but to raise to prominence the amount of *negotiation* that needs to take place to reach workable agreements and compromises among individual members of staff, particularly since, as the Primary School Staff Relationships project demonstrates, one irony of collaborative cultures is that disagreement is stronger and more frequent in schools with collaborative cultures than it is elsewhere. In collaborative cultures purposes, values and practice are discussed and challenged (Nias *et al.*, 1989; Fullan and Hargreaves, 1991). Collaborative schools are places where staff are open and trusting and are places where members of staff are not afraid to be critical of one another and themselves.

LEARNING

The nine ways in which staff learned from each other identified in the case example are not the only ways staff learned from one another. Others not included in that example are: touring the school, observing a colleague, curriculum review meetings, putting on concerts and dramatic productions. Although the different kinds of learning are important, as Little's notion of 'joint work' confirms, the scale and frequency with which they occur in a school is also significant. One conclusion of the Whole School Curriculum Development project is that the project team generally believe schools need more rather than fewer ways of fostering learning. A reliance on only one or two ways in which teachers learn is not sufficient; a rich mix is needed. Although we have not attempted any quantitative assessment of our data, our view is that senior staff in schools need to foster and sustain a high number of strategies by which teachers learn together and which are regularly and repeatedly used so as to develop a critical mass of them. Only then will the different ways become mutually supportive and so common that they seem almost natural to the staff.

STRUCTURE

The final characteristic to be highlighted concerns organizational structures. In recent years school improvers have set great store by calls for school development plans, and have typically been attracted to structured and systematic approaches to school development. Numerous charts and diagrams bear testimony to the linear thinking of many of the planners. Such an approach relies heavily upon formal structures and creates a strong sense of direction, clarity and certainty.

However, schools are also places of interacting interests, conflict and negotiation. As Shipman (1990) says, sometimes there is less partnership and more partisanship, in which case a degree of ambiguity can be helpful to all. At the same time, rigid and tight organizational structures can be restricting for individuals. A measure of looseness may be needed. In other words, learning schools are not always tight or organizationally 'tidy' places and the staff who work in them need to be tolerant of ambiguity. Indeed, alongside the plans, which create a clear picture of the goals at which we are aiming, needs to go a measure of flexibility. Learning schools are not soft and unfocused but neither are they hard and tight institutions. Informality abounds because it is the casual encounters and conversations that are as beneficial to teachers' learning as the formal arrangements. Moreover, learning is not always predictable and staff need some space in which to pursue the unexpected developments in their teaching and the children's learning. Learning needs to be opportunistic as well as planned. Learning cannot always be manufactured by mechanical means.

One reason why many schools adopt a strong sense of structure is that some staff, usually the senior ones, believe the structure will hold the school together. Such an outlook is only partially true. For sure it makes sense systematically to link together interlocking aspects of the school, as Fullan *et al.* (1990) show in their framework for classroom and school improvement. Here they pictorially present classroom improvement, teacher learning and school improvement as three cogs that all mesh together. It is an idea that broadly supports the notion presented earlier that there are different levels to the learning school.

Yet structures alone will not create a sense of cohesion. What really holds members of staff together is a sense of shared values. However, the development of shared beliefs takes time and requires a lot more than formal structures that invite staff to plan and evaluate together. For sure these play a part, but so too do other features, such as: leaders who promote their individual visions; discussions that enable all staff to contribute to establishing the school's mission; opportunities to see other staff at work; celebrations of success; recognition of others' efforts; interest in and awareness of colleagues. Formal structures should not dominate the school because informal patterns of interaction also play a vital part in the spread of educational ideas and beliefs. Time therefore needs to be preserved for informal interaction. If it is not, the formal meetings and planning sessions may swamp and stifle the informal ways in which staff collaborate and develop.

CONCLUSIONS

In concluding this chapter I have two comments to add. First, at a time when there is increasing devolution of power and responsibilities to schools, and the school is becoming the unit of development, it makes sense to focus upon schools and to try to understand how they develop and improve. The idea of the learning school attempts to do this. And the empirical evidence shows that the self-managing school can be a developing school. Indeed, the self-developing school and the learning school are one and the same. Both focus upon the processes and structures by which staff learn in order to improve the pupils' learning.

Second, because learning is an uncertain process which can create in some individuals feelings of doubt, uncertainty and, sometimes, a loss of confidence, it follows that a learning school might be an uncomfortable school in which to work. Learning is not always an easy process and it can bring with it emotional costs. To counterbalance the painful side of learning, such schools will need to be person-centred, sensitive and caring institutions; but then all schools should be that.

REFERENCES

Armstrong, M. (1980) *Closely Observed Children*. London: Writers and Readers.

Ball, S. (1987) *The Micro-Politics of the School*. London: Methuen.

Beare, H., Caldwell, J. and Millikan, R. (1989) *Creating an Excellent School*. London: Routledge.

Bennett, N. *et al.* (1984) *The Quality of Pupil Learning Experiences*. London: Lawrence Erlbaum Associates.

Caldwell, B. and Spinks, J. (1992) *Leading the Self-managing School*. London: Falmer Press.

Campbell, P. (1990) 'A cord of three strands', unpublished case study, Cambridge Institute of Education.

Campbell, P. and Southworth, G. (1990) 'Rethinking collegiality: teachers' views', paper presented at annual meeting of AERA. Boston, MA: Cambridge Institute of Education.

Conner, C. (1991) *Assessment and Testing in the Primary School*. London: Falmer Press.

DES (1977) *Ten Good Schools: A Secondary School Enquiry by HMI*. London: HMSO.

DES (1987) *Primary Schools: Some Aspects of Good Practice*. London: HMSO.

Desforge, C. and Cockburn, A. (1987) *Understanding the Mathematics Teacher*. London: Falmer Press.

Dewey, J. (1933) *How We Think: A Restatement of the Relation of Reflective Thinking to the Educative Process*. Chicago: Henry Regnery.

Fullan, M., Bennett, B. and Rolheiser-Bennett, C. (1990) 'Linking classroom and school improvement', *Educational Leadership*, 47(8), 13-19.

Fullan, M. and Hargreaves, A. (1991) *What's Worth Fighting For? Working Together for Your School*. Toronto: OISE.

Galton, M. (1989) *Teaching in the Primary School*. London: Fulton.

Galton, M. and Simon, B. (eds) (1980) *Progress and Performance in the Primary Classroom*. London: Routledge and Kegan Paul.

Hargreaves, A. (1990) 'Individualism and individuality: reinterpreting the teacher culture', paper presented at the annual meeting of AERA. Boston, MA.

Hargreaves, D. and Hopkins, D. (1991) *The Empowered School*. London: Cassell.

Holly, P. and Southworth, G. (1989) *The Developing School*. London: Falmer Press.

Holly, P. and Whitehead, D. (eds) (1984) 'Action-research in schools: getting it into perspective'. CARN Bulletin No. 6. Cambridge: Cambridge Institute of Education.

Hopkins, D. (1985) *A Teacher's Guide to Classroom Research*. Milton Keynes: Open University Press.

Hustler, D. *et al.* (1986) *Action Research in Classrooms and Schools*. London: Allen & Unwin.

Jenkins, H.O. (1991) *Getting It Right : A Handbook for Successful School Leadership*. Oxford, Blackwell.

Joyce, B. and Showers, B. (1980) 'Improving in-service training: the messages of research', *Educational Leadership*, 37(5), 379-86.

Lieberman, A. (1986) 'Collaborative research: working with, not working on', *Educational Leadership*, 43(5), 28-32.

Lieberman, A. (ed) (1990) *Schools as Collaborative Cultures: Creating the Future Now*. London: Falmer Press.

Little, J.W. (1985) 'Teachers as teacher advisers: the delicacy of collegial leadership', *Educational Leadership*, 43(3), 34-6.

Little, J.W. (1990) 'The persistence of privacy: autonomy and initiative in teachers' professional relations', *Teachers' College Record*, 9(4), 509-36.

Mortimore, P., Sammons, P., Stoll, L., Lewis, D. and Ecob, R. (1988) *School Matters: The Junior Years*. Wells: Open Books.

NCC (1989) *Curriculum Guidance One: A Framework for the Primary Curriculum*. York: NCC.

NCC (1989) *Curriculum Guidance Three: The Whole Curriculum*. York: NCC.

Nias, J. (1989) *Primary Teachers Talking*. London: Routledge.

Nias, J., Southworth, G. and Campbell, P. (1992) *Whole School Curriculum Development in Primary Schools*. London: Falmer Press.

Nias, J., Southworth, G. and Yeomans, R. (1989) *Staff Relationships in the Primary School*. London: Cassell.

Nixon, J. (1981) *A Teacher's Guide to Action Research*. London: Grant McIntyre.

Patterson, J.L., Purkey, S.C. and Parker, J.V. (1986) *Productive School Systems for a Non-rational World*. Alexandria, VA: ASCD.

Pollard, A. (1985) *The Social World of the Primary School*. London: Cassell.

Pollard, A. and Tann, S. (1987) *Reflective Teaching in the Primary School*. London: Cassell.

Reynolds, D. and Cuttance, P. (1992) *School Effectiveness: Research, Policy and Practice*. London: Cassell.

Rosenholtz, S.J. (1989) *Teachers' Workplace: The Social Organization of Schools*. New York: Teachers' College Press.

Rubin, L. (1978) *The In-service Education of Teachers: Trends, Processes, and Prescriptions*. Boston, MA: Allyn & Bacon.

Rowlands, S. (1984) *The Enquiring Classroom*. London: Falmer Press.

Schon, D. (1971) *Beyond the Stable State*. London: Temple Smith.

Schon, D. (1983) *The Reflective Practitioner*. London: Temple Smith.

Shipman, M. (1990) *In Search of Learning*. Oxford: Blackwell.

Southworth, G. (1990) 'Leadership, headship and effective primary schools', *School Organization*, 10(1), 3-16.

Stenhouse, L. (1975) *An Introduction to Curriculum Research and Development*. London: Heinemann.

Chapter 6

School Improvement in an ERA of Change

David Hopkins

The theme of this chapter is how the pressure for change can result in school improvement. Its title contains a deliberate pun, which by reference to the Educational Reform Acts (1986 and 1988) is intended to emphasize the point that change and improvement are not necessarily synonymous. Although it is true that external pressure is often the cause, or at least the impetus, for most educational change, this is not to imply that such change is desirable or easily achieved. Indeed, as will be seen later, some changes work, others do not. Too much change also produces 'overload', which in turn creates a cycle of dependency and sometimes paralysis; situations which are becoming all too familiar in British schools. Even when change is received enthusiastically, there is no guarantee that it will be satisfactorily implemented, or that it will result in enhanced outcomes, however broadly defined, for pupils or teachers. Student achievement must be the *raison d'être* for any educational change; yet because the process of translating policy into practice is so difficult to achieve, the reality of change, as opposed to the rhetoric of change, is often only loosely connected to the progress of pupils.

In this chapter I initially discuss the problematic nature of educational change and the hiatus between policy and practice. I then begin to develop an argument for regarding school improvement as the most appropriate means of achieving educational change. I first discuss the nature of school improvement knowledge and then describe the assumptions underlying the general approach. Using Bruce Joyce's (1991) metaphor of the 'doors to school improvement', I briefly review some of the various strategies for, or ways into, school improvement. I conclude the chapter by giving the example of how development planning, as a school improvement strategy, can assist schools in achieving their developmental priorities as well as changing aspects of their culture.

I should begin, however, by saying a few preliminary words about the phrase 'school improvement'. There are two senses in which it can be used. The first is the common sense meaning, which relates to general efforts to make schools better places for pupils and students to learn in. This is a sensible interpretation, but in this chapter I use the phrase in a more technical and specific way.

As I argue in some detail later, I regard school improvement as an approach to educational change that is concerned with process as well as outcomes. School improvement is about raising student achievement through enhancing the teaching-learning process and the conditions which support it. It is about strategies for improving the school's capacity for providing quality education. So those of us who work in the field of school improvement actively seek to enhance student outcomes through specific changes in teaching approaches and the curriculum, and through strengthening the school's organizational ability to support the work of teachers. School improvement cannot therefore be simply equated with educational change in general. Many externally (and some internally) imposed changes do not improve student outcomes, and most appear to neglect the importance of the culture and organization of the school as key factors in sustaining teacher and curriculum development. The main argument of this chapter is that we should consciously adopt a school improvement approach to educational change.

EDUCATIONAL CHANGE IN OECD COUNTRIES

Over the past ten years there has been a tremendous increase in the amount of change expected of schools. This increase in expectations has been accompanied by fundamental changes in the way schools are managed and governed. In most OECD countries (a term I prefer to the slightly pejorative phrase 'Western countries') there appear to be seemingly contradictory pressures for centralization (i.e. increasing government control over policy and direction) on the one hand, and decentralization (i.e. more responsibility for implementation, resource management and evaluation at the local level) on the other. This tension is making it very difficult for schools and local authorities to implement successfully innovations that make a real difference to the quality of schooling and pupil achievement. The key challenge, as a recent OECD report makes clear, is to find a balance between the increasing demands for centrally determined policy initiatives and quality control, and the encouragement of locally developed school improvement efforts. Three principal conclusions emerge from this report on decentralization and school improvement (OECD, 1989, p. 2):

1 The decentralization of decision-making as part of school improvement establishes new roles and responsibilities for senior education officials at the centre and for school leaders, teachers and parents at the school level. As new roles are assumed, tensions inevitably develop. Approaches need to be put in place to respond to these tensions.

2 Shifts of responsibility to the school level raise the possibility that some functions, formerly carried out at the centre, will not be effectively performed. Central authorities need to ensure, through guidance and support for pre-service, in-service, and community-based programmes, that those assuming new roles have developed the capacity to meet their new responsibilities. External support for schools, re-oriented to meet specific school-defined needs,

also must be sustained (even if the services are no longer provided by central authorities).

3 The management of change, whether at the centre or at the school level, requires a strategy which considers change as a dynamic and evolutionary process. Following from a clear vision of the expected results of the change, the strategy should anticipate tensions and difficulties but also allow for adaptations and adjustments as the change proceeds.

This type of analysis raises a number of questions about how central policy can be implemented and monitored, while leaving latitude for professional judgement at the school level: about the role of external support, the allocation of resources and the involvement of governors and parents. A general response to the dilemma of decentralization has been to give more responsibility to schools for their own management. Although this goes by different names in different countries — self-managing schools, site-based management, local management of schools, restructuring — the concept remains similar. Unfortunately, similarity does not imply clarity or specificity. Many of the policies seem to be either politically or ideologically inspired ('competition' is the only way to improve the system), or an *ad hoc* response to an immediate 'crisis' situation. Simply changing bureaucratic procedures or holding people more accountable *does not by itself* improve the quality of education for our young people.

The pathology of policy implementation has recently been described by Milbrey McLaughlin (1990) in her re-analysis of the large-scale 'Rand Change Agent' study undertaken in the USA in the mid to late 1970s. She found that many of the conclusions from the study still hold true today, and commented that:

A general finding of the Change Agent study that has become almost a truism is that it is exceedingly difficult for policy to change practice, especially across levels of government. Contrary to the one-to-one relationship assumed to exist between policy and practice, the Change Agent study demonstrated that the nature, amount, and pace of change at the local level was a product of local factors that were largely beyond the control of higher-level policymakers. (McLaughlin, 1990, p.12)

The Rand study also looked at the strategies that promoted educational improvement, and based on that analysis, McLaughlin (1990, p.12) developed a list of 'what does and does not work'. Strategies that were generally seen to be ineffective were:

- reliance on outside consultants;
- packaged management approaches;
- one-shot, pre-implementation training;
- pay for training;
- formal, summative evaluation;
- comprehensive, system-wide projects.

Those that were generally effective, especially when used together were:

- concrete, teacher-specific and extended training;
- classroom assistance from local staff;
- teacher observation of similar projects in other classrooms, schools or districts;
- regular project meetings that focused on practical issues;
- teacher participation in project decisions;
- local development of project materials;
- principals' (i.e. heads') participation in training.

As is apparent from these contrasting lists, the relationship between 'macro-level policies and micro-level behaviour' is paramount. According to McLaughlin (1990, p.12), this general observation has three specific implications:

- implementation dominates outcomes;
- policy cannot mandate what matters;
- local variability is the rule; uniformity is the exception.

There are obvious implications in these findings for policy formulation. They also serve to emphasize the point that much policy decision-making in education appears to be capricious and based more on ideology than educational substance. The main purpose of this broad sweep across the current field of educational change, however, has been to provide a context for the argument that there is a preferred way of meeting the challenge of educational change — through school improvement.

School improvement has already been defined as an approach to educational change that has the twin goals of enhancing student outcomes and strengthening the school's capacity for managing change. Unfortunately, the history of educational innovation is littered with the skeletons of innovations and changes whose implementers failed to recognize this key idea. The skeletons are usually the remains of single innovations, which may have been school-wide in so far as they aimed to affect all students, but were not school-deep because they ignored the process of change and the culture of the school. It is now well established that unless innovations take account of these two conditions their impact will be short-lived. To be successful, innovations need to be set within strategies that incorporate fundamental and lasting organizational change. Strategies are needed that directly address the culture of the school, and this is what school improvement is all about.

REFINING SCHOOL IMPROVEMENT KNOWLEDGE

School improvement approaches to educational change are action and developmentally oriented. They embody the long-term goal of moving towards the vision of the 'problem-solving' or 'thinking' or 'relatively autonomous' school. School improvement is about developing strategies for educational change that strengthen the school's organization, as well as implementing curriculum reforms. This obviously implies a very different way of thinking about change from the ubiquitous 'top-down' approach so popular with policy-makers. When the school is regarded as the 'centre' of change, then strategies for change need to take this new perspective into account.

This approach is exemplified in the work of the OECD-sponsored International School Improvement Project (ISIP) and the knowledge that emanated from it (see Hopkins, 1987, 1990). School improvement was defined in the ISIP as:

> a systematic, sustained effort aimed at change in learning conditions and other related internal conditions in one or more schools, with the ultimate aim of accomplishing educational goals more effectively.
> (Van Velzen *et al.*, 1985, p. 48)

This definition was derived from the practical and research experience of the past decade or so, which has supported three main conclusions. First, achieving change is much more a matter of implementation of new practices at the school level than it is of simply deciding to adopt them. Second, school improvement is a carefully planned and managed process that takes place over a period of possibly several years: change is a process, not an event. Third, it is very difficult to change education — even in a single classroom — without also changing the school organization. The co-operation of fellow teachers and the endorsement of the school leader are usually necessary too. These perspectives inform the ISIP approach to educational change, which rests on a number of assumptions.

The school as the centre of change. This means that external reforms need to be sensitive to the situation in individual schools, rather than assuming that all schools are the same. It also implies that school improvement efforts need to adopt a 'classroom-exceeding' perspective, without ignoring the classroom.

A systematic approach to change. School improvement is a carefully planned and managed process that takes place over a period of several years.

The 'internal conditions' of schools are a key focus for change. These include not only the teaching-learning activities used in the school, but also the school's procedures, role allocation and resource use that support the teaching-learning process.

Accomplishing educational goals more effectively. Generally speaking, educational goals are what a school is *supposed* to be doing for its students and society. More specifically, educational goals will reflect the particular mission of a school, and represent what the school itself regards as desirable. This suggests a broader definition of outcome than student scores on achievement tests, even though for some schools these may be pre-eminent. Schools also serve the more general developmental needs of students, the professional development of teachers and the needs of their communities.

A multi-level perspective. Although the school is the centre of change it does not act alone. The school is embedded in an educational system that has to work collaboratively or symbiotically if the highest degrees of quality are to be achieved. This means that the roles of teachers, heads, governors, parents, support people (advisers, higher education, consultants etc.) and local authorities should be defined, harnessed and committed to the process of school improvement.

Integrative implementation strategies. This implies a linkage between 'top-down' and 'bottom-up', remembering of course that both approaches can apply at a number of different levels in the system. Ideally, 'top-down' provides policy aims, an overall strategy and operational plans; this is complemented by a 'bottom-up' response involving diagnosis, priority goal setting and implementation. The former provides the framework, resources and a menu of alternatives; the latter provides energy and school-based implementation.

The drive towards institutionalization. Change is only successful when it has become part of the natural behaviour of teachers in the school. Implementation by itself is not enough.

It is this philosophy and approach that underpinned the International School Improvement Project. It emphasized that school improvement efforts are characterized by a dual emphasis on enhancing the school's capacity for change as well as implementing specific reforms, both of which have as their ultimate goal an increase in student achievement. School improvement is therefore about: (1) strengthening the school's organizational capacity, as well as (2) implementing educational reform. School improvement studies (3) propose a school-centred approach to educational change, and (4) take a broad view of student achievement.

In our own school improvement work we have attempted to distil this learning and practical experience into a number of 'principles', which seem to us to capture the essence of school improvement (Hopkins and Ainscow, 1992). They provide us with a philosophical and practical starting point. The schools in our project work from an assumption that they are most likely to strengthen their ability to provide quality education and enhanced outcomes for all pupils when they adopt ways of working that are consistent with the following ideas:

1 The main focus for action should be on teaching and learning in classrooms, in order that *all* students develop 'the intellectual and imaginative powers and competencies' that they need in as personalized a way as possible.

2 Such classroom practice can only be sustained through ongoing staff development.

3 Leadership should empower people (students, staff and community) to achieve their own and the school's purposes.

4 All members of a school community should actively build and share a common vision of its main purposes.

5 The school's current priorities should reflect its main purposes and its vision, and be generated through consultation.

6 Work on the current priorities should be based upon planning in order to manage the process of change.

7 The substance of staff development should be teaching skills, as well as the best available knowledge of curriculum content.

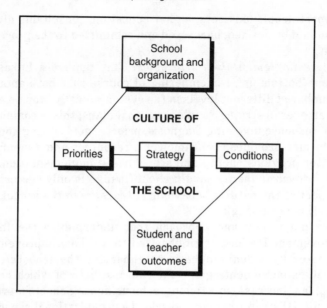

Figure 6.1 *The logic of school improvement*

8 Collaboration is a necessary condition for staff development and school improvement.

9 Processes of improvement should be informed by monitoring, feedback and reflection on the part of students as well as staff and, of course, the school.

10 Successful policy implementation occurs when groups of teachers adapt educational ideas to their own context and professional needs.

The significance of these principles lies in their synergism: together they are greater than the sum of their parts. And it is in this way that they should be regarded. They characterize an approach, rather than prescribe a course of action. The principles therefore inform what teachers do during school improvement work; they provide a touchstone for the various strategies they devise, and the behaviours they adopt. In the following sections we see how they underlie and fit into an overall strategy for school improvement.

THE LOGIC OF SCHOOL IMPROVEMENT

The knowledge described in the previous section is fine as far as it goes: but to be of much use to practitioners it needs to be cast in an action framework. Figure 6.1 contains the specific set of ideas on which we base our school improvement work and the interrelationship between them (for more detail see Hopkins *et al.*, in press). As such it too rests on a number of assumptions. In describing these assumptions we relate them to the main components of the diagram: i.e. outcomes for students and staff, school culture, the school's background and organization, the chosen developmental priorities, the conditions necessary to support such changes and the school improvement strategy.

The *first assumption* is that school improvement will result in *enhanced outcomes* for students and staff. We define 'outcomes' broadly, and there will obviously be variations in outcome according to the focus of the improvement effort. For students, the outcomes could be critical thinking, learning capacity, self-esteem and so on. For staff they could be collegiality, opportunities for professional learning and increased responsibility. The main point is, however, that those involved in school improvement must keep outcomes clearly in mind. This assumption, although perhaps uncontentious, needs emphasizing because many school improvement efforts lose their focus during implementation and as a result produce only frustration.

The *second assumption* is less obvious. School culture is the vital, yet neglected, dimension in the improvement process. When school improvement efforts are ineffective, it is often because they have ignored the *culture of the school.* Too often school improvement focuses on individual changes, discrete projects and individual teachers and classrooms rather than how these changes can fit in with and adapt the organization and ethos of the school. The culture of the school is a reflection of the norms and values of its members: 'it is the way we get things done around here'. School cultures are actively, though often unwittingly, constructed by their participants. The types of school cultures most supportive of school improvement efforts are those that: are collaborative; have high expectations for both students and staff; exhibit a consensus on values; support an orderly and secure environment; and encourage teachers to learn, take responsibility and work together. Research studies continue to accumulate to demonstrate the positive impact of culture on student achievement and teacher behaviour. It is of prime importance in any school improvement effort, because it holds the key to improving quality.

The *third assumption* is that the school's *background and organization* are key factors in the school improvement process. *Background* factors are those such as location, intake or buildings. They are 'givens', which are impossible or unlikely to change in the short or medium term and therefore provide the context within which change occurs. The school's *organizational* variables relate to internal features, such as their management arrangements, the level of staff collaboration, the style of leadership and staff morale. These variables are more amenable to change but are also 'given' at any particular point in time. Unfortunately most school improvement efforts address organizational factors, which are often the main inhibitors of change, as only explanatory factors. It is also interesting to note that a school's organizational structure is inevitably a reflection of its values; so there is a strong relationship between the school's organization and its culture.

The *fourth assumption* is that school improvement works best when there is a clear and practical focus for the development effort. These are the school's 'practices and policies', and they normally refer to some aspect of curriculum, assessment or classroom processes. As it is vital for the school's staff to feel 'ownership' of these developmental activities they need to be as practically focused as possible. Although the balance of activities will vary from school to school, *priorities for development* will inevitably be central to the mission of the school; relate to the current reform agenda; and lead to specific outcomes for students and staff.

The *fifth assumption* is that the *conditions* of school improvement are worked on at the same time as the curriculum or other priorities the school has set itself. In practice therefore the priorities will also: have implications for the school's management and organization; link to teaching and learning; contain an emphasis on evaluation and reflection; involve a programme of staff development.

It is these and similar activities that provide the conditions within which work on the priorities will flourish. In the list below, for example, are the conditions that we have been using in our Improving the Quality of Schooling project (Ainscow and Hopkins, 1992).

1.1 Forms of leadership that empower are established.

1.2 The school engages in a process of vision building.

1.3 Policies are developed that lead to action.

1.4 Development planning provides the overall framework for improvement.

1.5 Time is created for development

2.1 Staff development policies that link individual and institutional needs.

2.2 Staff development programmes that include various elements, such as theory, demonstrations, practice and feedback.

2.3 Staff development activities that take account of the change process.

2.4 Staff development strategies that promote individual learning (self-directed learning).

2.5 Staff development programmes that embrace teacher appraisal.

3.1 Task groups exist that are representative of the whole school.

3.2 Effective decision-making procedures are utilized.

3.3 All staff are made aware of decisions made in the task groups through a communication network.

4.1 Data are collected relevant to the school's development priorities.

4.2 These data are interpreted and used to inform planning processes.

4.3 All staff are aware of the procedures and ground rules for collecting data.

5.1 Teachers are proud of their craft and regard teaching as an art form.

5.2 Teachers are skilful managers of classrooms and of the individual learning of students.

5.3 Teachers work collaboratively to acquire a repertoire of teaching approaches or models.

5.4 School development supports teacher development through a central focus on the teaching-learning process.

6.1 Groups of staff meet together regularly to discuss aspects of their classroom practice.

6.2 Various members of staff co-ordinate activities related to school development priorities.

6.3 Individual teachers have established partnerships with colleagues who visit their classrooms to assist with professional development.

6.4 Effective use is made of available external support.

The *sixth assumption* is that a *school improvement strategy* needs to be developed in order to link priorities to the conditions. This is problematic because the strategy needs to affect not only what teachers do, but also outcomes, the school's culture and its organization. The strategy will need to be more or less powerful depending on the relative 'strength' of the other factors. In some cases, for example, the school's organizational structures may well need to be altered as part of the development process. This is difficult if the strategy only has an instructional focus.

Although it may be helpful conceptually and strategically to think of these three aspects of the overall strategy as distinct, in reality they coalesce. In practice, the priority or curriculum focus and the strategy combine in the minds of teachers to present a uniform reality. On a day-to-day basis school improvement is an amalgam of broad strategies, such as self-review, action planning and staff development, which link together the classroom and the school, *as well as* the more dynamic aspects of the change process. Given this complexity it is impossible to be prescriptive about the nature of such a strategy, particularly as it is composed of two interlinked but distinct aspects.

The first aspect is the *individual strategies*, such as collaborative inquiry, teacher appraisal, development planning, staff INSET, school evaluation and external support, which all receive strong empirical support as to their effectiveness. But they should be regarded more as possible ingredients for a recipe, that the school determines and then proceeds to mix, rather than as blueprints for action. There is also some indication that in combination they are even more powerful. Our evaluation of school improvement projects that linked school review to teacher appraisal, for example, showed major improvements in a school's curriculum and instruction in relatively short periods of time (Bollington and Hopkins, 1989). School development planning in particular, as we shall see later, appears to be one of those strategies that can link together a variety of school improvement approaches in a relatively seamless and holistic way, at least from the teacher's point of view.

When these strategies are embedded within the school's organization, they combine to form an internal infrastructure that supports the management of change. This *internal infrastructure* is the second aspect of the strategy. It refers, for example, to the way in which teachers work together, the organization of learning and the management arrangements employed by the school. In schools that are successful at managing the change process, this internal

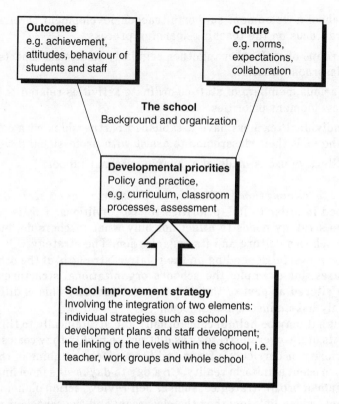

Figure 6.2 *A holistic approach to school improvement*

infrastructure links and integrates the individual strategies to provide a coherent framework for action that informs and supports the daily work of teachers.

In this section I have described the logic of school improvement in terms of a number of interlinked operating assumptions. In terms of doing school improvement however, one needs to know where to start. Figure 6.2 is a more prescriptive version of Figure 6.1, in so far as it suggests that one begins with a strategy that affects a chosen priority, which in turn and over time impacts upon student and teacher outcomes and the school's organization and culture. So far so good, but this still does not tell us which strategy to use. It is this question that provides the focus for the following section.

THE DOORS TO SCHOOL IMPROVEMENT

There is no one place to start with school improvement. It all depends on the aspirations and experience of the school and individuals involved. But as we have seen there are not only some principles to guide us but also some proven approaches. Bruce Joyce (1991) has recently reviewed various North American approaches to restructuring and school improvement, and finds them fragmented. He refers to these individual approaches as being 'doors' which can open or unlock the process of school improvement. Joyce (1991, p.59) concludes:

These proponents emphasize different aspects of school culture at the outset — in other words, they choose to open different doors to school improvement. Each door opens a passageway into the culture of the school. My examination of their work reveals the following five major emphases:

Collegiality: developing cohesive and professional relations within school faculties and connecting them more closely to their surrounding neighbourhoods.

Research: helping school faculties study research findings about effective school practices or instructional alternatives.

Site specific information: helping faculties collect and analyze data about their schools and their students' progress.

Curriculum initiatives: introducing changes within subject areas or, as in the case of the computer, across the curriculum areas.

Instructional initiatives: organizing teachers to study teaching skills and strategies.

All these emphases can eventually change the culture of the school substantially. Perhaps, if we look carefully at each door to school improvement, we can discover where each is likely to lead, how the passageways are connected, what proponents of any one approach can borrow from the others, and the costs and benefits of opening any one (or any combination) first.

Joyce argues that single approaches are unlikely to be as powerful an agent for school improvement as a synthesis. He says somewhat wryly that while schools are making up their minds about which door to open first they should be collecting information about themselves and trying to acquire an extra teaching strategy or two! His point is well taken: move into action while decision making, and make school improvement everyone's business.

The implicit assumption is that behind the door are a series of interconnecting pathways that lead inexorably to school improvement. Unfortunately, this is not so. Because of their singular nature, most school improvement strategies fail to a greater or lesser degree to affect the culture of the school. They tend to focus on individual changes, and individual teachers and classrooms, rather than how these changes can fit in with and adapt the organization and ethos of the school. As a consequence, when the door is opened it only leads into a cul-de-sac. This partially accounts for the uneven effect of most of our educational reforms.

To continue in this practical vein for a moment, it seems logical that if we are to overcome the problems of educational change already described, we need to find some way of integrating organizational and curriculum change within a coherent strategy. We need to find ways of opening the doors to school improvement simultaneously or consecutively and of linking together the pathways behind them.

There are a number of familiar 'doors' that we have passed through during the recent history of educational change in the UK, some of which are similar to those identified by Joyce. I regard his list as being illustrative rather than exclusive despite my attempt at translating from the American! A much opened door in the early 1980s was the one named school self-evaluation, which in some schools built on experiences gained from going through the teacher-based action research 'door'. Other 'doors' have been the 'discovery' of management training in 1983, changes in INSET funding in the mid-1980s, and categorically funded curriculum projects such as TVEI. The two Educational Reform Acts introduced new entrances, such as the increased role of governors, the devolution of financial control and the National Curriculum. There are of course many more examples of ways into school improvement: for example, an increasing number of schools are finding the prescriptions of the effective schools research a helpful starting point for their improvement efforts. In most cases, however, the research evidence suggests that such efforts will have limited impact on daily classroom life, unless some way is found to link them together.

What are needed are powerful and integrative implementation strategies that directly address the culture of the school. We have already noted that many strategies for school improvement tend to address single factors or innovations rather than whole-school issues. When strategies do encompass whole-school or cross-curricular issues they tend to be school-wide rather than school-deep. To paraphrase Fullan (1990, pp. 248-9), without a direct and primary focus on changes in the school's organization, it is unlikely that single innovations or specific projects will have much of an impact, and whatever impact there is will be short-lived. School improvement efforts which ignore these deeper organizational conditions are 'doomed to tinkering'. Strategies are needed that more directly address the culture of the school. The point is well made. Only the more comprehensive strategies have much of a chance of seriously achieving school improvement. It is to a description of one of these that we turn in the following section.

DEVELOPMENT PLANNING AND THE CULTURE OF THE SCHOOL

I hope that by now the argument is sufficiently clear to support my belief that successful change is predicated on modifications to and the enhancement of the culture of the school. The culture of the school is a reflection of the norms and values of its members. I share Rutter and colleagues' (1979, pp. 178-9) view that the characteristics of schools as social institutions *combine* to create a particular ethos, or set of values, attitudes and behaviours which are representative of the school as a whole, which are open to modification by the staff, rather than being fixed by external constraints.

The DES project on school development plans (SDP) was an attempt to develop a strategy that would, among other things, help governors, heads and staff to change the culture of their schools (see Hargreaves *et al.*, 1989; Hargreaves and Hopkins, 1991). In my admittedly biased opinion, development planning provides an exemplary illustration of a school improvement strategy, combining as it does curriculum change with modifications to the school's management arrangements. It is also a strategy that is becoming increasingly widespread in British schools as teachers and school leaders struggle to take control of the process of change.

Development planning, besides helping the school organize what it is already doing and what it needs to do in a more purposeful and coherent way, is about helping schools to manage innovation and change successfully. The distinctive feature of a development plan is that it brings together, in an overall plan, national and local policies and initiatives, the school's aim and values, its existing achievements and its needs for development. By co-ordinating aspects of planning which are otherwise separate, the school acquires a shared sense of direction and is able to control and manage the tasks of development and change. A development plan is easily described. Priorities for development are selected and planned in detail for one year and are supported by action plans or working documents for staff. The priorities for later years are sketched in outline to provide the longer-term programme (Hargreaves *et al.*, 1989, p. 4).

From our work with schools there appears to be a sequence of three stages that a school goes through as it more fully understands the process of development planning. When schools embark on development planning for the *first* time, attention is focused on the plan in the form of a document. People ask questions such as: What does a plan look like? What sort of document is it? What makes a development plan a good plan? Can you show us a plan to guide our own thinking? These are reasonable and understandable questions. Although they are the ones that first spring to mind, they are not the best place to begin (and in practice schools find it much easier than they imagine to write a plan as a document).

The *second* stage is when a school realizes that the process of development planning, rather than the plan as a product, is the key to success. The plan is no more than a statement of intentions: it is the quality of the process that determines success. The production of a good plan and its successful implementation depend upon a sound grasp of the processes involved. A wise choice of content for the plan as well as the means of implementing the plan successfully will be made only when the process of development planning is thoroughly understood.

The *third* stage is reached when there is a realization that the *management of planning* is the key to successful development planning. This may require a review of, and changes to, the school's existing management arrangements: i.e. the frameworks it establishes for itself, the way in which roles are clarified and allocated, and the way in which the school's partners work together. It is at this stage that the school understands that development planning's main purpose is to help create the conditions in which other innovations can flourish and be successfully implemented.

Not all schools find development planning easy. Schools face a double problem. They cannot remain as they now are if they are to implement recent reforms. But at the same time, schools also need to maintain some continuity with their present and previous practices. There is therefore for most schools a tension between development (change) and maintenance (stability and continuity). The problem is that schools tend to generate organizational structures that predispose them towards one or the other. Schools (or parts of schools) at the development extreme may be so over-confident in their innovative capacities that they take on too much too quickly. Schools at the maintenance extreme may either see little purpose in reform or have a poor record in managing innovation. Schools who can balance the demands of development and maintenance will find it most easy to engage in development planning.

We have used the term 'management arrangements' to describe this aspect of the culture of the school. Our descriptions of the three basic aspects or dimensions of the management arrangements are drawn from schools where development planning is most successful. The dimensions are common to all schools, large and small, primary, middle, secondary and special. The actual arrangements chosen to allow the tasks for each dimension to be accomplished will, however, be unique to the school. They may be used as a guide for a school to review the character and quality of its management arrangements. Space unfortunately precludes all but a cursory description of the three components. More detail can be found in Chapter 3 of Hargreaves and Hopkins (1991).

The first component consists of *frameworks* which guide the actions of all who are involved in the school. Examples of frameworks are the school's aims and policies, and the systems for decision-making and consultation. Without clear frameworks, the school would soon lapse into confusion and conflict.

Second, the management arrangements clarify *roles and responsibilities*. All who are involved in the school need to have a shared understanding of their respective roles and of who is taking responsibility for what. Well-designed frameworks are useless without clear roles and responsibilities.

Third, the management arrangements promote ways in which the people involved can *work together* so that each person finds his or her particular role enjoyable and rewarding, and at the same time the aims of the school as a whole can be achieved successfully. While the head undoubtedly plays the key role, management and the arrangements to support it are a collective activity and responsibility.

Through a review and revision of its management arrangements a school begins to transform its culture to support effective development planning. At the same time, the process of development planning will itself generate changes to the management arrangements and to the culture of the school. It is a matter of fine judgement to decide which aspects of the management arrangements need to be changed before beginning work on development planning. But it is unwise to delay just because conditions in the school do not seem wholly conducive — they rarely are. The work of development planning will itself help to promote better conditions.

In selecting and sequencing priorities for a development plan there is also another distinction to be borne in mind. Development planning involves two kinds of change: *root innovations* that generate the base on which other, or *branch innovations*, can be sustained. Strong roots to support the curriculum and teaching aspects of the development plan are provided by, for example, a well-developed staff development policy, or a history of collaborative work among the staff and with the school's partners. When such roots are lacking, there is a danger that some of the planned branch innovations will wither and die.

Because the management arrangements serve as a root to so many innovations, adjustments to them will be a strong candidate for an early priority in many schools. Recognizing that the appropriate management arrangements will evolve progressively to support new roles and relationships is itself a step in changing the culture of the school.

Let me conclude this section by outlining some guidelines for schools that wish to use development planning as a means of school improvement for cultural change. Schools embarking on development planning are most likely to lay foundations for future success when:

- they begin by reviewing their management arrangements
- the number of priorities chosen is very small;
- there are both root and branch innovations;
- branch innovations are restricted to those that cannot be postponed;
- root innovations are selected to support the inescapable branch innovations, and contain aspects of the management arrangements identified from the review.

CODA

Despite our increasingly sophisticated knowledge about the process of educational change, the school as an organization and the various strategies for improvement, student achievement still lags far behind society's expectations. The reasons for this are legion, but in conclusion let me briefly return to three themes that have provided the subtext for this chapter.

First, it seems to me that one of the major difficulties is the way in which school improvement knowledge is used. Knowledge of the type discussed in this chapter is not a panacea; at best it is informed advice that schools may wish to test out in their own situations, and policy-makers incorporate into their mandates. The advantage of school improvement strategies, however, is that they provide a means whereby this knowledge can be put to the test of practice. The knowledge is there not to control, but to inform and discipline practice.

Second, there is the realization that although we now know a lot more about school improvement there remains an element of serendipity in the achievement of educational quality. Schools are 'non-rational' organizations that are highly resistant to external pressure for change. Bruce Joyce captured this paradox nicely when he said that 'educational change is technically simple but socially complex'. It is the social complexity that militates against neat categorization and prescription. Yet this is why we must continue to pay attention, both in our policies and in our practices, to the social organization of schools, and to how they create their own cultures (Ainscow and Hopkins, 1992).

Finally, a word about politics. Educational change is usually the result of a political process at both the macro- and micro-levels. On the macro-political level centralized policies create the agenda, whereas at the micro-political level implementation determines outcomes. The implementation of policy is unpredictable because neither of these levels has, in reality, much influence on the other. Schools cannot determine national or local policy, although they can decide what *they* want to do. Similarly, policy-makers, although they may set the agenda, cannot control outcomes, because the process of implementation is mediated through many different school contexts. The hiatus between policy and practice inhibits student achievement. Unfortunately, in most systems the debate is too often dichotomous. There is a failure to realize that educational quality is a function of the dialectic between policy and practice, not the preserve of one or the other, although both have their part to play and their role to fulfil. It is time to recentre the debate on the process of schooling. The research evidence is unequivocal in maintaining that student achievement is positively related to school processes. It is here where policy is translated into practice and where the work of policy-makers and practitioners meets. It is with the specification of strategies for school improvement that the dialogue should begin.

In preparing this chapter I have drawn heavily from other pieces written (a few with colleagues) recently (in particular Ainscow and Hopkins, 1992; Hargreaves and Hopkins, 1991; Hopkins, 1990, 1991a; Hopkins and Ainscow, 1992; Hopkins et al., in press). I have done this because I have felt the need to clarify my thinking on the nature of school improvement, to put it down in one piece as economically as I could, and to share it with others. So I apologize to those few assiduous readers who find me repeating myself and crave their indulgence. I find that it is only through the process of writing, reflecting and re-writing that some clarity is eventually achieved.

REFERENCES

Ainscow, M. and Hopkins, D. (1992) 'Aboard the moving school', *Educational Leadership*, 50(3), 79-81.

Bollington, R. and Hopkins, D. (1989) 'School-based review — as a strategy for the implementation of teacher appraisal and school improvement', *Educational Change and Development*, 10, 8-17.

Fullan, M. (1990) 'Change processes in secondary schools: towards a more fundamental agenda', in M. McLaughlin *et al.* (eds), *The Contexts of Teaching in Secondary Schools*. New York: Teachers College Press.

Hargreaves, D. H. and Hopkins, D. (1991) *The Empowered School*. London: Cassell.

Hargreaves, D. H., Hopkins, D., Leask, M., Connolly, J. and Robinson, P. (1989) *Planning for School Development*. London: DES.

Hopkins, D. (1987) *Improving the Quality of Schooling*. Lewes: Falmer Press.

Hopkins, D. (1990) 'The International School Improvement Project and effective schooling: towards a synthesis', *School Organisation*, 10(2/3), 179-94.

Hopkins, D. (1991a) 'School improvement and the problem of educational change', in C. McLaughlin and M. Rouse (eds), *Supporting Schools*. London: Fulton.

Hopkins, D. (1991b) 'Changing school culture through development planning', in S. Brown and S. Riddell (eds), *School Effectiveness: An Account of Research Findings for Senior Management in Schools*. London: HMSO.

Hopkins, D. (1991c) *Process Indicators for School Improvement*. Paris: OECD-CERI INES Project.

Hopkins, D. and Ainscow, M. (1992) *IQEA Project Handbook*. Cambridge: University of Cambridge Institute of Education.

Hopkins, D., Ainscow, M. and West, M. (in press) *School Improvement in an ERA of Change*. London: Cassell.

Joyce, B. (1991) 'The doors to school improvement', *Educational Leadership*, May, 59-62.

McLaughlin, M. (1990) 'The Rand Change Agent Study revisited', *Educational Researcher*, 19(9), 11-16.

OECD (1989) *Decentralisation and School Improvement*. Paris: OECD-CERI.

Rutter, M., Maughan, B., Mortimore, P. and Ouston, J., with Smith, A. (1979) *Fifteen Thousand Hours*. Wells: Open Books.

Van Velzen, W., Miles, M., Ekholm, M., Hameyer, U. and Robin, D. (1985) *Making School Improvement Work*. Leuven: ACCO.

Chapter 7

Money, Monitoring and Management

Hywel Thomas and Alison Bullock

INTRODUCTION

Money, monitoring and management, and their implications for the curriculum experiences of children, are the themes of this chapter, and they will be examined in the context of resource planning at national, local and institutional levels. On *money*, the 1986 and 1988 Education Reform Acts require the provision of more information about the public funding of schools than has ever before been readily available in England and Wales. Adding to the 1986 Act's requirement that each LEA produce a statement of expenditure for each of its schools, the Local Management of Schools (LMS) provisions of the 1988 Act require each LEA to have a public and explicit formula setting out the means by which funds are allocated to schools. How this money is allocated in practice to different schools and children is the first theme that will be explored, drawing upon the work of a research project entitled 'The Funding of Schools after the 1988 Education Reform Act'. How the use of that money might be *monitored* is the focus of the second theme. Recent Education Acts have, *inter alia*, altered the role of LEAs in budgeting, staffing and administration. In the future, greater prominence will be given by LEAs, the Funding Agency for Schools (FAS) and the Office for Standards in Education (OFSTED) to functions of support, monitoring and evaluation. The chapter draws principally upon some completed research to suggest ways in which data on school costs and performance may provide means for informing the LEA in its quality monitoring role (Thomas, 1990). The use schools make of their *management* responsibilities in deploying resources is examined in the third theme and draws upon interviews with headteachers in locally managed schools. How these different facets of the processes of education planning affect levels of efficiency and equity is a component of the discussion of each theme and also contributes to the concluding section on planning for quality.

FUNDING THE SCHOOLS

Public funds provide by far the largest share of the finances of maintained schools in England and Wales and they are an essential component of school development. They provide much of the means upon which schools draw in order to meet their aims and objectives and, to an extent, they set limits to what can be achieved. Describing how these public funds are distributed makes explicit the preferences-in-practice of the planners who decide how much to allocate to different children and schools. One of the virtues of LMS, therefore, is that since April 1990 funds are being allocated to schools by LEAs on the basis of a public and explicit formula. This makes more explicit the judgements by LEAs about the funding implications of different educational needs. These include judgements of the needs of: children aged from 2 to 19 years; schools of different size; schools serving communities assessed as socially disadvantaged; and schools with children identified as having special educational needs but who are not statemented. This section draws upon the work of the 'Funding' project to reflect upon the planning of resource allocation within an LEA, using data on the funding of pupils according to age and the funding of schools of different size.

Schools in England and Wales are required to follow a National Curriculum, which specifies the programmes of study for all children from 5 to 16 years. How much money a school receives for providing for these children can differ widely (Bullock and Thomas, 1993a). In Table 7.1 we provide data on the allocations of funds to pupils at fifteen age intervals; in the contemporary jargon, these are age-weighted pupil units (AWPUs) and are the funding levels used in the financial year which ended in April 1991. We have data on AWPUs for 71 LEAs and show maximum, minimum and mean expenditures for the sample as a whole. Since the data on all 71 would be indigestible, however, we have selected ten cases to illustrate some general points. The choice was based upon AWPU8, normally the unit of lowest value in the 71 LEAs, and we have included in our sample all those LEAs where the AWPU8 was within 2 per cent of the group mean. The group mean was £800, so we include LEAs with a range of £784 to £816. While we begin our discussion with the set, we draw as necessary upon other examples.

The funds distributed on the basis of the AWPUs are not the whole budget of a school and we should be cautious about simplistic comparisons. In his early summary of schemes, George Thomas (1990) rightly warns that inter-LEA comparisons of AWPUs ignore the proportion of the General Schools' Budget which is delegated through the formula. An LEA may have AWPUs of a lower value than another but provide more support to schools through the non-delegated part of its budget. Differences may also arise because of the construction of a formula, the rules which determine the distribution of the Aggregated Schools' Budget (ASB). One LEA may allocate more of its ASB through the AWPU component of the formula compared with another, which may give more emphasis to non-AWPU special factors, such as additional funding for small schools. There are, however, some limits to these differences and government policy has been directed to reduce them further. In 1990 a minimum of 75 per cent of the ASB was allocated through the AWPU element of the formula and rose to 80 per cent in 1993. There are also differences in funding levels between LEAs, which arise because of the current arrangements for funding local government. For all these reasons, and because this chapter is not principally about funding, we shall largely avoid discussion here of inter-LEA comparisons (see Bullock and Thomas, 1993b for a fuller discussion). By including the maximum, minimum and mean data, however, we do indicate that there are very considerable differences

Table 7.1 *LEA funding (in £) at different ages (AWPUs)*

LEA	Age														
	4	5	6	7	8	9	10	11	12	13	14	15	16	17	18
Cleveland	856	856	856	814	814	814	814	1139	1139	1139	1453	1563	1917	1917	1917
Coventry	1064	803	803	795	795	795	799	1239	1239	1239	1594	1724	1732	1798	1798
Derbyshire	887	783	783	802	806	806	806	1135	1135	1135	1381	1497	1792	1803	1803
Isle of Wight	801	801	801	801	801	869	869	869	869	1302	1302	1392	2325[a]	2325[a]	2325[a]
North Yorks	861	816	816	792	792	792	792	1146	1146	1221	1435	1607	1921[b]	2062	2062
Redbridge	1031	804	804	804	804	804	804	1272	1272	1272	1525	1525	2148	2148	2148
Somerset	921	921	921	806	806	806	806	1133	1133	1133	1484	1591	1901	1901	1901
Sunderland	1124	827	799	799	799	799	799	1309	1309	1309	1368	1368	1664	1664	0
Tameside	1145	837	837	812	812	812	812	1170	1170	1170	1495	1609	1869	1934	1934
Warwickshire	789	789	789	789	789	789	789	1073	1073	1073	1436	1436	1862	1862	1862
Results for 71 LEAs															
Mean	935	840	831	804	800	810	820	1128	1148	1179	1383	1475	1843	1878	1865
Minimum	634	634	634	614	614	617	617	869	869	913	1105	1217	1428	1501	0
Maximum	1092	1092	1017	1025	935	987	1002	1468	1468	1468	1633	1901	2325	2325	2630

[a] A level, £2317; GCSE 6th Form, £2331.
[b] £1890 non-exam; £1952 exam.

between LEAs, which need to be better understood. Making comparisons within LEAs is somewhat less problematic, although we should be alert to specific circumstances which may explain notable differences. With these caveats, what can be said about these ten LEAs and the set from which they are drawn?

The ten were selected because their AWPUs for 8-year-olds (effectively National Curriculum Year 4) are close to the mean for the 71 LEAs. It is the least well funded year group, although these levels of funding are little different from the other junior school years. In eight of the ten LEAs, the lowest cash values are for 7-10-year-olds (NC Years 3 to 6) and, in this respect, they typify the larger set. The exceptions are Derbyshire and the Isle of Wight, where some infant years are less well funded. Why these LEAs differ in their view of the resource requirements of these year groups is a legitimate question, although of a lesser order, perhaps, than why the junior years should be the cheapest.

The overall chronological pattern is of a decline in funding levels for the junior years from the infant years and then substantial increases into the secondary years. This again is the pattern for the 71 LEAs, although the Isle of Wight and Warwickshire differ by not giving a premium to the early years by comparison with the junior years. Why?

The move from the primary to the secondary sector is demarcated by additional resources amounting to a mean of 38 per cent for 11-year-olds compared with 10-year-olds. Within the set of ten LEAs this ranges from zero in the Isle of Wight, explained no doubt by its pattern of school organization, to 64 per cent in Sunderland. Whatever historical explanations might explain the additional funding at 11 years, do they remain tenable in terms of differences in the requirements of the National Curriculum and the wider educational needs of the child? Will national and local planners begin to review these and other relative weights in the new curriculum and funding circumstances arising from the 1988 Education Reform Act?

The greatest relative differences in funding are those between the units for 8-year-olds and those for the 16-19-year-olds; here also there are sharp differences in intra-LEA ratios. In the Isle of Wight, for example, the value of AWPUI6 (£2325) is 2.9 times greater than the weighting of AWPU8 (£801). This compares with Sunderland where the value of AWPUI6 (£1664) is 2.08 times that of AWPU8 (£799). The summary data from the 71 LEAs in Table 7.1 show that the *minimum* value of AWPUI6 (£1428) is greater than the *maximum* value of any LEA's AWPU4 to AWPU10 (NC Years R to 6). While these inter-year differentials reflect the tradition of higher levels of resourcing for older children and raise questions about educational needs, the different *relative* judgements within LEAs suggest an area worthy of closer examination. It would also be pertinent to compare the funding levels of 16-19-year-olds in schools compared with further education, an area which will inevitably concern the new funding council as it merges sixth form and FE colleges.

A final example notes the different assumptions about the perceived needs of reception-year children (AWPU4) in different LEAs, our sample of ten having a range from £789 in Warwickshire to £1145 in Tameside.

Clearly, the comparative weights of all year groups is an area that would benefit from further examination with respect to the implied judgement of need. What are the rationales which underlie these differences, and are some more compelling than others in meeting contemporary needs? The differences and the similarities shown here raise questions about differences in local circumstances and in local interpretations of educational needs. One of the great merits of funding by formulae is that they make more public the preferences of policymakers and resource planners. They offer no answers but they suggest that, to the extent that resources contribute to the quality of educational experiences in schools for children of different ages, there are differences within and between LEAs which merit further investigation. They suggest a need for internal reviews within LEAs but also point to national reviews to understand better the differences which exist.

Similar observations can be made about differences in ways by which LEAs define and plan for the support of small schools. We have written about this elsewhere (Bullock and Thomas, 1992) and do not intend to repeat that material here. We only note here, therefore, differences in the definition of the small primary and secondary school in a small number of LEAs. In defining size for supplementary funding, for example, the number of pupils on roll (NOR) can be 150, 160, 200 and 250 in primary schools and 470, 600, 800 and 832 in secondary schools. These numbers may differ because of differences in the construction of formulae, but they provide *prima facie* evidence of quite different assumptions about the resource requirements of schools of different size. This is another area which would benefit from further investigation.

To compare levels of funding for different year groups or schools of different size and type is to concentrate upon inputs, recognizing that they tell us something about their implications for the scale and diversity of processes that schools may be able to provide. They tell us relatively little about the quality of those processes and even less about school outputs, although we may choose (unwisely) to intuit judgements about processes and outcomes from our information on inputs. In these respects, the study of provision gives us no direct information on the efficiency of schools, the concept that is central to this chapter's discussion of monitoring performance.

MONITORING PERFORMANCE

There is surely irony in the fact that once schools receive money allocated for the first time by an explicit and public formula they then have considerable freedom to reallocate it according to their judgement of need. Boundaries to this freedom exist, however, most notably with respect to statutory duties for the curriculum and testing. These statutory requirements provide standardized criteria by which some of the outcomes of schools might be compared. If the monitoring of these outcomes can, as a result of LMS, be more clearly linked with information on the disposition of resources it brings into sharper focus some of the relationships between inputs, processes and outputs, allowing consideration of the issue of educational efficiency.

Efficiency should not be equated with parsimony if, by that, we mean stin-

Table 7.2 *Selected cost and performance data on A-level provision in one LEA*

Institution	Range of courses offered annually	n subject entries p.a. for three years	Per capita cost of a subject entry (£)	Average A-level score standardized for intake	Cost-effectiveness on a progress criterion
Rossthwaite SFC	30-32	245	884	2.02	438
Weston SFC	30	298	920	2.10	438
Acreridge HS	15-18	79	1311	1.54	851
Beeches HS	16-18	156	841	1.72	489
Whitefield HS	15	50	1342	1.25	1074
Winson Heath HS	17	119	1097	1.72	638
Weston CoT	12-15	114	1065	1.88	566

giness. Efficient education is not an approach which feeds inputs through a productive process as cheaply as possible; it is, rather, cheapness in relation to a given end. A thoroughgoing efficiency study would involve, first, establishing the technical specification of the desired output and second, aiming to produce the desired output in the cheapest way possible. Output here should be recognized as measures of *learning value added*, which seek to take account of differences in the quality of inputs. We do not suggest that such thoroughgoing studies are either possible or desirable, a theme to which we shall return after setting out an example of an approach that links costs and performance data.

With suitable management information systems it is possible that monitoring schools after the 1988 Act could produce data which links costs and performance. This can be illustrated with data from an earlier study that compared the costs and performance of different types of institutions providing A-level courses (H. Thomas, 1990). Here, data are used from just one of the LEAs in that study so that what is produced allows an intra-LEA comparison; the costs shown represent those prevailing at the time the data were collected in the early 1980s. Table 7.2 includes data for each institution on the range of courses offered annually, the number of subject entries, unit cost data per subject entry, A-level outcomes standardized for intake and a cost-effectiveness criterion.

The first column shows the number of courses provided annually by each institution, the sixth form colleges clearly providing the wider choice. The second column shows that they also have the greater number of entries. Weston SFC had almost 300 subject entries each year, compared with 50 for Whitefield, the smallest school sixth form. The third column shows the unit cost of a subject entry, ranging from £884 at Rossthwaite to £1342 at Whitefield. In other words, the A-level subject provision for a three-subject A-level student would cost £2652 at Rossthwaite and £4026 at Whitefield. Yet the resourcing of 16-19-year-olds by the LEA was at about the same level in all the institutions covered by schools regulations. In effect, A-level provision in the schools was being subsidized by the resources provided to other parts of the school. Such subsidies were not marginal, as is evident from an analysis of the marginal costs for one of the sixth forms in the larger study, by no means the most costly. A-level subject provision for three cohorts of students took 20.12 full-time equivalent teachers, whereas the LEA's staffing rules provided 14.28 teachers for this part of the provision. In effect, the A-level programme at the school was subsidized by 5.84 teachers drawn from the 11 to 16 part of the school. A virtue of LMS is that, provided suitable information systems are developed, comparisons between what is provided and how it is used could be made using a currency which is more widely understood than pupil-teacher ratios and curriculum analyses.

The cost data alone illuminate the planners' dilemma on how best to allocate resources to achieve desirable educational ends. It provides worthwhile data for judgements about the equity of education provision. Is A-level provision in school sixth forms justified given the level of subsidy required to sustain an adequate range of subject provision? Can the loss of resources be justified for those students who do not stay in the sixth form? For them the subsidy to the sixth form is a once-and-for-all loss of access to resources ostensibly allocated for their education. Answers to such questions address equity considerations but lead into issues of educational efficiency.

Sixth form provision might be justified, for example, on the basis of examination outcomes or retention rates of groups of students who might not otherwise remain within full-time education. The examination outcomes shown in Table 7.2 suggest, however, that school sixth forms may be less effective than sixth form colleges as providers of A-level courses. What is unique about these data, however, is that they can be used to provide measures of efficiency as cost-effectiveness ratios. Linking data on performance — which represents value-added rather than raw outcome scores — to data on the per capita costs of providing the teaching programmes, a cost-effectiveness criterion is produced. The cost-effectiveness measures are given in the fifth column of Table 7.2 and show a wide range. Rossthwaite SFC and Weston SFC are the most cost-effective providers at 438 and Whitefield HS the least cost-effective provider at 1074. In other words, every A-level pass grade cost £438 at the two colleges and £1074 at Whitefield HS. In effect for every £1 spent at the sixth form colleges to obtain an A-level pass £2.45 was spent at Whitefield HS. It should be stressed that these cost-effectiveness ratios are measures of *efficiency* and not cheapness: they are not a measure of cost alone but of cost in relation to examination performance, after adjusting the data to take account of differences in the student intake as represented by their O-level and CSE qualifications.

We hope the example illustrates ways in which the monitoring functions of bodies such as LEAs can be developed in a post-1988 Act environment, where purposes are more focused upon these issues and where there will be more information on costs and performance. Such data should then contribute to the planning processes of LEAs and the FAS, assisting their evaluation of structures of provision as well as the performance of individual schools. The example only claims to be indicative of what might be done and it may be useful to reflect upon the limitations of what is presented. The efficiency criterion used in this example is drawn from the closed end of the evaluation continuum. Its selection, certainly its use by an LEA, reflects summative, formal, product-orientated approaches. It ignores 'non-pecuniary and psychic benefits . . . and the nature of the teaching-learning process' (Drake, 1982, pp.105-6). One might add that it also ignores any 'negative utility' (Sinden and Worrell, 1979, p. 34) arising from the experience of the course. Moreover, by not including other process and outcome measures, for example preparation for the different work environment of higher education as compared with schools, there is the risk that these other performance criteria might be 'assumed to be perfectly complementary and achieved in direct proportion to the target objectives' (Drake, 1982, p.113). To some extent, this can be avoided by making it clear that the cost-effectiveness ratios measure only those items which they purport to measure; the usefulness of the ratios then depends upon whether the selected objectives represent the preferences and rankings of those who would have a use for the information. What cannot be avoided, however, is that policy guidance based solely upon the analysis will have an unknown effect upon unmeasured outcomes.

There is, therefore, an urgent need to develop other ways of measuring pro-cesses and outcomes. Mortimore *et al.*'s (1988) study of 50 junior schools included measures of pupil self-esteem, for example, and it may be appropriate for LEAs to do more by way of collecting evidence on school processes and client views. Is it fanciful to wonder whether some recent legislative changes might not have occurred — or might have been different — if the education service had been able to provide regularly collected data which showed high levels of client satisfaction from the principal users of the service?

Monitoring should contribute to better planning but only if we are sensitive to the subjectivity associated with the selection and use of performance criteria. Cost-effectiveness analysis, therefore, is neither presented nor viewed as offering less subjectivity and less use of judgement. As Drake (1982, p. 121) notes, however, it does offer a greater quantity of information and, properly applied and presented, 'a more systematic and open application of judgement to decisions about the use of resources'. Analysis provides enhanced sources of information for policy-makers but data will always be incomplete and imperfect; they do not provide policy-makers with a decision.

What we do know, however, is that policy-makers will continue to make decisions. An issue, therefore, is how to make those decisions better informed in terms of the quality and relevance of the information they receive and also in terms of the sources of information. Devoting time to collecting the views of clients can contribute to the dialogue which should be a part of more open and accountable decision-making. That applies as much to the management processes of schools, to which we shall now turn.

SPENDING A SCHOOL BUDGET

The experience of managing the school's financial budget predates LMS in a small number of LEAs in England and Wales and this section draws upon interviews conducted in one of those LEAs. Six headteachers in secondary schools with full local management responsibilities were interviewed between autumn 1990 and spring 1991. In outlining the intention of each interview, it was explained that its purpose was to explore her or his view of the dif-ference between Local Financial Management (LFM) and LMS and, also, how relationships among 'stakeholders' were altering. There was no specific question on different ways in which the budget was being spent and the issues of resource choices discussed here arose from their replies and comments on the wider aspects of the interview.

Two of the headteachers emphasized differences in their awareness of choice under LMS by comparison with LFM. Mrs Duke began by recognizing that while different emphases in spending were possible under historic funding, 'there was, if you like, a hidden agenda of what ought to be spent on various matters. Now it is a much cleaner slate and, although there haven't been tremendous variations in what one would have done before, there is a greater capacity for there to be if the need arises.' Mr Bishop also made some early comments on the limited use of earlier freedom, suggesting that LMS gave 'a lot more freedom of action than we formerly had', which he also saw as creating a greater obligation 'to plan more effectively'.

This greater freedom was being used in relation to staffing in several of the schools. Mr Bishop and Mr Enfield both described changes in staffing allowances, one using honoraria to address some requirements and the other taking the opportunity to revise the management structure within the school. Mrs Duke and Mr Enfield were increasing their teaching establishment while Mr Adlington and Mr Carrington were reducing the number of teachers at the schools. These reductions arose because of the combined effect of enrolment changes and the change between historic and formula funding, although both schools had substantial reserves from LFM days which would have been allowed them to delay staffing reductions. At High Crest (Mr Adlington), staffing reductions were mainly achieved by 'natural movement' but a 'poor' teacher was encouraged to leave and there was also an unexpected early retirement. The non-replacement of teachers in some areas meant the school had to review the 'second string' subjects of staff and, although these were not used 'to any great degree, it was something we had to plan for; but it worked out very well'.

At Langford School, Mr Carrington declared some teachers compulsorily redundant while employing additional staff to meet changing curriculum requirements. Faced by a substantial gap between historic and formula funding, the need for a net loss of staff was unavoidable although, given the substantial reserves from LFM days, not essential in 1990. He spoke of the process:

> Running through it properly, keeping unions and staff informed all the way through; you can do what you like, it still hurts when the time comes. I had no problems with the unions; the unions did not take up any one case ... to be fair to your staff you're going to make redundant you really want to finish it by the beginning of April to give them a fair chance to get a job. You have to start the redundancy process somewhere at the end of January or beginning of February. At that time you don't know your budget, you also don't know how many children you've got coming in September; you can estimate but you can't know.

> To convince staff that it is necessary, you start with a curriculum survey and find out where your slack is and, of course, nobody ever

falls into nice little bundles. It is half a teacher there, a quarter of a teacher here and so forth. You then have to nominate, then you have to inform the governors, then you have to work all the way through the appeals procedure before you come to the point.... I was a union man and, therefore, at the very early stages.... I call in the unions to bring them into it at a very early level ... to be honest that's how we avoided the problems.

Asked further on the process of identifying staff, Mr Carrington again stressed the role of the curriculum audit: 'First you've got to look to see where the largest bundle occurs and that is usually fairly clear and obvious'. As more than one teacher will be working within that area, however, the qualitative judgement enters: 'you look at the staff and then you decide which would be the greatest loss to your school, which would be the least loss to your school. If we're talking honestly, it's also the quality of the teachers who are involved. But we do base it very solidly on that curriculum audit.'

The quality factor emerged again at Langford School when Mr Carrington replied to a question on the influence of teacher salary costs when making appointments. Did he look at costs?

No. That sounds very noble of me, but it isn't in fact because all our staff, the vast majority of our staff, are all established teachers and, therefore, you are talking of a variation of one or two thousand pounds, which isn't crucial ... I just appointed a head of chemistry, for example. I could have made it a B, I could have made it an A. I made it a C because, in my opinion, we needed a quality scientist to put more motivation, more drive, into the Science Department. So, I went for the C.... In an area like this, I don't care what facilities you've got, unless you've got teachers who can interest, motivate and control children, you're wasting your time, you're losing out. The quality of the teacher in this type of area is your greatest resource and there's no argument about that.

Heads did not disregard other resources when using their powers over the budget. Mr Enfield at Crossfield School noted the advantage of being able to increase funding for books and educational materials to meet the needs of new courses. At Langford, Mr Carrington outlined plans for delegating more funds to departments so that they could decide upon their own mix of spending on books, equipment, secretarial and technical support. At High Crest, Mr Adlington noted the spending of £10,000 annually for IT enhancement.

The quality of the premises is being improved in these schools. Mr Enfield at Crossfield School set out plans for spending on computer equipment for a new library and proposals to spend £25,000 on changing a classroom into a laboratory. Mr Adlington described a project for renewing the floor of a sports hall for £20,000.

In several interviews, mention was made of expenditure on what the heads often described as marketing. Typical is the allocation of funds to more lavish brochures. At Foregates, Mr Bishop referred to 'a much more up-market brochure. . . . A glossy'. At Crossfield, a new brochure was produced costing £6000: 'a super new school brochure but, then, I think if it brings in ten, it's paid for anyway'. At Langford, Mr Carrington referred to booklets and a brochure costing £2000. He also described the use of school concerts as means of attracting children from local junior schools and meeting the costs of hiring the buses.

Mrs Church, at Meadow School, drew attention to discussion and disagreement over spending about £5000 on the preparation of a 'more lavish school brochure to get more pupils into the school'. The issue led to a difference of view between the staff's finance committee and that of the governors, 'and there was strong feeling from at least one governor, a parent governor, that wherever possible all funding ought to be going towards pupil education in the narrow sense. Not on the environmental expenditure, for example and so on. It should be going on books and equipment at a time when people are saying there are not enough resources for schools.' This governor was swayed by the argument that five additional pupils would pay for the expenditure. The headteacher's own comments also reveal the positive aspect of 'marketing' as a means of improving positive communication:

> Yes, I thought there should be a brochure. I thought that. I have ambivalent views about marketing, perhaps the luxury of having ambivalent views simply because I haven't yet been a head of a school that has been under real threat as far as finance and numbers go. Time will tell. I do believe whole-heartedly in promoting the school in the community and, knowing the funding of the school at that stage, I thought that . . . money being allocated to producing something attractive that told the community, potential parents, visitors to the school about the range of things that the school did well, involving all sorts of pupils, was probably money well spent.

The dual purpose of marketing was also reflected in the comments of Mrs Duke at Southbridge. She argued that 'it's an LMS issue in that we have become more and more aware of the need to promote the school' but was 'not terribly keen on the word marketing as such. I think it is much more promoting the positive values of the school and identifying what is good.' At Southbridge, this has included reviewing relationships with the community, including local industry and feeder schools. It has also included looking at the decoration of the building and the quality of the school environment, as well as planning a new publication for parents in addition to the official handbook. Her approach rejected marketing if it meant 'amending a product and being very cut-throat with people in the area', but she took a much more positive view of marketing if it was concerned with communicating and educating:

> I think it is all right to amend a product if it is wrong but, I think, at the end of the day you have got to be quite certain of what your values are as a school and not amend those because of people out there. At a simplistic level, I think there are some people who don't send children to Southbridge because we don't have a blazer; well, frankly, I would rather they went elsewhere. It is cavalier of me but I think that, then,

you have got to have the role of educating parents . . . marketing what you are doing, what you believe in.

Linked to the various facets of marketing are relationships with industry and community, interests which also provide means by which schools can increase their budgets. Lettings, cash grants from local employers and support-in-kind from employers were all mentioned as means by which schools tried to improve their basic budgets. Compared with the LEA budget, however, none amounted to significant amounts.

CONCLUSION: PLANNING FOR QUALITY

While the quality of education provided in our schools is by no means entirely dependent upon the level of resources they receive, there is no doubt that resources are an essential component of that quality. In this chapter we have set out to examine some aspects of the relationship between the planning and allocation of resources and their consequence for educational opportunities.

We began with the basis on which funds are distributed to schools by LEAs. If resources matter, these allocations are of crucial significance in shaping the opportunities schools can provide for their children. The more public process for allocating those funds, as required by the 1988 Act, promises circumstances where the rationale for the funding of schools will be subject to more discussion and where the relationship between resources and educational needs will be more clearly articulated. Emerging is a system that does allow for easier comparison, more easily allowing questions to be asked about differences in funding of comparable children in different LEAs and different children in the same LEA. The more widely such information can be disseminated, the wider might be the debate about the desirable relationship between resources and needs. We are not suggesting a national formula that allows for no local diversity but setting out the benefits of a more open information system which, it is hoped, will require answers to questions about differentials in the funding of children ostensibly pursuing a National Curriculum.

Such questions are part of the monitoring processes, which are becoming increasingly prominent. The second part of the chapter argues for further work to be done in linking data on costs and performance. We argued above that such monitoring should contribute to better planning but only if we are sensitive to the subjectivity of the process and its place as a means of enhancing sources of information rather than providing decisions. Such work would shift the focus away from bogus efficiency studies, such as all too many from the Audit Commission, which have compared resource differences and then inferred efficiency conclusions. Cumming's (1971) remark might still be heeded: 'There need be no fears of naive productivity experts dominating the teachers' work if the teachers and educationists take pains to learn more of economics than economists know of education' (p.232).

In terms of their day-by-day experience, headteachers of locally managed schools may be better placed than most to become familiar with a proper relationship between resources and learning and to challenge the comments of 'naive productivity experts'. Do the accounts from the six headteachers of locally managed schools suggest that their approach to managing their budgets promises well for quality education? The choices we report include decisions on staffing, premises, educational materials, educational equipment and marketing. As might be expected, the language of explanation relates to the quality of provision for children; few would hurry to set out other justifications. Even spending on marketing is often expressed in terms of the educational value of communicating with parents and community. These accounts might suggest that delegating control over resources to schools has placed that responsibility in the right place. Such a conclusion would be premature.

Headteachers' are the only voices from schools which are heard in this chapter and heads are also among the principal beneficiaries of the redistribution of powers arising from the 1988 Act. This might make a positive perspective more likely, not least from a group already familiar with managing budgets. How others might view the quality consequences of the new resource planning arrangements in locally managed schools is as necessary a perspective before we can begin to draw conclusions about their effects. Outside the schools, what effects more public data on funding will have and how monitoring opportunities will be developed remain largely unknown. We know that planning for quality is different as a result of the 1988 Act but what we do not know is its effect upon quality.

We gratefully acknowledge the support of The Leverhulme Trust for their grant in support of the project 'The Funding of Schools after the 1988 Education Reform Act'.

REFERENCES

Bullock, A. D. and Thomas, H. (1992) 'School size and local management funding formulae', *Educational Management and Administration*, 20(1), 30-8.

Bullock, A. D. and Thomas, H. (1993a) 'Pupil-led funding and local management funding formulae', in M. Smith and H. Bush (eds), *Managing Schools in an Uncertain Environment: Resources, Marketing and Power*. Sheffield: Sheffield Hallam University for BEMAS.

Bullock, A. D. and Thomas, H. (1993b) 'Comparing school formula allocations: an exploration of some problems', in BERA Dialogues, *Local Management, Central Control: Schools in the Market Place*. Hyde Publications.

Cumming, C. (1971) *Studies in Educational Costs*. Edinburgh: Scottish Academic Press.

Drake, K. (1982) 'The cost-effectiveness of vocational training: a survey of British studies', *Economics of Education Review*, 2(2), 103-25.

Mortimore, P. *et al.* (1988) *School Matters: The Junior Years*. London: Open Books.

Sinden, J. A. and Worrell, A. C. (1979) *Unpriced Values: Decisions without Market Prices*. New York: John Wiley & Sons.

Thomas, G. (1990) *Setting up LMS. A study of Local Education Authorities' Submissions to the DES*. Milton Keynes: The Open University.

Thomas, H. (1990) *Education Costs and Performance: A Cost-effectiveness Analysis*. London: Cassell.

Chapter 8

The Multicultural Dimension of Quality and Equality

Carlton Duncan

INTRODUCTION

First, this chapter will, briefly, revisit some of the evidence and documentation which have indicated the plight of black children in terms of underachievement at school. It will be argued, thereafter, that one of the main factors contributing to black underachievement is the Eurocentric planned or formal curriculum, especially in schools which are mainly white. Finally, an attempt will be made to reach a compromise between those who would argue that the Education Reform Act 1988 (ERA) and its prescribed National Curriculum are against antiracism and multiculturalism and those whose views (as expounded by the author) are that there is enough legislative scope within the ERA and, indeed, in laws existing prior to the ERA for a purposeful antiracist and multicultural approach to the planned or formal National Curriculum.

BLACK UNDERACHIEVEMENT

Many researchers have compared black and white pupils' performances and they have very nearly always concluded that black pupils underachieve. In 1963 a small-scale study carried out by the Brent local authority showed that the performance of Afro-Caribbeans was much lower than that of white children in such important areas as reading, arithmetic and spelling. In the middle of the same decade Vernon (as quoted in Swann, 1985) compared white children's performances with those of Afro-Caribbean children in London and Hertfordshire and arrived at similar conclusions.

In the late 1960s further evidence of black pupils underachievement became available. The Inner London Education Authority researchers noted dissatisfaction with the performances of immigrant children. In 1966 and 1968 Little compared 9-year-olds of different racial groups in ILEA (Little, 1968), only to find that Afro-Caribbean children performed less well at primary school than white children from the same socio-economic backgrounds.

Several other pieces of research, such as Coard's work (Coard, 1971) and the London Borough of Redbridge Community Relations Council's report ('Cause for Concern, West Indian Pupils in Redbridge', Black People's Progressive

Association and Redbridge Community Relations Council, April 1978), continued to give this view right up to the publication of the Rampton and Swann Reports in 1981 and 1985. These two major initiatives in this area of education undertaken by the then Department of Education and Science (now Department for Education, or DFE) further established this fact of ethnic minority under-achievement. 'While we accept that there will perhaps always be some children who will underachieve and for various reasons will fail to reach their full potential our concern is that West Indian children as a group are underachieving in our education system' (Rampton, 1981, p.10). This interim finding was later restated and confirmed in the final report (Swann, 1985), and as part of the conclusion from the Eggleston Report (1984):

> There are social processes in both schools and society at large that work to counteract the efforts of these young people. In schools, both at and below sixth-form level, ethnic minority pupils may be placed on courses and entered for examinations at levels below those appropriate for their abilities and ambitions. Teachers may be unwilling to accept the existence of these processes or to ever redress them where they are aware of them. When schools fail then young black people can find it difficult.

THE CURRICULUM AS A VEHICLE FOR TRANSMITTING RACIST VALUES, ESPECIALLY IN TOTALLY OR MAINLY WHITE SCHOOLS

Prominent among the several factors identified as leading to this detrimental educational effect for non-white pupils is the racist Eurocentric nature of the school curriculum as practised in our schools.

This means problems for white children too. It stands to reason that if racism is a fact of all that we do in our schools — not to mention our homes, the media and the rest of society — the end effect will be to tarnish the minds, values and attitudes of those innocent white children who are entrusted to our care from an early age. Desmond Tutu once said, at a public gathering in Birmingham (at the official opening of the Nelson Mandela School), 'Children do not come into the world already hating and despising others. They learn these deeds.'

It is for this reason that it truly makes no sense when those colleagues who practise in all-white areas proclaim that they need not worry about antiracism and multiculturalism, since they 'haven't got any of the problem there'. The content of this statement is itself indicative of a major problem. To see black people only in terms of 'problems' reflects most seriously upon the nature of one's education. Furthermore, it has been the experience that these same colleagues will readily subscribe to the principles of equality and justice for all. It is, perhaps, not too unkind to say that this suggests a somewhat short-sighted position. Given that neither students nor teachers have a permanent hold on their positions at any moment, it might be realized that these white pupils will go on to positions of responsibility where they will be taking decisions that will affect the life chances of others, including blacks. Does it not make sense to prepare them well for this task now? Is it not an opportunity to prepare ambassadors for the causes to which we subscribe? Do we not have a duty as teachers to prepare our pupils for a world stage? Or do we simply prepare them for local insularity?

This view that all-white schools have 'no problem' was tested by the Rampton Inquiry. The Commissioners visited certain such schools in a particular area where the pupils seen admitted that they had no first-hand experience of black people. Yet the following are just some of the negative stereotypical opinions they held of black people.

> People from the West Indies mainly stay by themselves and don't mix with other people. Most West Indians live around the big cities like Coventry, Birmingham and Wolverhampton. Very few people live in the country. Back in the West Indies they live in shanty towns and eat coconuts all day.
>
> People from Africa are also black but you do not get many of them immigrating. In their country most of them live in the bush.
>
> I have learnt that a lot of the crime rate is due to the excess immigrants in the country. The immigrants who are mostly unemployed go around in gangs and commit violent crimes.
>
> When the immigrants come into Britain and complain, the Government should throw them out of Britain for good. Also, white people should have first choices about jobs.
>
> I have learnt that they are pulling this country down because they all depend on social security.

If we ignore the obvious contradiction embodied in the last two of these quotes and concentrate solely on the negative stereotypes, blatant misinformation and misconceptions, it is not then difficult to evaluate the 'no problem here' position. It also does not require major leaps in thought to understand why lessons planned and delivered by colleagues who might still feel that all is rosy in the 'White Highlands' must necessarily embody attitudinal and value problems for all our pupils as well as learning hindrances additionally for black children. Similarly, textbooks and other materials prepared by such teachers will reflect these obstacles.

David Wright of the University of East Anglia was making this very point when, following an examination of two standard geography textbooks, he became so appalled at their contents of racist views and negative stereotypes that he concluded:

> If teachers with sufficient expertise to be authors of standard textbooks write this insensitive material, what hope is there that other books, and other lessons, are less biased? At a conservative estimate 100,000 pupils have studied 'Man and his World'. Some of them are now policemen, teachers, social workers, others will soon qualify in these fields. What will their attitudes to race be? (Wright, 1983)

As far as the planned curriculum is concerned, an examination of all the subject areas covered within schools will show how subtly and how dangerously lurks an unwelcome diet of racial stereotypes.

Not only do our geography texts reveal the kind of stereotypes with which Wright was concerned, but their failure to include anything positive about so-called Third World countries and their peoples is a subtle way of doing the same thing: creating stereotype images of blacks in the minds of white youngsters, thus prolonging the myths and preconceptions, since these are the youngsters who will be tomorrow's teachers and authors of standard textbooks. For example, not many of our youngsters in schools would truly comprehend the economic relationship between Western civilization and Third World countries. Teachers have either wittingly or unwittingly portrayed the economic dependency as a one-way traffic. Little or nothing is told of the theft from Third World countries of their wealth, which has played a major part in Western development.

What our youngsters learn of is the dependency of Third World countries on the Western world for aid. They learn only of the poverty, the famines and the helplessness of the people. These are later or simultaneously confirmed in charity appeals via our television screens or advertisement posters at various key locations. Pupils are not taught that this state of affairs is largely the result of man's past and present inhumanity to man.

History, as it is taught, is perhaps more guilty of this line of inaccuracy than any other subject. Wilberforce and Lincoln have received eternal recognition for the parts they played in the emancipation of the slaves. The economic motivation behind their efforts is never mentioned in the textbooks or in the lessons. The roles played by the slaves themselves, black leaders such as Nanny and the Maroons, Harriet Tubman, Vassey, Gordon and others, are silently forgotten. Most of these black leaders made the supreme sacrifice with their lives. But the picture we transmit to young people is that blacks were enslaved by the whites who, themselves, took pity and emancipated them.

Already the works and achievements of Terry Waite are being vigorously told in schools and the media have told of all his brave expeditions and their outcomes. Yet the works of Martin Luther King and of Gandhi find no such parallel significance. Here lies the subtle but pernicious evil of racism in the curriculum. The effects of all this are to stunt the academic and social development of black young people and falsify white youngsters' perceptions of their black colleagues.

In recent days I stood and observed youngsters, at the behest of their teacher, recall a lesson they had been taught on the Crimea and the part played by Florence Nightingale. Brilliant recall it was, but though this was a multiracial classroom the opportunity to include the contributions of Mary Seacole was missed. This Jamaican lady's contribution to the Crimea was like that of Florence Nightingale, but greater in the sense that Mary Seacole was not sponsored — she was actually refused sponsorship on grounds of her colour and did everything under her own steam, using all her savings, which eventually led to her bankruptcy. Seacole is forgotten where schools and the nation generally are concerned. No one is allowed to forget the lady with the lamp. Our textbooks, lessons and hospital wards ensure that, and a glance at the back of an older £10 note will quickly remind one of her. In Scotland the note of similar value bears a reminder of slavery. Role models are an essential part of pupils' development.

For this reason the memory of Nightingale must always be kept alive and in the interest of equity and truth Seacole should be kept alive too.

The school's system must never lose sight of the fact that the influence of schools and teachers is very strong in relation to the formation of attitudes. Children very often, for example, contradict their parents, however learned, because 'teacher said so'. The planned curriculum is a powerful vehicle in the formation of attitudes. The opportunity must not be lost to ensure that black and white pupils develop positive attitudes about each other. A Eurocentric curriculum fails miserably to do that, as would a Black Studies approach to the curriculum. Therefore, what must be ensured by the school is that the curriculum is free of racism, whether by what it omits or what it includes. In short, an antiracist approach to the curriculum is absolutely vital.

In the teaching of food technology we sometimes forget that it is not so much a knowledge of being able to cook that we want to pass on to our pupils. In fact, it is about the science of diets that we want our pupils to learn. Pupils learn and develop their skills more readily and effectively in a context of relevance. The cuisine of any part of the world can be used to illustrate this science. Whatever the nature of the school or classroom, whether it is all-white, black or multiracial, the use of a variety of food will serve to meet the school's aim on diets. It will further destroy prejudices and preconceived myths of a negative nature about other people and their food; and in the multiracial classroom all pupils will have the benefit of relevance. To illustrate the kinds of attitude and development that take place in a situation where the teacher cares for all his or her pupils in the context of home economics as against one where this care is missing, I borrow two examples from a published discussion between Yvonne Collymore and myself (Collymore and Duncan, 1983). The first example is of a teacher who made some time in each lesson for the pupils to demonstrate a 'dish from home'.

> Each pupil had a turn to do this, and it meant close liaison with 'Mum' or 'Dad' to get the ingredients written down and learn the techniques. In one lesson where the topic had been pastry, an Indian girl skilfully demonstrated how to use pastry to make samosas. The class marvelled at how delicately they were wrapped, and how thinly the pastry was rolled; and everyone was keen to taste. No one felt 'put down' or patronised because their home culture was being focussed on as something exotic or foreign — everyone felt their home cooking had an equal place, and each had something to learn from the others. The liaison between home and school was encouraged because parents had a sense of being involved in what the school was doing, and felt their experience to be of value. On Open Day parents would more readily wish to come to a school with which they already had a close link.

The second example depicts an Afro-Caribbean student teacher who was asked by the pupils during her teaching practice to teach them Caribbean cookery.

The pupils had apparently made the same request of their cookery teacher some time before, but she had felt her own knowledge of Caribbean cookery to be inadequate to cope. The pupils had been refusing to pay for the food they cooked because they said that no one at home would eat English food, and it was only thrown away. When, with the teacher's agreement, the student began to teach Caribbean cookery, the head of department walked in and was furious. She apparently saw this as a 'lowering of standards' in a school which had always boasted good examination results.

It does not require an active imagination to realize the hurt and demotivation which would have followed the intervention of the head of department in this second example. It might be that we achieve our objective of teaching pupils to read or getting them through examinations, but at what cost? As caring teachers we must be concerned enough, beyond goals or objectives, to ponder the side-effects of our methods and materials. Many of our textbooks and much of our curriculum supporting materials are still of the type illustrated below.

To the conquest of nature through knowledge the contributions made by Asiatics have been negligible and by Africans (Egyptians excluded) non existent. The printing press and the telescope, the steam-engine, the internal combustion engine and the aeroplane, the telegraph and the telephone, wireless broadcasting and the cinematograph, the gramophone and television, together with all the leading discoveries in physiology, the circulation of the blood, the laws of respiration and the like, are the result of researches carried out by white men of European stock. (Fisher, 1984)

Perhaps in the future there will be some African history to teach. But at present there is none, or very little. There is only the history of Europeans in Africa. The rest is largely darkness ... and darkness is not a subject for history. (Trevor-Roper, 1966)

Perhaps she could finish her father's unfinished work. He had been interested in savages and backward races. Africa was the best place to find such people. ... Mary would go to Africa. She could go among the wildest savages she could find. She would spend her life studying cannibals. (Anon., 1968)

Apart from the inaccuracies, statements such as these tarnish the minds of white youths against their black peers. We see the true effects of such damaging inculcation in horrific racial discrimination in the job market, by the police and in every area of society that matters. The white children are destined to become the employers and the people in charge of selection. They are unlikely to employ savages or people of backward races. And this is the false and racist view of black people transmitted at school.

On the other hand statements such as those above do less than heighten black pupils' self-esteem and lift their hopes for the future. In a first-year art class at a South London secondary school the topic was a local street scene. Studying the work of an Afro-Caribbean girl, the art teacher asked,

'"Why don't you draw any black people in the picture?" "Miss, are we allowed to?" came the reply'. (Edmonds, 1973)

The mathematicians and the scientists readily deny that they and their subject areas can have the same effect on pupils as do other subject areas because, so they claim, their subjects are value free. Yet both mathematics and science are problem-solving subjects. Men and women, whoever they happen to be, wherever they happen to be, have problems and it is out of the solutions to these problems that bodies of knowledge called mathematics and science have developed. Yet in the classrooms these are constantly taught and illustrated with a Eurocentric bias.

The evidence-gathering exercises for both the Rampton and the Swann enquiries frequently revealed that black youngsters spent a disproportionate amount of their curriculum time on sports or some aspects of music. These are extremely important subject areas for the total development of any individual pupil. But the tendency is to stereotype black youngsters as being good at sports and music and nothing else, and so shift them from other classes to do more music or sports. No wonder they are good at these; no wonder they tend to do badly in other areas. What seems to happen is that blacks are labelled disruptive in English and mathematics and the like and are thus sent to be 'cooled off' in music and sports. What all pupils need is a balanced diet to allow maximum and varied chances for their potentials to develop.

Essentially, what is needed is that all teachers should adopt an antiracist and multicultural approach to the curriculum. Antiracism and multiculturalism are not limited to an understanding and enabling of ethnic minority cultures; essentially they are about the identification and eradication of racist values from the school curriculum and all other school activities.

THE EDUCATION REFORM ACT 1988, THE NATIONAL CURRICULUM, ANTIRACISM AND MULTICULTURALISM

There is a view that the Education Reform Act 1988 will have the effect of turning the clock back as far as multicultural education is concerned. This view is held largely because the Act is silent on this aspect of education and some believe and argue that most of the educational reforms of the 1980s are designed to pull education back to the right. It is not impossible to justify these views when we examine many of the provisions of the Act, the political context against which the reforms occurred and, indeed, the Government's response to the recommendation of the National Curriculum Council's English Working Report that pupils should read literature written by authors beyond the traditional set English texts. The Government's unwillingness to have this particular recommendation linked to attainment targets is, at least, suspicious in intent.

A further reason for feeling pessimistic in relation to multiculturalism is in connection with the National Curriculum Attainment Targets and associated testing and examination arrangements. It is felt that we could put children's examination chances at risk were we to persist with permeating the curriculum with a multicultural content. However, multiculturalism has gone too far, is too deeply rooted in the case of justice for even the most conservative of schools, governments or laws to justify turning back. Progress might be held up but no more. In any case, the committed practitioner can find much in the Act and its guidelines as well as in the resulting curriculum working parties' reports to justify continuing to adopt a multicultural stance with the curriculum.

> The curriculum for a maintained school satisfies the requirements of the [National Curriculum and Religious Education] if it is a balanced and broadly based curriculum which:
>
> (a) promotes the spiritual, moral, cultural, mental and physical development of pupils at the school and of society;
>
> (b) prepares such pupils for the opportunities, responsibilities and experiences of adult life. (ERA, 1988, s.2)

It is difficult to see how one might promote moral values and principles via the curriculum and at the same time retain its racist character. Similarly, the requirement to have regard for the culture of the pupils of the school and of society is a direct invitation to all schools to multiculturalize their curriculum.

Additionally, many of the National Curriculum Council's Subject Working Party Reports have advanced the need for teachers to build into the curriculum a multicultural dimension. This must be an important lead for practitioners, even if in some cases, such as mathematics, this guidance is only grudgingly given and in others, such as history, is totally absent.

If Section 2 of ERA is not enough legislative authority for us practitioners, then we might recall that nothing in the Act overrides the Race Relations Act 1976. The Race Relations Act had already decreed that local authorities had a duty to eliminate racial discrimination from their educational and other affairs.

> Without prejudice to their obligation to comply with any other provision of this Act, it shall be the duty of every local authority [under Local Management of Schools this applies to governors] to make appropriate arrangements with a view to securing that their various functions are carried out with due regard to the need:
>
> (a) to eliminate unlawful racial discrimination; and
>
> (b) to promote equality of opportunity, and good relations, between persons of different racial groups. (Race Relations Act, 1976, s.71)

CONCLUSION

The messages are that (a) black underachievement is not inevitable; (b) *high quality* in curriculum terms is never really attained unless the curriculum, among other qualities, is seen to do justice to all the peoples who go to make up our society; (c) all-white schools, in particular, must not hide behind the dangerous and inequitable falsity of the 'no problem here' scenario; (d) finally, the ERA and its National Curriculum prescription, far from being hindrances to antiracism and multiculturalism, are legal means by which these educational developments can justifiably permeate the entire National Curriculum and all else that happens in schools.

REFERENCES

Anon. (1968) *Reading on Red*, Book One, 7th edn. Edinburgh: Oliver and Boyd.

Coard, B. (1971) *How the West Indian Child Is Made Educationally Subnormal in the British School System*. London: New Beacon Books.

Collymore, Y. and Duncan, C. (1983) 'The answers? (Multicultural education discussed)', *New Home Economics*, 29(7), 20-1.

Edmonds, G. (1973) 'In search of heroes', *Guardian*, 2 May, p.18.

Eggleston, S.J. (1984) 'The educational and vocational experiences of 15-18 year old young people of minority ethnic group' (draft report submitted to the DES), Department of Education, University of Keele.

Fisher, H. (1984) *History of Europe*. London: Eyre and Spottiswoode.

Little, A. (1968) *The Education of Immigrant Pupils in Inner London Primary Schools*. London: Inner London Education Authority.

Rampton, A. (Chairman) (1981) *West Indian Children in Our Schools*, Cmnd 8273. London: HMSO.

Swann, Lord (Chairman) (1985) *Education for All*, Cmnd 9453. London: HMSO.

Trevor-Roper, H. (1966) *The Rise of Christian Europe*. London: Thames and Hudson.

Vernon, P. (1985) Environmental handicaps and intellectual development. An unpublished study, quoted in Rampton (1981), p.6.

Wright, D. (1983) 'The geography of race', *Times Educational Supplement*, 15 July, p.15.

Chapter 9

Equality and Quality: Approaches to Changes in the Management of Gender Issues

Gaby Weiner

> But I still insist, that not only the virtue, but the *knowledge* of the two
> sexes should be the same in nature, if not degree, and that women,
> considered not only as moral, but rational creatures, ought to
> endeavour to acquire human virtues (or perfections) by the *same* means
> as men, instead of being educated like a fanciful kind of *half*
> being — one of Rousseau's wild chimeras. (Wollstonecraft, 1792)

So wrote Mary Wollstonecraft at the end of the eighteenth century. As we can
see, the desire for greater equality and justice in education has been on the
political agenda for more than two centuries — since the Enlightenment when
such concepts were related to the ideas about *natural justice* in developing
democratic societies. Twentieth-century demands for greater equality have
likewise been predicated on the assumption that discrimination on the grounds
of sex, 'race', colour, religion, disability, sexuality or other irrelevant distinction
is contrary to natural justice and is therefore morally unacceptable. However,
the form these demands have taken has varied historically, according to the
particular priorities of the day.

Thus, in the 1950s and 1960s, concern was expressed about the class bias
of schooling, and particularly about secondary school allocation. This resulted
in moves towards non-selective, coeducational secondary schooling. At the
end of this period in Europe and the United States, an expanding economy
led to more employment opportunities and an expansion of higher education,
both of which included women. This increase in women's economic power and
independence contributed to the emergence of the women's liberation movement and a closer analysis of the social, political and economic inequalities
between the sexes. Similarly, the contemporary civil rights movement in the
United States began to push for greater equality, this time for black men and
women. Both these movements had a worldwide impact and contributed to a
deeper understanding of equality issues.

The 1980s and early 1990s have seen an extension of the meaning of equality
to include people with disabilities and issues around sexuality. But, in the main,

it has been a period of world recession in which conservative governments, in both Britain and the United States, have brought to a halt any major equality initiatives. Most recently, then, emphasis has been directed towards practical policy implementation and effective strategies for change so that the earlier gains are not dissipated.

In this chapter, I consider the developments of educational policy on gender in recent years. I focus, in particular, on the early achievements (and difficulties) of practitioners. I further consider the options for change currently available and, in particular, the importance of the curriculum and institutional policy-making in the quest for equality. I take a chronological approach in my discussion of gender issues because, in the heat of change processes such as we are experiencing now, all too often valuable work carried out in earlier times is discarded or ignored. My intention is to put on record some of the important work that has already been undertaken within the area of gender and education, and also to explore some of the theoretical frameworks which informed it.

Undoubtedly, pioneer authorities such as the Inner London Education Authority (ILEA) made vital contributions in encouraging equality initiatives through policy development, availability of resources and targeted funding (e.g. ILEA, 1986a, b); and the government funded Technical and Vocational Education Initiative (TVEI) programme generated some exploration of gender issues (see Millman and Weiner, 1987). None the less, it was teachers who were most committed to achieving greater equality and who were mainly responsible for the 'delivery' of equal opportunities in schools.

THE WORK OF THE PRACTITIONERS

Teachers have played a central role in the gender policy-making process, first in exploiting the emergence of sex equality as an official issue when education was included in the Sex Discrimination Act 1975. Their role was particularly important, at least from 1979 onwards, since according to Arnot (1987) central government was 'lukewarm' about its responsibility for promoting sex equality. It was thus left to committed teachers to force the pace by initiating their own projects and by putting pressure on local authorities and the teacher unions to provide support for equal opportunities work. Further, they continued to address girls' and women's issues in their higher degree dissertations and theses, and sustained, in a number of ways, a commitment to action and to challenge during the lean years of the market-led ideologies of Thatcherism.

During the 1980s, they developed knowledge, strategies and understanding of the issues that led to a more coherent approach to dealing with gender inequalities in schooling (and also with other areas of inequality, such as 'race' and special needs). In considering and analysing the range of teacher strategies, projects and initiatives of such 'pioneer' teachers, a number of areas of development were discernible.

The first sought to *problematize* gender as an educational issue in order to attract the attention of policy-makers. Feminist teachers aimed to persuade their colleagues (and employers) that educational inequality between the sexes was of mainstream educational concern. In order to achieve this, they needed to provide 'the hard facts of inequality' (Yates, 1985). So they reported on unequal school staffing patterns, sex stereotyping in texts and reading schemes, sex-specific patterns of subject choice at 13-plus, the unacceptability of traditional vocational and career choices, and so on. They also focused on the 'hidden curriculum', particularly on teacher attitudes. For example, they drew on research that showed that while teachers, in the main, believed that they treated boys and girls without prejudice, evidence pointed to the fact that this was not the case and girls were seriously disadvantaged (Clarricoates, 1978; Spender, 1980; Kelly, 1981; Stanworth, 1981). Emphasis was also placed on the activity of women in the labour force, particularly on the statistical unlikelihood of women remaining in the home for most of their adult lives (Avent, 1982).

Once the 'problem' of gender inequality had been established, immediate solutions or *change strategies* were demanded, strategies that could be readily injected into school life. A wide variety of recommendations were made, including:

- the creation of equal opportunities working parties and posts;
- revisions of school texts, reading schemes, examination questions and display materials;
- rearrangement of timetables to enable pupils to opt more easily for non-traditional subjects, such as physics for girls and modern languages for boys;
- appointment of female senior staff as a means of providing fresh role models for female pupils;
- encouraging wider career aspiration by inviting people in non-traditional jobs into school;
- changes to school organization by, for instance, 'de-sexing' registers and 'uni-sexing' school uniform.

Clearly, there was immense diversity in the strategies suggested and adopted. The main focus for teachers (as opposed to academics and researchers) was on *practical* change: how they could help reduce inequalities between the sexes by changing their own and their colleagues' perceptions and practice. Yet the diversity of teacher action did not stem merely from local or individual priorities. They were also based on critical differences in the perspectives of the teachers, themselves.

By the early 1980s a third stage was signalled by the emergence of *different teacher perspectives* to challenge traditional educational practices of gender differentiation. These may be broadly grouped into two categories: 'equal opportunities' approaches and 'anti-sexist' or 'girl-centred' approaches. There has been a full discussion about this categorization elsewhere (Weiner and Arnot, 1987). So, for the purposes of this chapter it is summarized in the following way. 'Equal opportunities' approaches are aimed at reforms on behalf of girls and women (and sometimes boys and men) within the existing educational structure, while 'anti-sexist' approaches are aimed at changing the unequal power relations between the sexes — in order to transform the patriarchal nature of school structures and curricula.

These differences became more visible in the strategies chosen to challenge sexism in schooling. The first group emphasized, for instance, persuading girls to go into science, textbook reform, a common curriculum and changing sex-stereotyped option choices. Those advocating more 'girl-centred' approaches, on the other hand, appeared more 'radical' in their challenge of male school knowledge. They considered what *her*story or girl-centred science might look like, monitored the male domination of classrooms and schools as a whole and addressed more contentious issues, such as sexuality, sexual harassment, heterosexuality and homophobia. Their stated concern was that of empowering female pupils and teachers in contrast to the more moderate aim of the first group, which was for female representation in the higher echelons of school and society. While both wanted to improve educational opportunities for girls and women, those advocating equal opportunities placed greatest emphasis on the need for consensual change through professional development. Those advocating an anti-sexist approach, in contrast, identified the need both to address the conflicting interests of women and men and for structural change in order to achieve significant progress.

However, by the mid-1980s, differences between activists began to diminish for two reasons; first, the increasing conservatism of government created the need for more co-ordinated approaches; second, new strategies emerged which combined the strengths of the various perspectives. Thus, more *coherent strategies* were developed, which adapted some of the more structural demands underpinning anti-sexist approaches, less for revolutionary change than for feasible and practical reform. First, connections were made between gender, race and class:

> Relationships between race, sex and class are dynamic and complex and
> have implications for classroom practice. If race, gender and class
> issues are compartmentalised, the teaching approaches and strategies
> developed for combatting racism, sexism and class bias will be limited
> and less effective than they might be. (Minhas, 1986)

Teachers thus developed policies to address racism and sexism across the curriculum; they focused on girls' reported experiences of racism in school as a basis for promoting change; and they designed a variety of activities for girls taking into account their ethnic group membership. They also looked at aspects of sexuality in and around school and organized conferences on sexism and sexuality for older secondary pupils. Workshops were arranged on assertion and confidence training for girls and school policy on sexual harassment was developed.

Other areas on which teachers now placed particular emphasis were:

- changing the content of such curriculum areas as history, social studies, science, religious education;
- making science, computing, technical subjects and mathematics more accessible to girls;
- exploring school policy on language, general organization and classroom management;

117

- developing equal opportunities policies in boys' schools;
- evaluating school library usage, practices and organization (ILEA, 1986a, b).

However, as I have written elsewhere (Weiner, 1989), there were noticeable omissions in much of the work mentioned above. For instance, only recently has any attention been devoted by feminist teachers to how to plan effectively for change (Myers, 1992). One consequence of this is that there has been a consistent failure to distinguish between long-term and short-term goals; that is, to differentiate between, say, the wider aim of changing pupil and teacher attitudes and the more simple tasks of de-sexing registers or developing non-sexist materials. Moreover, there have been few attempts to evaluate work on gender, possibly because, sometimes, merely to place gender on the school agenda has been a massive achievement. However, it is also evident that overly ambitious aims have necessarily meant that visible change has been slow to achieve.

NETWORKS AND PROJECTS

During the 1980s, a decade of increasing government hostility towards those (particularly local authorities) attempting to eradicate educational inequality, committed teachers (and other educationists) were compelled to look elsewhere for forms of support. They also had to draw on their own resources to develop more autonomous approaches to change.

Some initiated projects of their own, such as developing whole-school policy on a range of equality issues. Such *teacher-initiated projects*, whether by individuals or groups of teachers, were likely to be small-scale, and short-lived, with consequent problems of under-financing and resourcing. Moreover, the majority of the teachers involved were usually at the lower end of the school hierarchy, and from the secondary rather than the primary sector. Yet these projects were important in that they provided the main challenge to traditional educational assumptions about gender; and they also offered insights into how teachers could develop their own educational goals and implementation styles.

These teachers, who were trying to promote change from the 'inside', faced a number of difficult questions. First, how could they impress colleagues of the importance of gender as an educational issue, and convince the unconvinced? Second, what was the best way to promote change within an educational institution? How could change be 'managed' and what role might senior management take? Third, given the 'political' nature of the work, how far could teachers go in challenging gender differences in school?

Others became involved in *action research projects*, working collaboratively with educationists from different institutions. Thus, researchers, usually from higher education, joined teachers to intervene in the schooling process, for example on pupil subject choice or to develop curriculum materials. By working co-operatively to challenge inequalities in education, the traditional distance between researchers and academics, and teachers was also narrowed. The best-known projects of this kind focused on the curriculum choices of girls, and in particular their level of interest in science and technology. The 'Girls and

Technology Education' project (GATE) investigated ways of improving the curriculum and assessment of craft, design and technology (CDT), and developing 'good practice'. The 'Girls into Science and Technology' project (GIST), on the other hand, worked directly with teachers, attempting to reduce sex-stereotyping on the part of pupils and teachers, and promoting 'gender-fair' interaction in classrooms, so that girls would feel encouraged to study scientific subjects.

Alternative approaches involved helping teachers to become independent researchers. May and Rudduck (1983) conducted a project in first and middle schools in Norfolk. Their goal was to raise awareness about sex-stereotyping in the early school years by encouraging teachers to explore the dynamics of their schools and to enable them 'to understand better their own practice as a basis for informing future curricular decision'. Teachers volunteered for the project, and with the help of skilled researchers, designed and carried out investigations. May and Rudduck found the effects of such investigations difficult to assess. Would they have any long-term effect? Would the teachers continue with such research or put their skills to further use in the development of school policy? Could the data generated be useful for other schools?

Similar concerns confronted the 'Schools Council Sex Differentiation' project, which adopted the 'teacher-researcher' approach and did much to legitimize both the area and the method of producing innovation in schools (for a more detailed discussion of teachers as researchers, see Millman, 1987). Building on such projects, LEAs such as Brent and ILEA in London designed their in-service courses around the concept of teacher-researcher and, thus, involved a wide range of teachers from a variety of sectors in such activities.

Another strategy was to develop *contact and communication networks*, since the development of action research and teacher-initiated projects relied on access to information and advice about how to proceed. The existence of a network of teacher organizations was therefore critical in encouraging innovation and reform. Such networks included:

- teacher/subject groups, such as Women in History, Women in Geography, Girls and Mathematics (GAMMA), Women in Computing, Women in Economics etc.;
- women in education groups, organized locally, in Hull, Oxford, Manchester, Cambridge, London etc.;
- resource centres and newsletters, for example, the Women's Educational Resource Centre and the Women's Education Group with its journal *GEN*;
- publishing ventures, such as Pandora Press, the Open University's Gender and Education series, Virago etc.;
- learning materials, for example films, exhibitions, teaching and in-service packs on different subjects produced by such groups as GAMMA and Genderwatch.

Feminist teachers also came together in their *teacher unions*. Given the context of union work, they focused on different topics compared to the school-based initiatives, yet they faced similar obstacles — male-dominated union hierarchies, low status, inability to influence the union agenda etc.

By the end of the 1980s, the British educational agenda had been transformed. The passing of the Educational Reform Act (ERA) in 1988, which included the introduction of the National Curriculum and Local Management of Schools (LMS), signalled an attempt by government to break with the past. Certainly the introduction of a National Curriculum with the explicit aim of providing all children with the same curricular experiences seemed to address some of the feminist demands for a core curriculum. Yet the destruction of the metropolitan authorities — many of which had been pioneers in terms of equality initiatives — and the cash restraints of rate- and poll-capped authorities meant that much of the earlier work on gender now became heavily circumscribed. So, as already mentioned, it is important to remember earlier initiatives so that we do not have to 're-invent the wheel' in a few years time, when the political climate changes.

Some work, nevertheless, still continues: for example, teacher- and action-research, publications, networks and equal opportunities as part of professional development (Women in Higher Education Network, 1991). Ironically, as funding and support for specific initiatives have decreased, the rhetoric of equal opportunities has become more evident in mainstream educational and government publications. And local authorities and higher education institutions, seemingly, rush to call themselves equal opportunity employers.

POLICY DEVELOPMENTS: THE STORY SO FAR

In the final section of this chapter, I concentrate on current possibilities with particular reference to a recent programme of research with which I have been involved. Drawing on this work, which focuses on National Curriculum documentation and on equal opportunities policy-making generally, I suggest possible ways forward on the curriculum, pedagogical and professional fronts.

One programme of research concentrated on the scrutiny of National Curriculum texts (Burton and Weiner, 1990; Weiner, 1993). This involved looking particularly at the TGAT, English, mathematics, science, history and cross-curricular documentation, and was undertaken to try to identify both the overt and covert policy intentions of government. By close scrutiny of the texts, it was hoped that new meanings might emerge which hitherto had been invisible in the heat of policy introduction and implementation. We focused on equality issues in our study, and, in particular, on 'race' and gender issues. We identified the following themes.

The low priority given to equality issues in the documentation, in relation to both the formal and 'hidden' curriculum. For example, the final National Curriculum Mathematics Working Group report (1988) peremptorily dismisses the wide range of multicultural and antiracist strategies developed over the past decade. And, while there is a widespread rhetorical commitment to equal opportunities, scant attention is paid to the large body of research indicative of the endemic nature of racism, sexism and other forms of discrimination. Nor is any attention given to the whole-school or pedagogical approaches developed to counter such discrimination. Significantly, the Government's hostility to equality issues is further exposed by its failure to produce (as promised) specific cross-curricular advice on equality issues. Thus, *absence* from the documentation, i.e. what is left out, is possibly as important as what is kept in.

The National Curriculum does not apply equally to all pupils. While the legislation rules that there shall be a *common* set of subjects taught to all pupils, many students are likely to be excluded or differentially treated. These may be: children with disabilities for whom 'disapplication' may be sought; pupils taught in the private (or public school) sector to whom the legislation does not apply; girls who might choose to do the single rather than double science option; or inner city pupils whose schools will not have sufficient funding to resource the demands of the wider curriculum adequately.

The National Curriculum has a monocultural bias, despite some reference to the multiracial nature of British society. For example, the legislation requires that any new syllabus for religious education 'must reflect the fact that the religious traditions in this country are mainly Christian' (DES, 1989a), thus putting some schools in conflict with the 'minority' religions of their local communities (Troyna and Carrington, 1990). Another example is the pressure from government to increase the amount of *British* history in the school curriculum, giving teachers little choice but that: 'the programmes of study should have at the core the history of Britain, the record of its past and, in particular, its political, constitutional and cultural heritage' (National Curriculum History Working Group, 1990). Further, there is no topic devoted entirely to women and, as Gill (1990) points out, of the named individuals, white European males far outweigh any other representative group. National Curriculum history is still, it seems, to be the history of 'great' white men.

The documentation is over-prescriptive and bureaucratic, operating within an entirely new discursive framework with which government has sought to extend its power over teachers. It has thus sought to produce 'teacher-proof' curricula in the form of a continuous stream of glossy, persuasive literature that teachers are obliged to read, absorb and practise. It is stipulated that 'Teachers and schools will not be free to pick and choose, or to decide to modify the requirements for some pupils. . . . They can always do *more* than is required . . . but they must not do less' (DES, 1989b). Further, numerous new terms have been created specifically for the new curriculum arrangements (e.g. Programmes of Study, Key Stages, Statements of Attainment, Attainment Targets), each of which is feather-bedded by 'user-friendly' explanations of the precise specificity of its meaning. Parallels can be drawn between these developments in Britain and Apple's account of curriculum changes in the United States: 'The language of efficiency, production, standards, cost-effectiveness, job skills, work discipline, and so on — all defined by powerful groups and always threatening to become the dominant way we think about schooling — has begun to push aside concerns for a democratic curriculum, teacher autonomy, and class, gender, and race equality' (Apple, 1986).

It is difficult, at the time of writing, to evaluate how teachers are coping with the changes arising from the ERA. Certainly there seem to have been positive benefits, e.g. more science and technology being taught in the primary school. But the very complicated assessment regulations, the overloading of the curriculum, the lack of resources for effective implementation, the reduced influence of local authorities and the lack of priority of equality issues are all indicative of the difficulties we are still facing in trying to keep equality issues on the educational map.

What, then, are the possibilities of extending equal opportunities practice given the changes described above? It seems to me that there is some room for manoeuvre. As Ball (1990) remarks in the last paragraph of his book on British education policy, the battle is far from over: 'it is crucial to recognise that the analysis of the noise and heat of reform and the making of national policy still begs questions about the implementation and realisation of reform in schools and classrooms. The struggles over interpretation and accommodation go on'.

THE AGENDA FOR THE 1990s

It seems vital that we both maintain our critique of existing school practices and offer new challenges to meet the changing circumstances of schooling. In my view, we have at least four areas of action available: challenging curriculum content, reviewing pedagogy and the hidden curriculum, in our roles as professionals, and in policy-making.

As we have seen, teachers have had considerable experience of collaborating with, and building on the work of, curriculum developers and academics to create *girl- or woman-centred curricula*. This work could be extended and incorporated into the National Curriculum. Teachers might have to learn to think creatively, for example by putting together sections on 'government and social reform' and 'Victorian mothers and fathers' in the history curriculum to organize a substantial enquiry into girls' and women's lives in Victorian times. Or school-designed history units could utilize feminist, oral and documentary history methods to explore the lives of women as well as men in local communities. Extra resources (and energy) will clearly need to be found to ensure the effective teaching of these 'additions' to an already overcrowded syllabus — but the possibilities, none the less, will be available.

If teachers are to be effective in their challenge to (as well as their 'delivery' of) the new curriculum and other arrangements arising out of ERA, they will need to be able to work with colleagues to develop and exchange a wide range of source materials. Collaborative curriculum development and team teaching (significantly, not encouraged in the documentation) and a commitment from the school staffs to tackling educational inequalities will be important. Teachers will also need to develop *alternative pedagogical approaches* that enable students to derive meaning from the curriculum offered to them. These might include adoption of materials-based or independent learning approaches, collaborative investigative work, or small group discussion of 'contentious' issues, etc. Students, it is hoped, will then be able to see the importance and relevance of education to their lives, and be encouraged to adopt a more critical view of the academic 'truths' that they find in their school texts. Collaboration with teachers in higher education is also likely to be valuable; for example, in the development of appropriate teaching materials, or in order to extend professional skills or personal development, or to gain external support for any work.

There is also potential for teachers in their roles as professionals. One of the greatest successes of feminist teachers in the past, as we have seen, has been their ability to create lasting networks for communication and support. However, there are other possibilities for collective as well as individual action. At a policy level, teachers concerned about gender issues are likely to continue to group together to lobby for changes in the curriculum as well as other areas of education. They may wish to develop critiques of existing forms of school knowledge for discussion within their schools or for publication in the educational press or journals. Collaboration with parents and colleagues may lead to changes in school curricula or organization, if only at local level. The arrangement of seminars and conferences as means of exchanging information about developments in equality policies and practices in Britain and in other countries is likely to prove mutually supportive. Teachers will, no doubt, continue to work in their trade unions to fight for better career opportunities for women teachers.

Continued attention also needs to be paid to school structures and school policies. Certainly the advent of the National Curriculum has stimulated more frequent use of whole-school policy-making. A recent project with which I have been involved explored the career paths and management styles of women and black and ethnic minority managers in educational institutions (including schools) and has indicated further possibilities for progress (Powney and Weiner, 1992). While pointing to the endemic nature of sexism and racism at institutional level, constructive recommendations were made about the importance of democratic management styles, representation at senior level of under-represented groups and institutional commitment to, and policy on, equal opportunities. Additionally, proper staff recruitment and promotion procedures, monitoring of equal opportunities policies, posts of responsibility for equal opportunities, and policies on student access are all cited as vital to any programme of change (Burton and Weiner, 1993).

CONCLUSIONS

In this chapter I have attempted to provide an overview of the experiences gained in recent years from efforts made to challenge inequalities relating to gender in education. It is true, currently, that times are hard and that teachers, in particular, may feel that there are few possibilities available for autonomous action. However, I hope that some of the rich variety of suggestions and strategies I have described will provide an incentive for the renewal of practice, both institutionally and in the classroom, which will make educational equality more achievable in the 1990s.

REFERENCES

Apple, M. W. (1986) *Teachers and Texts: A Political Economy of Class and Gender Relations in Education.* New York: Routledge and Kegan Paul.

Arnot, M. (1987) 'Political lip-service or radical reform? Central government responses to sex equality as a policy issue', in M. Arnot and G. Weiner (eds), *Gender and the Politics of Schooling*. London: Hutchinson.

Avent, C. (1982) 'Careers education and guidance', *Secondary Education Journal*, 12(2), 6-7.

Ball, S. J. (1990) *Politics and Policy Making in Education*. London: Routledge.

Burton, L. and Weiner, G. (1990) 'Social justice and the National Curriculum', *Research Papers in Education*, 5(3), 203-28.

Burton, L. and Weiner, G. (1993) 'From rhetoric to reality: strategies for developing a social justice approach to educational decision-making', in I. Siraj-Blatchford (ed.), *'Race', Gender and the Education of Teachers*. Milton Keynes: Open University Press.

Clarricoates, K. (1978) 'Dinosaurs in the classroom: a re-examination of some aspects of the hidden curriculum in primary schools', *Women's Studies International Quarterly*, 1, 4.

DES (1989a) *The Education Reform Act 1988: The School Curriculum and Assessment: Circular 5/89*. London: HMSO.

DES (1989b) *National Curriculum: From Policy to Practice*. London: HMSO.

Gill, D. (1990) 'Response on behalf of Hackney teachers to the National Curriculum History Working Group Final Report', submission to DES.

ILEA (1986a) *Primary Matters*. London: Inner London Education Authority.

ILEA (1986b) *Secondary Issues*. London: Inner London Education Authority.

Kelly, A. (1981) *The Missing Half: Girls and Science Education*. Manchester: Manchester University Press.

May, N. and Rudduck, J. (1983) *Sex Stereotyping and the Early Years of Schooling*. Norwich: University of East Anglia Centre for Applied Research in Education.

Millman, V. (1987) 'Teacher as researcher: a new tradition for research on gender', in G. Weiner and M. Arnot (eds), *Gender under Scrutiny*. London: Hutchinson.

Millman, V. and Weiner, G. (1987) 'Engendering equal opportunities: the case of TVEI', in D. Gleason (ed.), *TVEI and Secondary Education: A Critical Approach*. Milton Keynes: Open University Press.

Minhas, R. (1986) 'Race, gender and class — making the connections', in *Secondary Matters*. London: ILEA.

Myers, K. (1992) *Genderwatch*. Cambridge: Cambridge University Press.

National Curriculum History Working Group (1990) *Final Report*. London: DES.

National Curriculum Mathematics Working Group (1988) *Final Report*. London: DES.

Powney, J. and Weiner, G. (1992) 'Outside of the norm: equity and management in educational institutions: project report', School of Education and Health Studies, South Bank University, London.

Spender, D. (1980) *Man Made Language*. London: Routledge and Kegan Paul.

Stanworth, M. (1981) *Gender and Schooling: A Study of Sexual Division in the Classroom*. London: Hutchinson.

Troyna, B. and Carrington, B. (1990) *Education, Racism and Reform*. London: Routledge.

Weiner, G. (1989) 'Feminism, equal opportunities and vocationalism: the changing context', in H. Burchell and V. Millman (eds), *Changing Perspectives on Gender: New Initiatives in Secondary Education*. Milton Keynes: Open University Press.

Weiner, G. (1993) 'Shell-shock or sisterhood: English school history and feminist practice', in M. Arnot and K. Weiler (eds), *Feminism and Social Justice in Education*. London: Falmer Press.

Weiner, G. and Arnot, M. (1987) 'Teachers and gender politics', in M. Arnot and G. Weiner (eds), *Gender and the Politics of Schooling*. London: Hutchinson.

Wollstonecraft, M. (1792) *A Vindication of the Rights of Women* (reprinted in A. Rossi (ed.), *The Feminist Papers*. New York: Bantam).

Women in Higher Education Network (1991) *Access and After: Conference Report*. Nottingham: WHEN.

Yates, L. (1985) 'Is girl-friendly schooling really what girls need?', in J. Whyte, R. Deem, L. Kant and M. Cruickshank (eds), *Girl Friendly Schooling*. London: Methuen.

Chapter 10

Quality and Equality in Education: The Denial of Disability Culture

Bob Findlay

INTRODUCTION

The general theme of this book is an exploration of issues around quality and equality in education. I want to try to look at these issues from what I shall call a 'disability rights perspective', which means providing an examination of the existing set of dominant ideologies and practices associated with disability and considering how, as well as why, they have impacted on the educational needs and rights of people with disabilities.[1] My starting-point will be to ask what is meant by 'disability' in the first place.

I will argue that the dominant ideologies and practices associated with disability present 'disability' as a 'personal tragedy'. The impact of these ideologies and practices is such that people with disabilities believe that members of their social group are offered an inferior quality of education, which is often provided in a segregated manner.

Organizations of people with disabilities have challenged these ideologies and practices by offering a radical critique of the individualized personal tragedy approach to disability. This critique shows that from a disability rights perspective the question of disability has to be addressed as a form of social oppression. My exploration of the issues around quality and equality will operate through the adoption of this framework.

Much of my presentation will deal with the social creation of disabling barriers within the educational systems. However, in addition to the material disabling barriers that exist, I want to suggest that the societal perceptions of people with disabilities socially construct an oppressive identity for them. This means they are subjected to what I regard to be a 'systematic denial' of not only their basic human rights, but also the right to develop a positive identity with the recognition of a distinct culture. I will suggest that this systematic denial supports, and is also informed by, the dominant approach towards disability which, taken together, helps to create the disabling barriers people with disabilities encounter. The disabling barriers people with disabilities encounter are evident within the educational system and the Education Act of 1981 has not been implemented to the extent that it has succeeded in shifting the educational culture towards integration even in the narrowest sense of the word.

Having considered the question of the denial of a disability culture, I will show how the development of the notion of 'special educational needs' is an example of how some dominant ideologies have tried to add a social dimension to their approach but without making a qualitative change in the overall addressing of the issues. This development has had contradictory implications for children with disabilities: on the positive side it has helped to shift the emphasis away from a purely medical focus on 'educational need'; but on the down side it maintains disability as a 'personal tragedy'.

My concluding comments will seek to challenge current thinking on what 'integration' means and how it is applied. I will ask what the implications will be for the educational system as disability activists articulate the need to acknowledge and embrace the concept of a 'disability culture'. Will we see pressure on the educational system to undertake a radical critique of the National Curriculum and to include a disability perspective within it?

To reach these questions, we need to return to the beginning, and acknowledge the fact that more than one definition of disability exists within British society. It is usually taken for granted that there is common agreement as to what disability actually is and, as a result, who is subject to it. The truth, of course, is very different!

WHAT DO WE MEAN BY 'DISABILITY'?

Since the 1970s a growing number of people with disabilities have questioned the main societal perceptions of disability and the professional and social practices which flow from them. Through this questioning, a radical critique has emerged that has helped to provide one of the cornerstones on which the self-organization of people with disabilities has been built. Disability was redefined as a political issue, which resulted in the formation of the British Disability Movement.[2] From within its ranks, writers such as Finkelstein (1980) and Oliver (1983) have argued that there is in existence within British society a social construction of disability. Michael Oliver has explained that definitions of disability are not universal: 'In short, disability does not have meanings which are similar in all cultures, nor indeed within the same culture is there always agreement about what disability actually is' (Oliver, 1983, p. 33). I would agree with Oliver that meanings given to 'disability' are not 'fixed', but I would go further by suggesting that they are, in fact, historically specific. There are a number of determining factors which can produce societal or cultural definitions of disability:

> The type of economy is a factor with its varying production units, need
> for manpower, amount of surplus and its mode of distribution. The
> social structure is important, whether egalitarian or hierarchical, how it
> defines achievement, how it values age and sex. (Hanks and Hanks,
> 1980, p. 13)

By acknowledging that 'disability' can have more than one meaning people with disabilities created the space for themselves to explore the historical roots of the social perceptions of disability that have informed the current dominant definition of disability within society. Within the Disability Movement there continues to be a debate concerning the periodization of the social construction of disability and key events, but I intend here to present my own view.

From the rise of industrialization society underwent a deep transformation and this produced new social groups with specific roles. To restructure to such an extent, the ruling classes within society had to establish clear norms and values; therefore, the social and economic changes were matched by ideological ones. A crucial factor in determining the arrival of 'the disabled' [sic] as a distinct social group was the emergence of the notion of 'normality'. The idea of normality played a significant role in drawing the contours around what was considered 'acceptable' and excluding what was not. The rise of the institution and subsequent popularity of the workhouse and asylum were part of the process that saw people deemed to be 'different' ultimately 'removed from the public gaze' because they were thought to be offensive or incapable. The question of an individual's social use-value, especially in terms of his or her contribution to the labour process, has always been a key determinator in defining 'disability'.

The nineteenth century saw the transformation from 'the cripple' to 'the hapless cripple' and finally 'the disabled'. To understand this shift and the significant rupture with the past, more attention needs to be paid to the role of the philanthropic and eugenicist movements in the shaping of the lives of people with disabilities. The growth of an imperialist ideology has as one of its components the eugenicist movement. The promotion of the purity of the race and the concern that the nation might not have soldiers fit and healthy enough to carry the flag were popular sentiments prior to the First World War. The war, it could be argued, became a watershed in the social construction of disability.

The perversity of war is such that medical technology tends to advance by leaps and bounds; rehabilitation became a major new factor in warfare. The circle was also complete. Disability became a medical issue via a medicalized social evaluation of what was considered 'functionally normal' in terms of social roles. Hence, the *less* the ability to function like a 'normal person' (able-bodied), the *more* 'disabled' (abnormal) one was judged to be. The aim of rehabilitation, therefore, was to restore an individual to as near a state of normality as possible. This medical approach to disability had important social and ideological implications too. The focus was the individual who had become the *victim* of war and was expected and encouraged by the rehabilitation process either to *overcome* or to *come to terms with* disability. Disability was articulated as a negative and tragic experience because it was seen as a *loss* both in terms of functional capability, and with regard to able-bodied normality. The language and imagery socially constructed conflated together notions of illness and disability. Even today the media insists of talking about people *suffering* from disability.

The emergence of dominant perceptions and sets of practices has never been satisfactorily addressed by historians, but should that really surprise us? People with disabilities, generally speaking, are absent from history because they are not considered as active social actors. This is the backdrop to the 'personal tragedy theory'.

THE PERSONAL TRAGEDY THEORY

Disability activists have given the dominant ideologies a number of names, ranging from the medical model and the administrative model, through to the personal tragedy model. It is my view that the different names reflect the sites of influence or specific aspects of the dominant ideologies and practices at work and, therefore, I believe Michael Oliver is right to refer to the personal tragedy theory as a catch-all. How does the personal tragedy theory impact on the education system? To begin to understand this it is necessary to see how it has developed since the early days of the century. Peter Leonard explains:

> Within this perspective able-bodied experts — doctors, teachers, social workers — may feel free to concentrate on explanations of the feelings and aspirations of handicapped people [sic] in terms of the supposed psychopathology, 'reactions to personal tragedy' to be understood within a specialised 'psychology of disability'. One result of this powerful external definition of their situation is that it tends to suggest that people with disabilities cannot live worthwhile, active lives and that their capabilities can only be defined through medical and social expertise, for their own is bound to be 'subjective'. (Leonard, 1984, p. 188)

The above quotation has as its focus the central core of the dominant ideologies surrounding disability, but it is extremely important to understand that the impact of ideology lies in the ways in which it informs both social and professional practices while, at the same time, being legitimated by these practices. It is generally recognized that the medical professionals were the prime developers of the theory, but we must not forget how other professionals gave their support or were influenced by the medical world. Len Barton explains that:

> Also, the existence of such a powerful group of experts, who were viewed as definers of need, resulted in an increased demand for their services. The effectiveness of their influence can be seen in that it was only in 1970 that the education of severely handicapped children became the official responsibility of the Department of Education and Science. It was previously under the control of the Department of Health and Social Services. (Barton, 1986, p. 277)

If the professionals have been the 'definers of need', how have their theories and practices been employed to achieve their objectives? As Léonard states, by seeing 'disability' as a negative consequence of a specific condition, everything about that individual becomes 'problematized', thus requiring professionals to intervene to deal 'with the problem'. The individual takes on the imposed 'disabled' identity, which allows the experts to 'take control over them'.

The personal tragedy approach engages with other dominant ideologies operating within the educational system, and through these connections it is not long before a child with a 'difference' is labelled. By confering the 'disabled' identity on to a child it is immediately set apart from its able-bodied counterparts. The setting apart can be done in a variety of ways, but traditionally it was through the division between normality and abnormality. The social evaluation of 'functional loss' first establishes that the child has broken with normality and then helps to decide what implications flow from this.

The measurement of 'functional loss' will allow experts to decide to what degree they can *translate* 'disability' into negative features which require management. The focus on individuals as *having something wrong with them* means that the management of 'their needs' is conducted through policies which demand adjustment or conformity to the norms and expectations set by able-bodied people. The 'disabled' identity suggests non-conformity and therefore invites members of society to view those considered 'disabled' to be a burden and, as a consequence, allocated to a dependent role. Having been allocated a dependent role, the individual is at the mercy of the professionals who determine his or her lifestyle in terms of levels of care required. By problematizing the individual, the personal tragedy model creates a distance between that person, his or her needs and lifestyle and his or her able-bodied counterparts.

Failure, by individuals, to bridge this distance results in everything about those individuals being negatively assessed. Their non-conformity and assumed need of care increases the 'difference' which sets them apart. The management of 'their needs' becomes specialized and outside the mainstream. Historically, therefore, the educational needs of children with disabilities have been evaluated differently from those of their able-bodied counterparts. The medicalization of their lifestyles has allowed professionals to impose priorities on them, which usually relegate 'education' to a poor second. The management of these other priorities is generally speaking not considered to be the responsibility of mainstream provision and, therefore, 'special' provisions are created.

To conclude, the personal tragedy approach 'blames the victim' and avoids taking a close look at the norms, values and structures which socially construct 'disability' as non-conformity. Disability activists argue that the dominant ideologies and practices lead to people with disabilities having to deal with the implications of society seeing able-bodied lifestyles as being the only valid ones and that those led by people with disabilities are a problem or inferior. The result of the dominant societal view is the creation of a form of social oppression.

How does this impact on the existing educational system? Does it mean confronting difficult questions, such as who is education designed for and who decides what values and expectations are called upon to establish meaningful goals? There is a strong feeling among people with disabilities that given the existence of social oppression, it is clear that the educational system is structured to fail them as a specific social group.

THE SOCIAL OPPRESSION THEORY

The articulation of disability as a form of social oppression was first put forward by the Union of Physically Impaired against Segregation in 1976 in the following terms:

> In our view, it is society which disables physically impaired people. Disability is something imposed on top of our impairments by the way we are unnecessarily isolated and excluded from full participation in

society. . . . Thus we define impairment as lacking part of or all of a
limb, organism or mechanism of the body; and disability as the
disadvantage or restriction of activity caused by a contemporary social
organisation which takes little or no account of people who have
physical impairments and thus excludes them from mainstream social
activity. Physical disability is therefore a particular form of social
oppression. (UPIAS, 1976, pp. 3-4)

This definition of disability remains the dominant one inside the Disability
Movement although others exist and I, personally, feel unhappy with this one
for a number of reasons. Colin Barnes, for example, writes: 'Impairment is
generally regarded as a neutral term' (Barnes, 1990, p. 3). There are people, like
myself, who believe the term cannot be 'neutral' because it carries with it social
and cultural meanings that frame the individual as being 'other than normal'.
With the term carrying these assumed negative meanings I believe it would
appear extremely difficult for people to use the notion as a basis for a positive
self-image! The key point is to *accept* and not to *deny* our 'differences' but
from within a framework that does not allow the *cause* of our 'difference' to be
presented in ways which can devalue or oppressively define us. Many, including
myself, prefer the term 'condition', even though it too has limitations.

While accepting that disability is about the disadvantage or restriction of
activity experienced by those of us considered impaired or having a condition,
I believe it is now accepted that disability is far more pervasive in terms of
its social and cultural dynamics. This why I believe the UPIAS analysis is too
narrow.

Disability is not just about preventing people from engaging in activity
(using this term in the widest possible contex), but it includes the imposition of
a false and damaging identity that robs us of any social meaning other than the
ones that are externally given. Thus, as 'the disabled' [*sic*], we can be viewed
as dependent creatures who can be brave or courageous, a far cry from being
regarded as an oppressed social group who are denied basic human rights. Our
'existence' is, generally speaking, either denied or discounted. What this means
is that, *in the first instance*, our social groups' marginalization and exclusion are
not due to the fact that 'contemporary social organization takes no or little
account' of us, but because of the very ways in which it *does* take us into
account!

Whether one agrees with the majority view or the one I advocate, the main
point remains the same: the focus of people with disabilities' disadvantage and
oppression has to be seen as the values and structures of society, not their own
individual characteristics. Thus, the social oppression approach seeks to question how society evaluates and marginalizes people with disabilities. The *cause*
of disability is not the absence of 'normality', but how notions of 'normality'
negate the existence and acceptance of 'difference' and create oppressive social
relations as a result. The disability is experienced through the subjection of
differential and unequal treatment caused by society's failure to acknowledge
and meet the needs generated by people with a variety of conditions.

The people with disabilities experience oppression daily. However, the

British Council of Organizations of Disabled People have explained the important role the special school system plays:

> The special education system, then, is one of the main channels for disseminating the predominant able-bodied/minded perception of the world and ensuring that disabled school leavers are socially immature and isolated. This isolation results in passive acceptance of social discrimination, lack of skills in facing the tasks of adulthood and ignorance about the main social issues of our time. All this reinforces the 'eternal children' myth and ensures at the same time disabled school leavers lack the skills for overcoming the myth. (BCODP, 1986, p. 6)

The able-bodied/minded perception of the world is not an abstract concept but a material reality. Because society assumes that people with disabilities are passive, non-active and cared for through special provisions, their needs are not catered for or valued when the social organization of society is planned and carried out. Token or 'special' provision is often an afterthought that highlights difference and maintains segregation.

Disability activists argue that the real problems people with disabilities face are both socially constructed *and* created. A person, for example, has a visual disability when confronted by an environment designed for sighted people. The loss of sight is an undeniable reality, but whereas the personal tragedy approach would identify this as the cause of the 'problem' for the individual, the social oppression approach would focus on the problems caused by a lack of facilities available to that individual to assist his or her participation in activities. There needs to be greater awareness of and identification of disabling barriers. These barriers can be organizational or structural, environmental, cultural or attitudinal.

An inaccessible classroom, for example, is a disabling barrier to a person with limited mobility, but the cause of the disadvantage is not the fact that the individual cannot walk or climb steps, but rather, is the building design not facilitating people with limited mobility. Whether a child can or cannot enter a mainstream school is often debated in terms of meeting 'special educational needs' but this usually hides, or denies, the real disabling barriers, which are the lack of resources to, for example, employ a classroom assistant to support that child.

Thus, how disability is addressed is a crucial political and a human rights issue. The personal tragedy model imposes a negative oppressive identity on to a social group who are marginalized as a consequence and the marginalization of the social group maintains this identity. The social oppression model, on the other hand, offers a way of breaking free of this negative circle by changing the focus of attention and asserting the right of members of this oppressed social group to construct their own positive identity.

THE DENIAL OF DISABILITY CULTURE

Defining disability has become a site of struggle because of the impact it has had on the ability of people with disabilities to take control over their own identity and lifestyle and to articulate a distinct culture. People with disabilities argue that their experiences are, more often than not, subjected to able-bodied people's interpretation. The language and imagery employed reflects the societal view of disability as tragedy or problem and, therefore, people with disabilities are either 'hidden from view' or presented through stereotypes constructed by professionals, media and charities.[3] It is rare, therefore, to view positive images of people with disabilities. Alan Sutherland wrote:

> The Disabled are generally understood to be a small, clearly defined section of society, quite distinct from the public at large — poor dependent creatures, immediately recognisable as physically different from normal people. (Sutherland, 1981, p. 13)

Societal perceptions and treatment of people with disabilities help to determine who they are, what they are and what they are incapable of! There is a growing recognition among people with disabilities that in order to dismantle the disabling barriers they face there is the need to organize collectively and build a positive new identity for themselves. This identity must come from a decisive break with any negative comparison with able-bodied people. Other oppresed groups have acknowledged that the processes involved in forging or articulating positive self-images and identities have played a major role in challenging the nature of their oppression. Simon Brisenden articulated the importance of the concept of 'disability culture' when he wrote:

> The idea of disability culture begins with the recognition that we are valuable people in ourselves, and that we need not avoid each other or hide behind the cloak of false integration. We no longer need to build our lives on a denial and devaluing of our background and the experiences of pain and triumph, sadness and joy, which form the reality of our upbringing. Disability culture is being built upon a ruthless honesty about the people we are and the role we play in society. (Brisenden, 1990, p. 63)

The idea of a disability culture is threatening to both people with disabilities and able-bodied people alike because it questions completely the rules of the game we have historically been taught to play. Brisenden confronted this by writing:

> The idea of a culture of people with disabilities, a set of common experiences and aspirations belonging to us all, seems to undermine everything you have achieved. It seems to threaten the basis upon which you live. If you have struggled and fought to become assimilated, to merge with the majority, you do not want this achievement to be knocked, you do not want to be reminded of what you have left behind. (Brisenden, 1990, p. 63)

With the dominant approach to disability demanding conformity to able-bodied norms and ways of doing, it follows that the goals set will aim to 'unproblematize' and encourage a striving for 'normality'. Against this backdrop it is perhaps understandable why people with disabilities are willing to accept the status quo and avoid being seen and treated as 'them'. Disability activists break with the status quo by demanding a change of agenda. In recent years there has been a debate over Wolfensberger's development of 'normalization'. Tony Booth highlights a concern I have:

> It is apparent that he views society as a unified cultural whole rather than as containing competing groups which are culturally, morally and politically diverse. In assuming that the notion of what is normal is unproblematic he leaves it to be defined by the dominant group of which the advocate of normalisation may well be a member. (Booth, 1988)

I see this as extremely problematic and therefore do not consider it a useful model to work with. It also fails to address the question of sub-cultures which exist among people with disabilities. Many advocates of normalization would find themselves up against a powerful section of the deaf community, for example. Normalization would be viewed as an imposition of an alien culture on to deaf people. It is interesting to consider at this point a paradox which currently affects the politics of disability. There is a debate taking place within the deaf community as to whether or not they can identify with the Disability Movement.

Many deaf people do not see themselves as 'disabled', especially through the dominant perceptions of the word, but argue instead that they are a linguistic minority who have their own culture. There are others, however, who support the view that there is a distinct culture but maintain that this does not mean they are separate from a wider oppressed social group who experience disability. The paradox is, of course, that the segment of the social group that has done the most to understand and promote the idea of disability culture believes, generally speaking, that it is outside of it.

Nevertheless, if one considers the historical background to the teaching of deaf children, one can see how the educationalists have oppressed them by demanding oralism (conforming to normality) and denying their right to their own cultural language (signing). Deaf people have gone through many of the battles some people with disabilities are just engaging in. However, both groups offer the same challenge: why should people strive to lead lifestyles which are alien to them and risk being penalized when they fail? The challenge being made by people with disabilities is a fundamental one that goes beyond simply saying to society, accept our 'difference' positively; it is revealing the fact that people with disabilities have begun *a celebration of difference*. The world is being turned on its head! The struggle is on to create a new social worth that is not based on accommodation or assimilation to able-bodiedness, but is situated within an articulation of self-pride and self-determination over what is seen as a valid lifestyle.

The overall impact of the concept of a disability culture remains largely unknown at present because it is still relatively new, but I believe we have already seen an indication of what it might mean. The Disability Movement has begun to develop social and cultural activities that confront how activities have been hitherto organized. Direct action has been used to protest against inaccessible public transport and demonstrations have been held to protest at the patronage fostered by national charities and mass media. Disability activists have also developed disability equality training to assist professionals and others to alter their practice.

Richard Rieser and Micheline Mason (1990) suggest that the question of the invisibility of disability issues inside the structures of society will become an increased target for attention as disability culture becomes more recognized. The rejection of accommodation and assimilation has already led people with disabilities to question past held positions on the notion of integration. Some of the processes unfolding have a similar ring to the ones gone through by black people. Consider the ideas being articulated by Simon Brisenden in the following quotation, and compare them with views expressed by the South African black activist Steve Biko. Brisenden wrote:

> Out of the recognition of our value comes the ability to organise ourselves, to put on events, to mobilise our forces, to produce works of art, to run workshops and newsletters and generally to get together and share the common language of our experiences. Only people who value themselves, and listen carefully to their own voices, have a culture of their own rather than a secondhand culture gifted to them as the price of a silent acquiescence to unthinking 'normality'. (Brisenden, 1990, p. 63)

Biko stated:

> Briefly defined therefore, Black Consciousness is in essence the realization by the black man of the need to rally together with his brothers around the cause of their oppression — the blackness of their skin — and to operate as a group in order to rid themselves of the shackles that bind them to perpetual servitude. It seeks to demonstrate the lie that black is an aberration from the 'normal' which is white. It is a manifestation of a new realisation that by seeking to run away from themselves and to emulate the white man, blacks are insulting the intelligence of whoever created them black. (Biko, 1989, p. 63)

By placing disability culture and black consciousness side by side I am not seeking a crude comparison; the connections exist in terms of how oppressed social groups articulate their *awakening* to the challenge of their oppression and their assertion of the right to a self-defined identity. The recognition of these connections has led people with disabilities to draw heavily on the ideas expressed by other oppressed groups and transform them for their own use. The debate about integrated or segregated schooling takes on a fresh perspective when the issue of disability culture is introduced. Most of the past discussions I have witnessed have merely focused on either the merits or practicalities involved and the issues around rights and cultural identity have been ignored. Personally, I cannot help reflecting on the approach to integration expressed by Biko:

> The concept of integration, whose virtues are often extolled in white liberal circles, is full of unquestioned assumptions that embrace white

values. It is a concept long defined by whites and never examined by blacks. It is based on the assumption that all is well with the system apart from some degree of mismanagement by irrational conservatives at the top.... This is white man's integration — an integration based on exploitative values. It is integration in which black will compete with black, using each other as rungs up a step-ladder leading them to white values. It is an integration in which the black man will have to prove himself in terms of these values before meriting acceptance and ultimate assimilation, and in which the poor will grow poorer and the rich richer in a country where the poor have always been black. (Biko, 1989, p. 107)

The substitution of able-bodied people for white and people with disabilities for black would produce an apt description of this existing approach to the integration of people with disabilities in society. The 'acknowledgement' of the need to integrate people with disabilities into society, especially within the framework of education and employment opportunities, has been based on the premise that it will only happen if additional resources can be found to meet people's 'special needs'. The past decade, therefore, has seen a preoccupation with the notion of 'special needs' and the education system has led the way in this development. I want to suggest that this maintains rather than questions the present status quo and, if kept in use, will not assist the introduction of the concept of disability culture into the education system.

The denial of disability culture means that the values, interests, rights and lifestyles favoured by people with disabilities are ignored or not considered. Equality in education for people with disabilities can only be presently understood in the terms of access to able-bodied people's agendas. To discover images and perceptions of the world, as offered in the classroom, which were not viewed through the eyes of an able-bodied person is rare. Imagine, for example, a topic on the history of transportation that included the changing face of the wheelchair or a discussion on the inaccessibility of buses due to poor design.

Until there is a shift towards the incorporation of disability issues into mainstream provision, no qualitative shift towards integration will occur. The incorporation must be guided by people with disabilities to ensure that issues around equality and quality are addressed. Currently, 'integration' is about having children with disabilities placed in mainstream schools; it is never considered in terms of changing the 'special' school status to include able-bodied children — now that would be challenging!

Under the influence of disability culture the debate inside the Disability Movement on integration in terms of education has shifted ground in recent years. The subject is no longer a simple issue of segregated provision being all wrong and integrated provision always being the way ahead. Blind people, for example, have begun to assess their educational needs in terms of the pros and cons of existing provision and quality in comparison with the prospects under 'special educational needs' within mainstream provision. The segregated provision had the edge in their opinion. What should we conclude from this? First, the issue of integration is complex and needs a new political focus. Steve Biko's perspective was:

> If ... by integration you mean there shall be free participation by all members of society, catering for the full expression of the self in a freely changing society as determined by the will of the people, then I am with you. (Biko, 1989, pp. 38-9)

In other words, the dominant culture of society must acknowledge and respond to the sub-cultures being developed by people with disabilities. This shift in acceptance will at the same time influence that dominant culture and, it is hoped, assist in building a multicultural society.

SPECIAL EDUCATIONAL NEEDS

If one accepts the argument that there has been a systematic denial of a disability culture, what are the implications for the educational system? To answer this question we need to return to the issue of 'special educational needs' and try to discover the role this concept plays. Will it assist in introducing the notion of a disability culture or is it itself a disabling barrier?

Currently, the education system addresses 'disability' purely as an external (individualized) factor introduced from the outside and thus requiring 'management'. I have already noted that it was only in the 1970s that the Department of Education and Science took over from Health and Social Services, so it is obvious that until the past decade the 'management' of the educational needs of children with disabilities had a medical bias.

The Warnock Committee had the following terms of reference: 'To review educational provision ... for children and young people *handicapped by disabilities* of body or mind' (Warnock, 1978, p. 1). Through its work, the Committee recommended that the ten medical categories of 'handicap' be replaced by the broader notion of 'special needs'. Why was this change considered so important? Lady Warnock said:

> To describe someone as handicapped conveys nothing of the type of education help, and hence provision, that is required. We wish to see a more positive approach, and we have adopted the concept of special educational needs, seen not in terms of a particular disability that a child may have, but in relation to everything about him, his abilities as well as his disabilities — indeed all the factors which may impinge on his educational progress. (Warnock, 1978, p. 37)

What we see here is the shift within the dominant ideologies associated with disability. Instead of having a focus on impairment or disability (identification and measurement of functional loss) leading to fixed assumptions about an individual's needs, the focus is switched to disability or handicap (measurement of functional loss within set social environments), which means addressing 'learning difficulties' as being where:

(a) he has a significantly greater difficulty in learning than the majority of children of his age; or

(b) he has a disability which either *prevents or hinders him from making use of educational facilities of a kind generally provided in schools*, within the area of the local authority concerned, for children of his age. (Warnock, 1978, p. 1; emphasis added)

Within the Warnock Report 'disability' was still negatively situated within the individual and considered the *cause* of his or her ultimate disadvantage *vis-à-vis* 'normal' educational provision. It breaks with the traditional approach over the recognition that the introduction of additional social factors might reduce or remove the 'handicapping factors' involved. The introduction of this shift was meant to signal the establishment of a new 'management' of the needs of children with disabilities within a more progressive framework. The medical aspects were no longer seen as the priority concern and the 'handicapping factors', now defined as 'special educational needs', had taken their place.

There are problems with this. First, the dominant perception of disability remains unchallenged, which means that despite attempts to see 'special needs' as resulting from social barriers, the cause will still be viewed by many educationalists as the child's medical condition (see Swann, 1987, p. 183). Second, the fact that a child is seen as having *'special* needs' reinforces the idea that the child is set apart by the difference or should be viewed as a 'problem'. It is suggested by people with disabilities that the adoption of the concept 'special needs' has only resulted in substituting one negative label for another and therefore has done nothing positive in terms of influencing societal perceptions of children with disabilities.

Many have said that to refer to children as having 'special needs' is better than saying they are 'handicapped', but others, especially those with the experience of disability, are not convinced. Oliver, for example, suggests that the acid test is not what label is employed, but how a child's needs and rights are met. The opposition to the labels 'handicap' and 'special needs' arises from the recognition that they assist in the legitimatization of a negative evaluation of 'difference'. Thus, the dual identity people with disabilities have is because of how their 'difference' is both viewed and made sense of by others or themselves. As I have suggested throughout this chapter the articulation of 'difference' via the dominant ideologies of disability results in a negative appraisal of the social group's needs and rights. However, it is important to stress that being viewed as 'different' is not in itself a bad thing. The articulation of 'difference' as a positive experience — which is the underlying message contained within the development of a disability culture — offers the possibility of changing the agenda altogether. Without this happening I believe one has to agree with the critics of the Warnock Report.

Critics of the report argue that a strong medical/psychological emphasis underpins it. Having witnessed the statementing process, I would support this view. It is equally true to say that the notion of 'special educational needs' is open to interpretation that lends itself to being largely a tool of administrative convenience, which fosters bureaucratization and reinforces the power of professional judgement. The Education Act 1981 has not delivered the goods and ensured access for children with disabilities into mainstream provision. The statementing process, which was designed to identify 'special educational needs', has been used to *police* the educational resources made available and, therefore, rather than being an enabling factor often becomes one of the 'handicapping factors' children and parents have to overcome!

In my opinion the Education Act 1981 offers little concrete evidence of a shift towards true integration and a challenge to the disabling barriers within the education system. The Act was not concerned with the issue of equal opportunities. Nor did it address the wider cultural implications of moving towards integration. Therefore it has been left to individual authorities and schools to adopt and develop good practice.

CONCLUSION

I have been extremely negative and critical of the education system as far as children with disabilities are concerned. It would have been possible to give positive examples of schools moving towards integration but I decided instead to offer a generalized account of what is taking place. It is extremely difficult to measure the quality of education offered to children with disabilities without first addressing issues around their oppression. The fact that 'disability' is treated as a 'special educational needs' issue distorts any chance of a serious or informed debate initiated around the question of quality.

The educational reforms of the past decade have failed to address the real questions being asked by parents of children with disabilities — if anything the reforms have only succeeded in increasing concern. We must add to this the continued denial of disability as a cultural and political issue, which means that the education system is incapable of positively 'including' disability as an educational issue within the National Curriculum. It has been left to disability activists and pro-integrationists to show how this might be done (see Rieser and Mason, 1990).

The twin issues of quality and equality are important and I welcome the work being done to raise standards, but this said, I must question whose standards we are working with and for what purpose. Are people with disabilities to be involved or not?

NOTES

1 I have elected to use the term 'people with disabilities' rather than the more commonly used 'disabled people'. In taking this decision I am supporting a minority view inside the Disability Movement, who feel the term 'people with disabilities' reclaims the historical definition of 'with disabilities', which signalled the imposition of a disadvantage through the absence of power and social worth. They also see difficulties in transforming 'disabled people' into a positive group identity.

2 The British Disability Movement or Disabled People's Movement is a phrase used to describe the self-organized disability groups who adhere to the social oppression theory of disability and engage in campaigns to raise civil rights issues.

3 The British Council of Organizations of Disabled People has produced

a pamphlet called *Disabling Imagery and the Media* (1992), which examines the major disabling stereotyped images used by the media and many charities.

REFERENCES

Barnes, C. (1990) *Cabbage Syndrome*. Lewes: Falmer.

Barton, L. (1986) 'The politics of special educational needs', *Disability, Handicap & Society*, 1(3), 273-90.

Barton, L. (ed.) (1988) *The Politics of Special Educational Needs*. Lewes: Falmer.

Biko, S. (1989) *I Write What I Like*. Harmondsworth: Penguin.

Booth, T. (1988) 'Challenging concepts of integration,' in L. Barton, *The Politics of Special Educational Needs*. Lewes: Falmer.

Brisenden, S. (1990) 'What is disability culture?' in R. Reiser and M. Mason (eds), *Disability Equality in the Classroom: A Human Rights Issue*. London: ILEA.

British Council of Organizations of Disabled People (1986) *Disabled Young People Living Independently*. London: BCODP.

Finkelstein, V. (1980) *Attitudes and Disabled People: Issues for Discussion*. New York: World Rehabilitation Fund.

Hanks, J. and Hanks, L. (1980) 'The physically handicapped in certain non-occidental societies', in W. Philip and J. Rosenberg (eds), *Social Scientists and the Physically Handicapped*. London: Arno Press.

Leonard, P. (1984) *Personality and Ideology*. London: Macmillan.

Oliver, M. (1983) *Social Work with Disabled People*. London: Macmillan.

Oliver, M. (1990) *The Politics of Disablement*. London: Macmillan.

Rieser, R. and Mason, M. (eds) (1990) *Disability Equality in the Classroom: A Human Rights Issue*. London: ILEA.

Sutherland, A. (1981) *Disabled We Stand*. London: Souvenir Press.

Swann, W. (1987) *Including Pupils with Disabilities*. Milton Keynes: Open University Press.

Union of Physically Impaired against Segregation (1976) *Fundamental Principles of Disability*. London: UPIAS.

Warnock Report (1978) *Special Educational Needs*. London: HMSO.

Wood, P. (1981) *International Classification of Impairments, Disabilities and Handicaps*. Geneva: World Health Organization.

Chapter 11

Performance Indicators, Value Added and Quality Assurance

Carol Fitz-Gibbon

One of the more important tasks for managers in the 1990s will be to collect systematic information about the performance of the units that they are managing. In other words management in the 1990s almost certainly implies the setting up of performance indicator systems. These systems will take time and cost money, because the collection, analysis and interpretation of data are exceedingly time consuming activities. This will be time and money well spent only if the performance of the system is improved by the existence of the performance indicators. It follows that one of the most important characteristics of performance indicators should be that their impact on the system should be beneficial. Whether or not the impact is beneficial may rest crucially on two actions taken by management: the particular indicators chosen and the manner in which they are used.

MEASUREMENT GIVES MESSAGES: THE IMPORTANCE OF CHOOSING THE RIGHT INDICATORS

The choice of performance indicators represents a signal from management as to the features of the system that are of most concern. Consider the tragedy of the cross-channel ferry called the *Herald of Free Enterprise*. It might well have been the case that the time taken to cross the channel and return was carefully monitored, because of the need to adhere to a strict timetable and to make as many crossings as possible, so that each crossing represented a maximum intake of money into the system. This monitoring would have acted as a signal to operators to concentrate on a rapid turn-round in each port. If, concurrently, there was no systematic monitoring of what might be called 'near misses', such as leaving port with the bow doors open, then less attention would be paid to that feature of the system than to the speed of turn-round. The consequences of such monitoring could be disastrous in terms of safety. The design of beneficial performance indicators is surely one of the most onerous and demanding responsibilities placed on management.

THE MANNER OF USE OF INDICATORS

Not only must the choice of indicator be made carefully but the conditions of reporting of the indicator may also be vital in determining the effect it has on the system. In the airline industry, for example, pilots can report 'near misses'; that is, situations in which, although no accident happened, planes were flying too close for comfort or some evasive action was needed to avoid an accident. Pilots do not need to give their names, so that 'near misses' are not held against them. If the system required that pilots gave their names then it could be seen in terms of punitive surveillance and the self-report aspect would be in jeopardy. Since the report of 'near misses' can only be made by those aware of these incidents, it is exceedingly sensible to make sure that such information *is* collected, rather than to set up a system in which data would simply not be produced or would be corrupted.

The philosophy behind the confidential reporting of 'near misses' is that these potential accident situations arise from *faults in the system rather than faults attributable to individuals*. Is this a principle that can be applied generally to complicated systems, such as airlines, education or cross-channel ferries? W. Edwards Deming believes it is, suggesting that most inefficiency is due to defects in the system rather than indolence or unwillingness on the part of employees. If the system is at fault, the system needs monitoring in order to set it right. The monitoring must be based on good data and that often requires some confidentiality so that the temptation to make the data simply *look* good is not built into the system. Highly punitive surveillance systems simply become corrupted. This was evident in Eastern Europe in a widespread manner, with phoney targets and phoney feedback of the extent to which targets were being met. The consequence was an economic system full of disinformation and exceedingly ineffective.

EXAMPLES OF INDICATORS IN USE IN EDUCATION

We need, then, to set up systems of performance indicators in which the indicators are chosen so that their use produces a beneficial impact on the system. This requires a careful choice of indicators and of the methods by which they are reported and used. With these considerations in mind, let us consider some performance indicators that are recommended for use in education in such documents as the Coopers & Lybrand report, *Local Management of Schools* (Coopers & Lybrand, 1988). One kind of indicator is the percentage of students achieving a pass or a particular grade. In its worst form this indicator may be the 'percentage pass rate', measured by the percentage of those entered for the exam who obtain a passing grade. The impact of a percentage pass rate indicator is unfortunate in a number of ways. Logically, percentage pass rates should be expected to encourage teachers to push out of their classes students who are likely to fail, whether or not it is in the student's interest to be encouraged to leave the class or not. Logically, a percentage pass rate should encourage teachers to concentrate their teaching on the borderline students. The students heading towards an A or a B are unlikely to end up failing and can therefore be neglected. The teacher should concentrate on improving the pass rate by ensuring the borderline candidates get through the examination. If these logical approaches to 'fixing' the indicator were adopted the result would be unfair practice: pupils would not be treated equally. The consequence for some students of failing to obtain their As may be as grave as for other students of failing to pass the examination at all. To encourage fair practice, performance indicators must be chosen so that each pupil counts equally in the computation. If the percentage reported as an indicator is not of those entered for the examination but of the year group there are still unfortunate implications in the publication of percentages attaining various grades. In colleges, where enrolment is fluid, they face the problem of wanting enrolment for the money but not wanting students who are going to fail and damage the performance indicators.

Of course these problems can be exaggerated. If the drop-out rate is also monitored, the temptation to push students out of a course as the exam draws nearer will be moderated by a desire not to worsen the drop-out indicator. These considerations suggest that to monitor a system adequately a fair number of performance indicators will be needed. Indeed, the use of a large number of indicators may be fairer and more beneficial in the long term than concentrating on one or two indicators. There is always the danger, however, that only a simple indicator like the percentage pass rate will be reported in meetings or in the press. It would therefore be wise to choose a good single indicator which can be emphasized and the use of which would be least damaging. The kind of value-added indicators used in the A Level Information System (ALIS) project, and widely used in research on school effectiveness, treat each pupil as equally important. By also taking into account the most important influences on the examinations, the indicators are probably the best single indicators available.

Another example of an indicator that could have unfortunate effects is the relative rating used in Scotland (Kelly, 1976; Fitz-Gibbon, 1992). The relative ratings provide comparisons between the performance of different departments within the same institution. The relative rating indicator takes account of the two dominant influences on examination results in each subject: the difficulty of the examination in that subject and the general aptitude of students enrolled in the course. This system is a sophisticated development of a practice used in many schools, that of looking at the grades in one subject in comparison with the grades the same students attained in other subjects. While it is an interesting and sophisticated statistic the impact could be unfortunate in that it places departments in competition with each other. The maths department will be placed in competition with the physics department because they share the same students. The maths department should logically load students with maths homework to encourage them to neglect their physics, because if physics performance declined the maths department could get a better relative rating.

An interesting feature of relative ratings, however, is that they tend to correlate about 0.70 with measures of 'value added'. Value added indicators show the extent to which students are gaining examination results relatively better or relatively worse than similar students elsewhere studying the same subject. In other words, departments which are *relatively* effective in their school tend to be those which are effective *in comparison with other departments in the same subject in other schools*. Value added indicators compare maths departments with other maths departments, physics departments with other physics departments and so on, in all the institutions participating in the performance indicator system. It should be noted that if schools were uniformly good or bad the correlation of value added with relative ratings would be close to zero. The high correlation illustrates a point made many times in the ALIS project: departments differ substantially even within the same school.

Now that the Scottish Examination Board, in conjunction with the Scottish Office Education Department, is producing relative rating indicators for just about every department of every school in Scotland, it will be very interesting indeed to find out how this information is used in schools. Here is a prime need for careful qualitative research. How do headteachers interpret the data? To whom do they communicate the data? With what messages are the data communicated? Do those to whom the data are communicated interpret the messages correctly, misinterpret the data, accept the data, find them interesting, find them useful, find them threatening? The same questions need to be asked about the reception and use of the ALIS data.

DESIGNING MONITORING SYSTEMS

We have considered up to now existing indicator systems, but in many situations indicator systems do not as yet exist and must be created. The creation of indicator systems must obviously take account of the need for the indicators to have a beneficial impact.

In the first instance, decisions have to be made about which outcomes need to be monitored. A system in which the outcomes are not monitored is flying blind, totally unable to set reasonable targets or know whether it is doing well or doing badly. *The measurement of outcomes is absolutely fundamental to the monitoring of the performance of a system.* The outcomes that are measured must be chosen carefully. Clearly they must be outcomes over which the system has some influence. This may seem obvious but it has been suggested that delinquency rates should be collected school by school. This would be reasonable if it had been shown that schools had an influence on delinquency rates. It *has* been shown that delinquency rates vary from school to school, but so does the incidence of leukaemia. Until the causes or mechanisms are understood it would seem unfair to regard staff as responsible for delinquency rates in their school. 'No accountability without causality' might be a rallying cry.

An example of an indicator that may be susceptible to some distortion is the truancy rate. As one head remarked, commenting on the requirement to publish truancy rates: 'It's quite simple: from now on we won't have any truants. It's all a matter of definition.' Another corruptible indicator may well be the results of Key Stage assessments, assessment done by teachers and reported so that, in this era of competition, we can see how well they are teaching. The extent of checking required to verify testing conditions and marking standards make the Standard Assessment Tasks (SATs), as proposed, unworkable except as a system resting on 'scout's honour'. In a framework of competition and unemployment, grave misgivings about the validity of publicly reported SAT results would seem to be reasonable. Confidential use of well-tested items from the

Assessment of Performance Unit might have provided valued feedback to teachers, but the proposed system of public reporting of teacher-marked performance lacks credibility. It is a system that also provides little in the way of safeguards against bias. (This discussion of SATs was written about a year before their collapse and their subsequent revision by Sir Ron Dearing.)

In the measurement of outcomes many managers and researchers look at whole-school indicators, such as the sum total of examination results produced by a year group. This aggregate sum may be of passing interest but the managers will need to know the contributions made by each department. Furthermore, it is the departments that are the units that are managed to provide the education that results in the examination passes. The departments, therefore, need indicators.

There is much reliance currently placed on the provision of raw data. League tables are drawn from information on the number of students achieving various grades, which must now be published. We need to repeat, again and again, the following idea. That is, we need to teach this idea to politicians and to the public.

FOUR KINDS OF DATA

There are four kinds of data.

Raw data are simple to understand, but often almost impossible to interpret. For example, if we know that 10 per cent of students attained an A at GCSE level in English we know what this information means but we do not know what it implies. The attempt to evaluate or interpret this information often leads to a second kind of data.

Comparative data. The 10 per cent As may be compared with the national rate at which As are attained. This adds to the body of information, but interpretation and evaluation of the data are still very difficult. The comparison with a national average raises the question: Is it reasonable to expect this school to attain results in line with the national average? Or should its results be better? Should its results be worse? This kind of question leads on to the third kind of data.

Residuals or adjusted data. This kind of data could also be called *fair comparative* data or *contextualized* data. Although it represents an intrusion of what might be seen as statistical jargon, I will use the term 'residuals' for this third kind of data because the term itself carries important implications. A residual is defined as the difference between the result obtained and the result predicted from measurements of factors known to be correlated with the outcomes. The results that could reasonably have been expected in an examination, for example, can be predicted from a knowledge of the pattern of results across many institutions in that subject, for that year, and a knowledge of the intake characteristics of students. The residual is the difference between an actual and a predicted grade. The computation of 'residuals' basically is the calculation of what is left over after taking account of important factors which influence the results and over which the school and staff have little control. The school and staff have little control over the prior achievement, ability and interest of

145

students. If these are measured two years before an examination, say, they form an important baseline against which to judge the examination results. The change from two years earlier is often called the value added and the techniques of measuring value added are the techniques of obtaining residuals (a better term than value added would be relative value added). The argument is then made that the performance indicator which best represents the examination effectiveness of a department is the average residual obtained in the department. If the average residual is positive it implies that students on the whole obtained higher grades than would have been predicted on the basis of their prior achievement and other factors that have been taken into account. In the A Level Information System (ALIS), for example, we also take into account home background and scores on a specially administered aptitude test (the International Test of Developed Abilities). Gender is also an important factor in performance and seems to have systematic effects across the A level results.

Residuals are as close as we generally get to fair performance indicators but it must be emphasized that the residual is *what is left over* after certain factors have been taken into account (to the extent that they can be taken into account) by the measurements available in the system. There are many factors influencing the outcomes that are not measured and are not, therefore, taken into account. The effect of some of these factors will be present in the residuals, and the effects of the errors of measurement will also be present in the residuals. Only a part of the residual can be seen as indicating the 'effect' of the department on students' performance in the examinations. A fundamental principle in measurement is that all measurements contain error and some estimate of this error is what makes a measurement scientific. In the case of residuals the amount of error involved in their estimation is computable and indeed in the ALIS project we report average residuals for departments with an error indicated alongside as a warning against the over-interpretation of small differences.

Experimental data. There is a fourth kind of data, which is rarely available in the system. If it were available it would provide the most conclusive and the most fair evidence of effectiveness. The fourth kind of data arises not from surveys, passive observation of the way the system is working with all the problems inherent in the built-in self-selection mechanisms in various courses and various schools, but from randomized experimental assignment. In other words, if we ran clinical trials, as is done in medicine, the resulting data would be the Gold Standard Data, those derived from controlled experiments. It is sometimes said that experiments are impossible in education. This position is far from accurate. There have been controlled experiments, yielding very important cost-benefit analyses of various interventions, most notably in the area of early childhood education (Lazar *et al.*, 1977). Furthermore, the ideal of undertaking 'reforms as experiments' (Campbell, 1969), in order quickly and accurately to evaluate their impact, must eventually be adopted if progress in social science is to be sufficiently rapid and accurate to achieve the kind of society that we would like for our grandchildren. However, this issue of experimentation cannot be further explored in the confines of this chapter. It is simply an issue that must be raised again and again until people, especially policy-makers, begin to recognize and understand the implications. The classical best-seller in educational research, Campbell and Stanley's *Experimental and Quasi-experimental Designs for Research* (1966), should be a required textbook in all research methods courses.

How, then, should educational managers approach the design of performance indicator systems? The system needs to be designed in the framework of a rationale. Goals have to be identified, and factors that have an impact on those goals also need to be identified so that we have the basis for producing fair performance indicators or residuals. Achieving these steps represents much, but there is one further important step to take: to add process variables in order to investigate, through the system, possible ways of achieving improvements.

To illustrate, rather sketchily, the procedures adopted in developing an indicator system, I will outline three systems: the A-Level Information System, a monitoring system for BTEC and a year 11 indicator system. For each one we need to consider the outcomes, the covariates that predict those outcomes and that we need to take into account in order to make the comparisons between outcomes fair, and the processes that are of interest in their own right or in order to examine their effects on the outcomes.

THE A LEVEL INFORMATION SYSTEM (ALIS)

Outcomes/goals

Consensus on goals is not difficult to achieve among A-level teachers and managers. Five major outcomes are monitored yearly in the ALIS project: examination results, students' attitude to the subject, students' attitude to the institution, students' aspirations *vis-à-vis* higher education and participation in extramural activities (the last being an indicator of the quality of life in the sixth form). These goals reflect the notion that in addition to getting reasonable examination results teachers hope that students enjoy their time in the sixth form and have a broadly educational experience.

Covariates

The factors which are taken into account in evaluating these outcomes are prior achievement, gender, ethnicity and socio-economic status. It is found in general, however, that as a matter of empirical fact the socio-economic status of students adds little to the prediction of A-level grades when there is some measure of prior achievement available. In any case, adjustment of indicators for socio-economic status is also problematic in that it implies that less is expected of equally able students if they are from poorer backgrounds. This is not a desirable message. In the ALIS project, therefore, the major indicator is based on the prediction of A levels from GCSE results. Additional tables taking account of other factors are available but the main table rests on this simple measure of value added.

Process variables

In addition to these outcome variables and their covariates the data collected from students by questionnaires contain students' estimates of the frequency of use of various teaching and learning activities, such as dictating notes, working in pairs and presenting work to the class. In order to generate ideas about the kind of teaching that might be effective these process variables are related both to students' outcomes on examinations and to students' attitudes to the subjects.

THE BTEC INFORMATION SYSTEM
Outcomes

The BTEC-awarded grades and measures of satisfaction similar to those in the ALIS project are the outcomes monitored. It might be thought that qualifications provided by the Business and Technician Education Council would not relate to prior achievement in academic subjects such as GCSE. It is true that the correlations between GCSE and BTEC grades are weaker than those between GCSE and A levels but they are far from negligible and too large to be neglected when looking at the performance of *groups*, as opposed to *individuals*. The correlations between GCSE and vocational qualifications reflect the general finding that prior achievement measures representing general aptitude are good predictors of performance in a variety of situations, including in jobs (Hunter and Hunter, 1984) and in obtaining vocational qualifications.

Covariates

These are prior achievement, gender, socio-economic status and ethnicity. A major feature in the BTEC Information System lies in the *process* variables assessed on the questionnaire. BTEC has developed careful quality assurance procedures in terms of the provision of resources, time, materials and computers to be made available in institutions running their courses. The questionnaires obtain students' perceptions on the adequacy of the resources available on particular courses. This provides interesting and important comparative feedback for course providers and for BTEC moderators.

A YEAR 11 INDICATOR SYSTEM (YELLIS)

The outcomes of concern in year 11 are somewhat different from those at A level. Examination results (GCSEs) are of course a matter of prime concern. In addition, schools wish to know if students feel safe at school and, if not, where it is that they do not feel safe. Schools wish to know if students are responding well to target setting and individual action planning, and other such procedures urged on teachers. As at A levels, schools are interested in students' responses to various subjects and the extent to which they enjoy the school experience, get along with staff and get along with other pupils. Other important outcomes relate to career choices and aspirations. Covariates present a problem as there are no examinations prior to GCSE. We have used Raven's Standard Progressive Matrices and, also, a maths test and vocabulary test. These are used along with measures of 'cultural capital' (Bordieu and Passeron, 1977), gender and ethnicity. By monitoring these outcomes schools may be able to improve. At least the monitoring will make them aware if the situation starts to deteriorate. It may also be found that some schools are producing better outcomes than others, in which case studies ought to be made of the management practices, resource allocations, structural arrangements, ecology of the building and other aspects that may contribute to the positive outcomes.

WE'VE ONLY JUST BEGUN

Performance monitoring will be the growth area in the 1990s. This was predictable from the steadily increasing availability of computers and, indeed, education as a discipline comes late into an era of performance indicators. Such indicators have been used for some years now in other public services (or what were previously public services), such as the water industry, the railways and hospitals. We need, as a profession, as researchers, as managers, as policy-makers, to work together to produce indicator systems that improve education rather than cause damage. We need to monitor the monitoring.

REFERENCES

Bordieu, P. and Passeron, J. C. (1977) *Reproduction: In Education, Society and Culture*. London: Sage SES.

Campbell, D. T. (1969) 'Reforms as experiments', *American Psychologist*, 24, 409-29.

Campbell, D. T. and Stanley, J. C. (1966) *Experimental and Quasi-experimental Designs for Research*. Chicago: Rand McNally.

Coopers & Lybrand (1988) *Local Management of Schools*. London: HMSO.

Fitz-Gibbon, C. T. (1992) *Performance Indicators and Examination Analyses* (Interchange number 11). Edinburgh: Scottish Office Education Department.

Hunter, J. E. and Hunter, R. F. (1984) 'Validity and utility of alternative predictors of job performance', *Psychological Bulletin*, 96(1), 72-98.

Kelly, A. (1976) 'A study of the comparability of external examinations in different subjects', *Research in Education*, 6, 50-63.

Lazar, I., Hubbell, V. R., Murray, H., Rosche, M and Royce, J. (1977) *The Persistence of Pre-school Effects: A Long Term Follow-up of Fourteen Infant and Pre-school Experiments*. Ithaca, NY: Community Service Laboratory, New York State College of Human Ecology.

Chapter 12

Educational Quality and Student Achievement

Harvey Goldstein

INTRODUCTION

Recent years have seen increasing international concern with the measurement of school performance, usually interpreted as the performance of *individual* schools rather than the performance of a whole school system. There has been considerable investment in the development of school performance indicators by both national governments and international agencies, such as the OECD. At the same time, there has been an increasing attempt at linkage between the performance of schools and other educational institutions and the general performance of national economies. Perhaps unsurprisingly, this has been strongest in countries such as the UK, whose economies are perceived as weakening and increasingly uncompetitive.

The most common kind of performance indicator, and in many cases the only one, is that based upon measured student achievements, for example in the form of exam or test results. Indeed, in the UK it is now government policy to measure the quality of schools by the average exam or test results of their students and to relate the fortunes of a school to these results via parental choice mechanisms.

There are several issues that arise from all this. First, the crude equating of school performance with economic performance requires careful scrutiny. A simple association (even if this could be demonstrated reliably) does not imply cause and effect. A declining economy might well be responsible for poorer school performance, for example by the inability or unwillingness of the weaker economies to provide higher levels of resources for education. Alternatively, both might be caused by complex interactions of social and political factors. By the same token it cannot be concluded that a particular form of curriculum organization is causally related to economic performance simply because it is found in some countries that are considered economically successful.

Second, it is naive to assume that improving performance on test scores will necessarily improve the 'skills' of a workforce and hence economic performance. The evidence, such as it is (Wolf *et al.*, 1990), suggests that attainment in the workplace is only weakly associated with success at school, and the same is true for the performance of higher education students.

Third, the real difficulty with the use of student achievement to assess the performance of schools is that it is a very indirect measure of the effects that schools may have. Almost all the research in this area has demonstrated that the factors which affect student achievement are largely outside the immediate control of the school. In particular, the single most important determinant of exam or test performance at the end of a period of schooling is the achievement of the student at the start of the period. Given the selective nature of most school systems, the average outcome performance will therefore reflect the intake achievements of the students and associated policies. Unless this can be properly taken into account, the use of student achievements to measure the quality or effectiveness of schools is invalid.

In this chapter I want to explore, in particular, the ways in which student achievement could be used to say something about school quality. I start with an attempt at a categorization of assessment by its purposes.

THE PURPOSES OF ASSESSMENT

Let me distinguish four major uses of educational assessment.

1 As certification, to provide entry to employment or a further stage of education.

2 To promote learning by establishing what a student's strengths and weaknesses may be.

3 To understand those factors which promote learning by carrying out research into performance.

4 As a screening instrument to identify schools or departments which may be poor promoters of learning.

I argue that these four functions serve distinct purposes and require distinct approaches. An integrated assessment policy will need to address the relative importance of these functions and the links between them.

Certification

In the UK external examinations provide the principal individual selection mechanism, which enjoys the confidence of its users. At present the GCSE is the major examination at the end of compulsory schooling and affects the structure of the curriculum at least from the age of 14.

The promotion of learning

The use of assessment to promote individual learning is quite different from its other uses. This 'diagnostic' function needs to probe each student in depth to expose weaknesses as well as strengths, over a wide range of activities. As such it has to encourage openness and honesty so that these can be appraised and acted upon. It is inconsistent with certification, which encourages students to minimize their weaknesses and exaggerate their strengths. It is also inconsistent with any system that is used to judge schools or teachers, for similar reasons. Since our present system of national assessment is primarily one whose intention is to provide such comparative judgements, it cannot legitimately be considered as adequate for any kind of diagnostic function. The effective omission of the diagnostic function from the present national assessment system is serious because that function is likely to be downgraded in importance.

An important aspect of diagnostic or formative assessment is that it measures progress. The progress made by a student, from a given starting point, is amenable to teaching. By contrast, the student's achievement at any particular time is only partly determined by what happens in school: it is also, and perhaps predominantly, affected by environmental, social and biological factors, over which schools have little control. By concentrating on progress, and shifting emphasis away from assessment at a single occasion, we can move towards what legitimately can be expected from schools and teachers.

Monitoring the system

I shall discuss below why external assessment systems are unsuitable for comparing schools. Nevertheless, external assessment can help our understanding of the factors that promote learning, and long-term research on this needs to be encouraged. A useful model here is the Assessment of Performance Unit (APU), although that had serious deficiencies in terms of the limited range of pupil and curriculum information collected. Using a sample, the functioning of a varied curriculum can be monitored and analysed.

Because they are conducted on a sample only, such assessments are unlikely to impose a large burden on schools or students. Nor can the results be used to label or rank schools or LEAs. They are, however, one means by which the impact of different approaches to implementing the National Curriculum can be studied. They are able to collect information about a wide range of academic and non-academic activities and the circumstances in which these occur. Thus the achievements of pupils may be studied in relation to the contexts in which schooling occurs: in particular, the way in which changes in curriculum, resources, etc. are seen to affect those achievements. More than any other assessment activity, such assessments provide a systematic means for judging the effects of educational innovation and change. If the notion of 'monitoring standards' is to have any useful content, this activity would be an important means of providing it. It can be said to underline a philosophy of co-operative rather than competitive enterprise in the sense that the lessons learnt from it are then available for the benefit of all.

Comparing institutions

As I have already indicated, the research evidence suggests that the earlier achievement of students is the most powerful predictor of their later achievement. It is clear, however, that the proposals of the present Government for reporting school assessment results are unfair because these 'raw' results will reflect largely the achievements of the students when they enter a school. Furthermore, there is an inherent instability in attempts to rank schools based upon average school results, even when it is possible to take account of socio-economic or intake achievement scores (Woodhouse and Goldstein, 1988). Any

Table 12.1 *Rankings*

LEA	Raw score	Model A	Model B	Model C
Harrow	1	1	1	4
Barnet	2	2	35	27
Coventry	59	5	7	1
Haringey	90	91	79	66

attempt to do so, whether by a formal analysis or an informal procedure such as suggested by the Task Group on Assessment and Testing (Black, 1988), will lead only to lengthy and inconclusive debate which will throw little light upon the genuine reasons for any school differences. In particular it may well ignore genuine excellence and overlook genuine failure in a quest for simple league tables.

THE RESEARCH EVIDENCE

Table 12.1 is extracted from Woodhouse and Goldstein (1988) and shows the results of an aggregate analysis of LEA achievement data. The first column shows the LEA rankings based simply on the proportion of students with five or more O level passes. The other three columns show the rankings derived from analyses that attempt to adjust for various socio-economic factors, so as to try to compensate for variations in these factors between LEAs. These three analyses are statistically 'equivalent' in the sense that they predict or explain exam performance equally well, but they differ in terms of the detailed way in which the socio-economic factors are modelled. As is clear, the rankings vary widely, and this underlines the inherent instability of such 'aggregate level' analyses.

It is now generally agreed by most researchers that comparisons between schools should be based upon analyses on individual student data rather than school averages. The use of so-called 'multi-level' models in analyses of achievement has pointed to the depth of information that it is possible to extract. Nuttall *et al.* (1989) analysed examination data from the Inner London Education Authority and showed that schools differed along several dimensions. They differed in terms of the achievements of different ethnic groups, in terms of the initial intake of their students and in terms of the gender difference in examination achievement.

Table 12.2 shows some selected results from an analysis of 1988 exam results using a simple scoring system based on the grades obtained by students, whereby a grade A obtains seven points, B six points, etc. Intake achievement is measured by verbal reasoning band membership (1, 2 or 3), so that the differences given for the remaining factors are adjusted for intake, albeit somewhat crudely. Thus Bangladeshi students on average are 4.1 points higher than English, Scottish or Welsh students. Some school 'contextual' factors are also present. Thus, for example, for every 10 per cent increase in the band 1 students, there is an average 1.2 points increase in score.

It is also clear that the largest differences are those associated with intake

Table 12.2   *ILEA 1988 exams analysis, adjusted overall effects*

Factor	Estimate	Standard error
%FSM	− 0.0955	0.028
%WI	− 0.0741	0.031
%VRI	0.161	0.059
Denom. (CE – maint.)	2.197	1.019
Denom. (RC – maint.)	2.939	0.796
Gender (girls – boys)	3.509	0.322
VR1 – VR3	22.33	0.339
VR2 – VR3	10.1	0.288
Caribbean – ESW	− 0.191	0.321
S.E. Asian – ESW	7.867	0.769
Bangladeshi – ESW	4.146	0.824
Pakistani – ESW	8.7	0.928

Between-school variation.
VR1 – VR3 standard deviation = 4.1

achievement. Those in the top 25 per cent (band 1) are 22 points ahead of the bottom 25 per cent (band 3) on average. In addition we find that this difference between band 1 and band 3 varies from school to school and the standard deviation of these between-school differences is 4.1. Thus some schools will produce a much larger difference between these groups than others.

For each school we can calculate a 'residual', which is in effect the average difference between the observed and predicted exam scores. This, provisionally, is assumed to represent the 'value added' by the school. For each school we can also estimate residuals for students in each of the three bands and hence produce a value added ranking for each band. Figure 12.1 shows these ranks for band 1 and band 3 students. It is clear that while there are some schools that appear to do badly or well for both types of student, there are others that do much better for band 1 than band 3 students and vice versa. The implication is that the performance of schools depends in part on the characteristics of their students and a single overall ranking cannot represent the inherent complexity.

Caveats

It is clear that a prerequisite for a fair comparison of schools is to be able to take account of intake achievement and to analyse individual student data. While these basic requirements for useful school comparisons are recognized, we are still a long way from being able to prescribe a standard analysis which can be adopted routinely to provide definitive school comparisons. Rather, such analyses as are possible must be regarded as research tools. Statements about individual schools will be tentative, and the whole exercise should be regarded as a screening procedure that could indicate which schools might repay further study. It follows that an exercise of this kind should be carried out in co-operation with schools, inspectors and advisers and in a spirit of co-operation and support rather than one where public judgement is made while ignoring the underlying uncertainties.

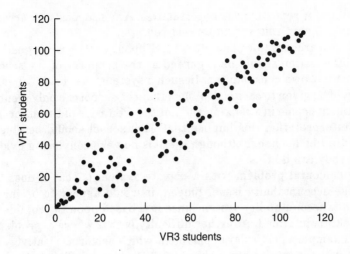

Figure 12.1 *School rankings for VR groups*

Apart from anything else, there are three technical reasons for exercising caution over the use of these 'multi-level' intake-adjusted analyses. The first of these follows from the fact that, apart from the most extreme residuals, it is usually impossible statistically to separate schools. In other words, in terms of significance tests or sets of confidence intervals, the sampling variation associated with the estimates is relatively large and does not justify a full ranking.

The second difficulty is similar to the one that arises in the analysis of aggregate data, namely that small changes to the model, for example transforming the scale of the exam score, will change some of the ranks.

The final difficulty is that the results for a set of schools will apply to a cohort which entered the schools some years earlier, five in the case of secondary school exam results. Since schools vary over time (Nuttall *et al.*, 1989), the usefulness to parents of the results about a cohort several years previously must be very questionable.

ASSESSMENT FOR ACCOUNTABILITY

Although I have argued in the previous section that the comparison of schools should be done in a way that avoids simple-minded judgements, there is certainly some validity in requiring schools to be accountable for the way they educate their pupils. The real issue is who is to carry out that accountability function and to have responsibility for interpreting findings.

It will, no doubt, always be possible to argue that any particular procedure has flaws, no matter how sophisticated the analysis which underpins it. What becomes important then is to find ways of indicating the uncertainty to be attached to any conclusions, both the inherent statistical uncertainty and the uncertainty over what precisely it is useful to measure. If public judgements are to be made it is essential that effort has to be put into tackling this issue. It follows that whoever has the responsibility for interpreting findings also has responsibility for reporting the uncertainties. Any proposals for accountability systems that ignore this should be resisted.

Some researchers (for example, Fitz-Gibbon, 1991) have argued that comparative information should be regarded as the property of the schools themselves, for their own consumption. In such a system, the results of value added analyses will be given to each school such that the school can only identify where its departments come in a ranking and not the identities of the other schools. In terms of interpretation this implies that each school should be able to judge the uncertainties for itself, although there is no very convincing evidence that generally they can do this.

A fundamental problem with a private system is that it does not really address the accountability issue. Indeed, it would appear to be incompatible with a public accountability system since it is based upon the confidentiality of the information provided. A further difficulty is that where a 'problem' is identified, for example a particular department which performs relatively poorly, in general it will not be clear how this is to be evaluated. This is because of the absence of an independent external body to investigate the performance alongside that of other schools, taking into account factors that may emerge during such an investigation. As soon as such a body is introduced into the system it moves towards becoming a publicly accountable system.

The unease that many feel about publicly accountable systems seems to stem partly from the current educational climate, where the political *intention* would appear to be that of punishing the relatively poor performers rather than helping them to understand their situation. Nevertheless, this should not deter us from considering how to set up accountability systems, using the best possible techniques and making all the necessary caveats. To argue that only a privately accountable system is needed ignores the legitimate concerns over accountability. It also, ironically, may serve to strengthen the current educational philosophy of the Government, as follows.

The essence of a private system is that it aims to enable each school to take action to improve its relative performance. In a system such as the present, which is highly competitive, inevitably there will be a tendency for schools to focus on achieving good performances in raw examination and test results since these are publicly what count. If a private system of reporting were successful in enabling schools to improve their performances, it does not follow that they will improve the overall quality of the education they provide. Furthermore, because a private system almost inevitably is inimical to serious attempts to develop publicly accountable value added systems, it may well achieve the end result of leaving unchallenged the publication of raw 'league tables' with all their unwelcome consequences.

CONCLUSIONS

There are, no doubt, many reasons why the Government, and in many cases opposition politicians too, are in favour of the public display of test scores and exam results for schools. The results are relatively inexpensive to compile and the status that public exams possess provides a useful platform. Nevertheless, despite the apparent simplicity and populist appeal, the use of such results for comparisons between schools is fraught with problems. At the very best they might be useful as a screening instrument for use by schools and LEAs to identify possible problems and successes, although only in the long term when analysed using individual pupil data with suitable adjustments for intake. At worst they will provide misleading information to parents and others who may then use it to make judgements that will be unfair, inefficient and educationally destructive.

Even for those who would advocate a market-place ideology for schooling, exam-based league tables can hardly constitute a rational approach to implementing such a market. If, despite all this, such league tables continue to be taken seriously by governments, the profession will need to find suitable ways of educating the public about their shortcomings, and especially the uncertainties which inhere even with the most sophisticated procedures.

Finally, I suspect that in all of this there is a hidden agenda which is rarely made explicit. As I have argued, raw exam results reflect largely the intake achievement of the students, and I would suggest that it is in fact just this information that the politicians wish to convey. Their supposition is that parents will want to choose schools where the average intake achievement is high, because they feel that this will tend to raise the achievements of their children and also because it is seen as a surrogate measure of high social status. While the latter may have some validity, and thus have an appeal for some parents, the former belief is more problematical, and is certainly not the case for all kinds of students.

If there really is such an agenda then what we are seeing is a covert and somewhat disreputable attempt at social engineering on a large scale.

REFERENCES

Black, P. (1988) *National Curriculum: Task Group on Assessment and Testing.* London: Department of Education and Science.

Fitz-Gibbon, C. T. (1991) 'Multilevel modelling in an indicator system', in S. W. Raudenbush and J. D. Willms (eds), *Schools, Classrooms and Pupils: International Studies of Schooling from a Multilevel Perspective.* San Diego: Academic Press.

Nuttall, D. L., Goldstein, H., Prosser, R. and Rasbash, J. (1989) 'Differential school effectiveness', *International Journal of Educational Research*, 13, 769-76.

Wolf, A., Kelson, M. and Silver, R. (1990) *Learning in Context: Patterns of Skills Transfer and Training Implications.* London: The Training Agency.

Woodhouse, G. and Goldstein, H. (1988) 'Educational performance indicators and LEA league tables', *Oxford Review of Education*, 14, 301-19.

Chapter 13

Planning for Quality

Trevor Edinborough

INTRODUCTION

> 'We don't need time to plan — it's wasted time; time we could be using to do the things we know we have to do but don't have enough time to do.'

> 'We don't have enough time to plan and prioritize — both are important if we are to make real progress.'

Are these two comments from two different colleagues having alternative views? No, they are two comments from the same colleague — one made before our first planning conference and one made a year later. The two statements taken together underline the nature of our progress and the changing of attitudes and practices towards structured development based on increasingly clear management principles.

The school concerned has chosen to devote considerable energy to the development of strategies for monitoring and evaluation based on the central focus of school development planning. It subscribes to the view that 'the purpose of development planning is to improve the quality of teaching and learning in a school through the successful management of innovation and change' (Hargreaves and Hopkins, 1991). In doing so it has followed a path that has been greatly informed by the strategy for quality development being pursued by Birmingham Education Authority. The quality development strategy is now increasingly well established in over 150 schools in the city and has three key purposes:

- improving the quality of learning and teaching;
- proving to fulfil accountability requirements;
- learning — the development of a learning community expressed through a commitment to increase knowledge and understanding by engaging in curricular and other forms of research and development (Ribbins, 1992).

What follows is essentially a case study that sets out to chart one particular school's work towards greater quality. The chapter will seek to identify and explore each of five development stages that the school has experienced over recent years, alongside the learning acquired from each stage. Before I embark upon that task, however, it is appropriate to provide a brief account of the context.

CONTEXT

The school is an 11 to 16 co-educational school with a five-form entry, serving a wide and extremely diverse 'catchment area'. The majority of pupils come from areas at the heart of the city. The LEA strategy for quality development began with a pilot phase, though this particular school was not part of that pilot. However, the headteacher was closely associated with the implementation of the pilot programme and the developments beyond the pilot phase. Schools that are beginning to adopt the quality development strategy have, as part of their entitlement, the opportunity to undertake training via an Advanced Certificate in Education course, which has as it focus the quality development approach to monitoring and evaluation in schools. A member of staff in the case study school participated in such training immediately after the pilot phase.

STAGES OF DEVELOPMENT

In pursuing this case study it is appropriate to spend a short time detailing, in broad terms, the stages of change the school has undergone, or is undergoing. In this a particular focus will rest on the last three of the stages. Throughout it all, however, it will be important for the reader to have a view of the principles which are guiding the developmental path, and the learning acquired at each stage.

First, the five stages have all been greatly clarified with the benefit of hindsight. One suspects that while the stages have been identified in relation to this particular school there may well be points of reference for other schools. Hindsight is of course a wonderfully precise science and it would be reassuring to be able to report that the stages have worked out exactly as planned; would that it were so! However, it is possible to outline five broad stages, which might usefully be labelled thus:

1 Internal agendas/external opportunities.
2 External agendas/management of changes.
3 Development planning.
4 Quality and development planning.
5 Quality, development and inspection.

Stage 1 — Internal agendas/external opportunities

This represents the period before 1988 — or more precisely the period before the Education Reform Act. How far this stage extends before 1988 is perhaps of little significance here but it is significant that for this school, as indeed for all other LEA-maintained schools, this period represented a time when the change agendas were largely being set by the schools themselves. Of course there were exceptions and there were major changes during this period; for example, the change that brought about GCSE and further back the raising of the school-leaving age. However, by and large there was a considerable degree of autonomy as far as the school's capacity to embark upon change was concerned. This is not to say that there were no change agents external to the school; what is different from today's context, however, is that the change agents that were in existence before 1988 — stage 1 — sought to provide opportunities rather than compel institutions to change. The onset of the Technical and Vocational Education Initiative via the pilot programme is an example of such a strategy. There were therefore various pressures for schools to embark upon change but in the main schools could: first, decide for their own reasons what changes were to be courted; second, embark upon them one at a time; third, consolidate and integrate specific change issues before pursuing other items of change. This is not to say that schools were static and not to imply that the case study school was that either. In this school there was a considerable track record of imaginative and effective curriculum innovation and change. The school was a successful TVEI pilot school. It initiated and led an innovative Mode 3 English scheme, which was subsequently taken up by very many schools within and beyond the authority. It was involved in the Oracy Project. It had development groups centred on particular areas of work, for example junior-secondary liaison. It was in short a school that sought to become a learning community in the fullest meaning in the sense that curriculum research and development was at the very forefront of the work of the staff. While stage 1 represented a period when schools could avoid change this was certainly not the case in this particular school and, further, the work that was undertaken during stage 1 was crucial in setting the context for subsequent stages.

During this stage of development the school acquired significant skills related to the management of change and furthermore the capacity to be innovative, creative and evaluative.

Stage 2 — External agendas/management of changes

Since the Education Reform Act of 1988 all that was typified by stage 1 went by the board — or at least almost all of it. Stage 2 was the beginning in earnest of the dominance of external change agendas. The Education Reform Act ensured that the Government was in a position to inflict its collective will in a way that had hitherto been unprecedented. No longer was there to be a reliance on the provision of opportunities without compulsion. As a consequence the pace of change quickened, as too did the scale of change — both to levels that were previously unheard of. What is more, the control over both the scale and the pace of change was very firmly in hands external to the schools.

The school at the centre of this case study responded in a number of ways. In the first instance it moved to a more significant task culture than it had previously experienced. The development groups that were almost standing committees in the school management system moved away from broad areas of interest to specific tasks and very specific topics. In essence the development groups were replaced by task groups, each of which was given a particular brief to consider a particular topic in a particular way, which is not the same as dictating what the outcome should be. The task culture was a focus partly because of management changes within the school and partly as a survivalist response to the changed context within which the school was operating.

During this stage we developed some skills relating to the management of change and increasingly sought to manage change, but we were in some respects still at the stage where we were managing individual changes rather than a coherent and cohesive policy for development.

It was a particularly interesting time when our pressured circumstances led us to look for other contexts in which there had been a particular focus on the management of change. As a result we embarked upon a seemingly flirtatious relationship with industry as we sought to find models that we could adapt to our own context. While we learnt much we also concluded that it was our responsibility to create and develop the model that would suit this particular school.

It was a difficult and yet challenging time during the course of which we learned a great deal. We became convinced that the management culture was central to our capacity to undertake effective and sustainable change and development. More especially we learnt:

- about the importance of time scales in getting things done;
- about the need for a task culture;
- about the need for action;
- about working collaboratively;
- about co-ordinated and managed development.

As you might expect we learned these lessons sometimes through a process of painful developmental growth — a nice way of saying we made some pretty major blunders. Take, for example, the requirement to produce a National Curriculum development plan, which we did in 1989. The plan was a great success — written by the senior management team and delivered to the staff — a significant product which signalled the supremacy of product over process. There is little wonder that our National Curriculum development took place in spite of the plan rather than because of it. We began to understand that the processes we used to arrive at the development plan were every bit as important as the ultimate plan, if we were serious about delivering on the planned objectives.

As has already been stated the school elected to have development planning at the heart of its work. It subscribed to the quality development strategy's preferred model for development planning — a model that draws heavily on the work of Peter Holly. In such a model it is vital that participants identify 'where they are now'. It is also useful to ask a supplementary question, namely 'How did we get to this stage?' The two stages above are perhaps most important because the school needed to understand the stages it had undergone and the learning acquired.

Stage 3 — Development planning

Development planning began in earnest with the arrival of the so-called 'Purple Book' (*Planning for School Development*: Hargreaves *et al.*, 1989) — although its chances at the time of arrival didn't appear to be too high. It looked for all the world as if here was another classic example of someone else's needs about to take up a major amount of time, energy and effort. The Purple Book, with its reported view that a development plan 'helps to relieve the stress on teachers caused by the pace of change', was something less than convincing and the 'Getting started' section had the opposite of the desired effect. The whole issue was consigned to the pending tray — more aptly described as the 'leave it there long enough and it will go away tray'. Yet the requirement to engage in school development planning was in itself a watershed of sorts, because as it emerged from the pending tray a number of fundamental questions were asked:

- Why are we having to do this?
- What is the significance of the due date, 30 June?
- How might we do this, with whom and when?
- Most of all, how can this task best be tailored to the needs of the school?

The initial questions all had easy answers because they were all in the negative. A more careful examination led us to address the task with greater creativity and ultimately to begin to list the principles that would guide this aspect of our work. The principles are not in themselves original but the process of drawing together the sometimes very obvious into a set of guidelines was fundamental; fundamental not only in that they enabled us to have a means of moving forward but also in that the listing of the principles required us to relearn and collate the lessons that had been learned from previous work. The compiling of the list was vital in establishing the values which were at the heart of the institution, and in developing the view that the management culture was not merely a statement of how the headteacher worked — the management culture affected everybody.

Those principles are worth listing here but the reader should remember that the listing is not finite and that it provides an attempt to define the management culture.

1 Teachers are the key resource in any school and it is the teachers who empower and enable pupils to access their entitlements in meaningful, productive and creative ways. However, teachers also need to be empowered and enabled and that is a primary function of school management.

2 The route to effective and sustainable development and growth is via collaboration and participation. Without either, key capabilities are lost. Therefore openness is essential in the management of the school.

3 A task culture is essential — with clear, shared and agreed values and goals, and a clear acknowledgement of time scales. Opportunities therefore have to be created to enable shared values and goals to be defined.

4 Working in teams is crucial. In any real development path there is a

vital need for evaluation in both formative and summative senses. These functions are better carried out in an analytically critical manner that seeks to move away from the 'cult of the individual' and all the inherent threats and obstacles.

5 Management is about matching resources to meet agreed targets and goals, and any school development planning process needs to encompass the harnessing of resources to agreed goals. This also needs to be an overt process so that all those with whom there has been collaboration, and from whom there has been participation, can see the process and identify the effect of that matching of resources.

6 A senior management team needs to engage in decision-making and to do so it needs to come from a very well informed base. Colleagues need to know that the management team have all the appropriate information before them and that they have actually used the information in arriving at a decision.

7 In enabling and empowering teachers there is a need to release colleagues' creative professional energy. One of the requirements for that to be possible is that colleagues need to feel that their views, judgements and ideas are respected and valued.

8 School development planning is about learning and teaching. All that we do is to serve that central purpose and thus evaluative tools need to be geared at all times to that central purpose. If one cannot honestly state that whatever issue is being targeted is actually likely to improve teaching and learning then one has to ask why it is taking time, energy and effort to pursue.

From that period of reflection and consequent set of guiding principles three significant developments followed.

First, consideration was given to the planning cycle or spiral (call it what you will) — essentially what will happen when. Figure 13.1 details the overall planning cycle and is on the whole self-explanatory. It should, however, be said at this stage that the teaching staff had instituted an annual staff conference back in 1988. The staff conference is held immediately following the half-term break in October or November each year. It runs over two consecutive days, is off site and seeks to launch development issues. Prior to the launching of school development planning, the conference had been the vehicle for launching curriculum review (1988), and launching the development of assessment processes (1989). Within the planning cycle, therefore, staff conference was both an appropriate feature and a particularly well timed one.

Second, consideration was given to action planning. Reference is made in Reid et al. (1987) to the need to turn 'serious goodwill' into organized and efficient action. One of the reasons that there is seemingly so much serious goodwill that has remained at that level is that we have not always planned in detail how we will expect to arrive at our objectives. Action planning was therefore deemed to be essential if teams were to deliver. Furthermore, action planning had to be reported if the senior management team were to engage in

Improving Education

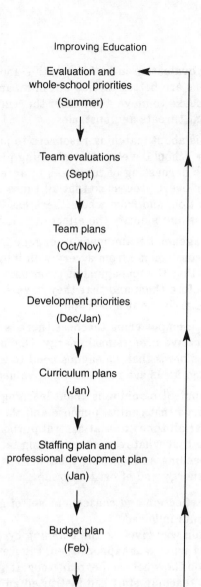

Figure 13.1 *The planning cycle*

informed decision-making and in the matching of resources. Otherwise what was the point of engaging in planning? Once plans were agreed there needed to be a means of ensuring that they were given the best possible opportunity to succeed.

In devising an action planning process, therefore, there was an overt desire to have a means of collecting and using planning documents. There was also an overt agenda of requiring teams to ensure that they went through fundamentally important stages — again to ensure that the targets were the right targets and that they were given the best possible opportunity to be fulfilled, and that the process was undertaken collaboratively by those people who were to be

164

instrumental in bringing about the change. The planning process was therefore essentially a four-stage process, each stage of which ended with a summative document for onward submission. The stages are:

1 Areas for development. Through consideration of evaluations alongside internal and external development needs, teams arrived at a prioritized list of areas for development. The list emerging was to be prioritized by the originating team on the basis of what could be achieved during the lifetime of the action plan — a 12-month period.

2 Defining specific targets. Areas of development had to be translated into targets. The notion of the 'quality gap' (Ribbins and Burridge, 1992) was introduced. Where are we now? Where do we want to be? What do we have to do now in order to get nearer to where we want to be?

3 Routes. Having defined the target(s) it is crucial that each team maps out the individual and precise steps that will be taken in order to arrive at the target. Who will do what, when, how and with whom? Fundamental to this stage was the requirement to determine who will be responsible for leading the development towards each target. Roles and responsibilities need to be clear, agreed and known.

4 Costs. If the target is to be achieved what costs — in the widest sense — need to be taken into account? What professional development needs will arise? What additional spending may be needed? What are the implications for meeting and development time? What needs are likely to be created for the curriculum plan to encompass? Are there likely to be any information technology needs?

Third, consideration was given to the 'contracting stages'. Simply put, once teams had agreed on their targets there was a need for agreement beyond the teams before there could be a shared commitment to the resourcing and other implications.

What came out of all of that was an awareness that school development planning was a process, and a process that was much more important than the product — the school development plan. If the processes are right then there is a real chance that a school will achieve its objectives, and indeed will be clearer what its objectives are. We also began to understand what we started to call action points: the place where action would, could and should be taken on particular aspects of the life of the school. Such action points would also provide bases for accountability, and should therefore have certain resource and decision-making capabilities commensurate with the responsibilities and accountabilities.

Stage 4 — Quality and development planning

Stage 3 was now well established in the school but was missing a vital component — that is, there was little evidence of systematic rigour in monitoring and evaluation. In stage 4 we sought to move the development planning processes on to engage in monitoring and evaluation in a systematic and rigorous way based on the principle of supported self-evaluation. In order to achieve movement on this very critical yet emotive issue we needed to raise awareness of the role and value of monitoring and evaluation, place it within the 1990s context, suggest what such a policy might mean for the school and engage in turning the rhetoric into practical strategies.

The chosen strategy was that of success criteria around which everything else appeared to hinge. In order to deliver on success criteria within the by now well established planning process the linkage was made with the target setting stage. Colleagues were asked first, using the quality gap approach, to determine an outline target. The target setting stage had by and large caused little if any difficulty. However, in setting the target teams had not been required to define standards — to define in more precise terms what was meant by success in that particular issue. With the onset of success criteria as part of the planning process teams were now required to be more specific, and at times did not find the process very easy. During this part of the process teams needed to establish both the success criteria related to each target and the evidence base that would be used to demonstrate effectiveness. In order to do so and to guide thinking three prompts were suggested:

1 How will this target improve teaching and learning?
2 How will I know if it has improved teaching and learning?
3 How will we know if the target has been achieved?

In accepting that 'Guilt can be the unintended legacy of confused criteria' (Handy and Aitken, 1986), colleagues were asked to define the quality of success they were looking for. They were also required to look for affirmation that success was being achieved and through the evidence base to determine what needs to be done next. When the success criteria, and the evidence base, had been established and agreed it was then necessary to look back at the target and be clear that the outline target would actually produce the desired and detailed effect. If not the target was wrong and needed amending.

This sounds all very simple but it is in fact no easy task, and it is not possible to state that the planning process, including success criteria, is yet fully and systematically established. While there is great cause for optimism in this respect we have to see the processes through for some time to establish whether or not our primary target of a systematic and rigorous strategy for monitoring and evaluation, based on supported self-evaluation, has been achieved.

Stage 5 — Quality development and national inspection

While we were engaged in the development of strategies for pursuing monitoring and evaluation the agenda began to change somewhat, with the growing awareness of the scope and shape of the then proposed national inspection. Two other factors prompted a further development of our strategy: our interest in the national standards associated with the investors in people scheme; and feedback, which further indicated that not enough emphasis had been placed on whole-school direction and whole-school targets. Teams felt that they were effecting their planning against an uncertain backcloth.

In relation to national inspection there was an anxiety that the process of inspection would lead us to abandon firmly held views about what empowers a school to achieve greater quality. While inspection may serve to provide a focus for further development, little will have been achieved in the long term unless there is a firmly established means for developing from the experience. In short there was tension between inspection as a form of evaluation and supported self-evaluation as a means of bringing about further progress.

Throughout our development path the annual staff conference has played a significant role; in this particular stage the staff conference will be shown to have played a pivotal role. In attempting to ensure that all colleagues had an awareness of the issues that stretched before us, and ensuring that staff had a means of addressing the issues, we used both pre-conference publications and the conference discussions. In pre-conference documentation the issues were addressed, centred on three key themes: public accountability, 'raising standards' and national inspection. The publication went on to propose whole-school purpose, goals and targets.

During the conference purpose, goals and targets were discussed and debated, and before teams embarked upon their own target setting and action planning whole school targets were modified and issued. The targets are related to purpose and goals and reflect staff evaluation of the issues that need to be addressed. Our strategy for developing quality was therefore used to address impending national inspection. In taking those issues forward we are also using our strategy for developing quality and remaining true to the principles detailed above.

In engaging all staff in the debate on purpose, goals and targets we have also taken ourselves a little further down the road towards success as investors in people. In publishing the outcome and in constructing action plans we will have begun to assert that national inspection and our internal strategies for self-evaluation have a compatibility that was not immediately understood by all.

CONCLUSIONS

In conclusion, this particular school has chosen to base its quest for greater quality on the school development planning processes — not because we were told we had to, but because of the developmental stages we had gone through. In getting to that stage we have gone through stages 1 and 2, where we learned many lessons and acquired a number of guiding principles in order that we could customize school development planning processes for the school. In establishing those processes (stage 3) we quickly learned that we needed to move on into the field of monitoring and evaluation. We have begun to do so, and from a firm belief that the sustainable way to a learning community, in the fullest sense, is via a self-evaluative route. In choosing that route, however, we should point out that self-evaluation is not the cosy option some would have us believe, particularly if one takes the widest possible view of what constitutes a school community. It can be a harsh learning process but it is one that can lead to more effective and targeted growth through a capacity for analytical evaluation at individual, team and whole-school level. Effectively done it provides the opportunity to evaluate critically, learn from the evaluation, and thereby set in train activities for growth and development.

It is also acknowledged that schools are not to be left to develop quality via the sole strategy of supported self-evaluation. Stage 5 in our development acknowledges that fact, while also seeking to remain true to our principles for sustained and effective growth and development. Inspection will provide further evaluation, which the school's established processes can utilize to stimulate the subsequent moves towards greater quality. In electing to focus on development planning as the primary vehicle for the development of quality we do not seek to ignore other useful and complementary strategies. Indeed it is our intention to seek to create an ongoing and ever-changing school 'statement of health', which will contain evidence, qualitative and quantitative, from a range of different sources, both internal and external. We have some way to go but we have come a long way. Above all we have learned that producing a school development plan alone will be unlikely to result in the improved quality sought by all stakeholders. The processes, the ethos and the management culture all need to be given very careful consideration if any school is serious about the development of quality. A school development plan, without careful attention to and if necessary modification of the management culture and ethos of the school, is no more likely to succeed than previous attempts at the management of change and development. When the two are effectively co-habiting then the prospects for sustainable quality are greatly enhanced.

There remains much to do but much has been achieved. It has to be said, however, that in our seeking to work collaboratively with colleagues in establishing future directions, the majority of the work has centred on teaching staff. Support staff have not been greatly involved in the processes outlined above. That is a serious omission and one we intend to correct.

Finally, it needs to be said that the commitment to the pursuit of quality rests with all my colleagues — our success is their success, our progress is their progress. Without their willingness to engage in school development planning in an effective way, none of the above would be possible; nor would any of the above lead to the greater development and definition of quality. Because there is that collective commitment the optimism expressed above must be well placed.

REFERENCES

Handy, C. and Aitken, R. (1986) *Understanding Schools as Organisations.* Harmondsworth: Penguin Books.

Hargreaves, D. H. and Hopkins, D. (1991) *The Empowered School.* London: Cassell.

Hargreaves, D. H., Hopkins, D., Leask, M., Connolly, J. and Robinson, P. (1989) *Planning for School Development. Advice to Governors, Headteachers, and Teachers.* London: Department of Education and Science.

Reid, K., Hopkins, D. and Holly, P. (1987) *Towards the Effective School.* Oxford: Blackwell.

Ribbins, P. (1992) *Improving, Proving and Learning in Schools. Evaluation of a Pilot Initiative in Quality Development.* Birmingham: Centre for Education Management and Policy Studies, The University of Birmingham.

Ribbins, P. and Burridge, E. (1992) 'Improving schools: an approach to quality in Birmingham', in H. Tomlinson (ed.), *The Search for Standards.* London: Longman.

Chapter 14

Networking Quality: The Issue Is Quality Improvement

Ian Cleland

The purpose of this chapter is to argue that the concept of quality is not static and that not only does agreement about what is 'quality' change over time but also it often depends upon the individual values of those who undertake the role of quality assessors. As a consequence, I believe, efforts to define a static quality standard are doomed to failure. The nationally accepted standard BS 5750 or its European or international equivalents validate systems rather than product quality. This would seem to accept that quality in product derives more from the way in which people work than from product definition. Systems and processes that support and sustain good practice and are themselves the product of such practice are founded, I believe, on the shared values of the participants or partners in the activity. These shared values are the product of a climate that has grown from the interaction of people who have a shared purpose to achieve agreed objectives but who are also committed to their improvement.

The networking of quality leads thereby to its improvement and should operate at all levels of the organization and within all other agencies with which it interacts. During the 1980s, Dudley Local Education Authority undertook a planned programme of improvement founded upon the need to facilitate collaborative development. It created a structural framework based on networking, evolved a philosophy for review (inspection) based upon partnership, and developed a process for school and individual improvement which has permeated the whole authority. As will be shown later, the concept of the development network has achieved significant results not only in the areas of shared values and the quality of relationships but also in the improvement of performance.

The current preoccupation with quality is to be applauded; unfortunately, there is a tendency for quality to be defined in the terms of the auditor. This has its place but if it is allowed to become the major plank of the quality movement, it will detract from the significant improvement that has occurred in British education during the past decade. The impetus for improvement provided by TVEI, GCSE and the principles, if not yet the practice, of the National Curriculum complemented by the liberalizing of teacher in-service provision has, in my experience, been of significant benefit. The addition of purely audit-based practice allied to the administrative burdens created by LMS could well constrain rather than facilitate school improvement.

We must also remember that, until comparatively recently, the British education system has been based upon the measurement of failure, not success. Indeed, our whole national culture is one of deficiency. The quality movement can either reinforce this or assist in the creation of a new culture founded upon positive attitudes and where improvement, no matter how incremental, is valued. The concept and reality of the quality network gives a confidence to its partners that enables them to accept risk when required, to plan and invest for the longer term and to recognize the value of collaboration and teamwork. The positive attitudes engendered do produce improvement. The process helps to ensure that existing quality is recognized and that the quality of the purpose to be achieved is defined in terms that facilitate its achievement or allow failure to be used as a learning experience.

THE QUALITY MOVEMENT

There is no doubt that the current preoccupation with quality issues is long overdue. It is quite salutary to learn that by 1986-87 about one-third of local authorities had no formal methods of monitoring overall quality in their schools and colleges (Nubesnuick, 1991). It was also clear at this time, as Stillman and Grant's (1989) research showed, that the management and delivery of the practice where some formal monitoring took place often lacked rigour. The impact of the 1988 Education Reform Act led to DES Circular 7/88 which, in the context of the above, understated the fact that 'LEAs will need up to date information regarding the performance of schools'. This need was further articulated by CIPFA (1986) concerning the relationship between good management and information to inform policy, and by Coopers & Lybrand (1988), who advocated inspection, school reports and performance indicators.

This welcome commitment to improve quality was, unfortunately, if not falling upon stony ground, certainly falling upon ground that was unprepared. It was unprepared because there was no consistent philosophy of managing quality that integrated both quantitative and qualitative processes. As a result, the pressures to respond to the new ERA were and are in danger of pushing quality issues into a more simplistic and quantifiable direction. The performance indicator was readily accepted as the way forward by many. AMA Education Committee (1987) commented on their value and the DES pilot scheme was based upon this premise. Fortunately, those involved in the DES pilot quickly appreciated that most of the key indicators cannot be measured statistically. Bainbridge (1990), reporting on the Dudley pilot, indicated that the top fifteen PIs identified by headteachers, such as parental involvement and pupil motivation, could not be accurately measured. As a result, the DES guidelines were founded upon indicators that 'helped' observers to judge whether learning had been effective and left considerable scope for qualitative interpretation.

The need for such qualitative judgement based on inspectoral experience was recognized by Coopers & Lybrand (1988) although, as Derek Esp (1988)

171

indicated, these judgements must be made in the context of clear aims and criteria for evaluation. However, the key issue was emphasized by the Society of Chief Inspectors and Advisers (1989) who highlighted the partnership between the school and the adviser in which external review is complemented by school self-evaluation. The ongoing and integrated nature of this partnership, with its core functions of review, advice, support and development, is at the heart of quality improvement. Wilcox (1989) argues quite rightly that it is the systematic and planned application of these components of quality review that will promote improvement.

If we are to assure quality in education, notice does need to be taken of the wider context. As the Audit Commission commented in 1989, planning and management are vital. There is a need to ensure that school development plans relate to those of the LEA, mediated by the advisory service. Yet, as the Audit Commission showed, very few advisory services have clear aims related to those of the LEA. We could go further and ask how many of them have aims related to the development planning needs of schools. The management of quality assurance is, therefore, a central issue, as is the training and development of advisers for the complex interface role that they should ideally perform in carrying out this function.

A comment by a Chief Adviser from a case study in the EMIE-sponsored research by NFER, *Promoting Quality in Schools and Colleges*, perhaps sums up the inadequacy of current management and training for advisers. 'I don't know where the initiative for monitoring and initiating changes has come from.' This is further supported by the general lack of a shared perception of the relationship between advice and inspection or an agreement regarding the time required for formal review and inspection. There is also lack of a clear under-standing of the relationship between local advisers and inspectors (LAI) and their DES colleagues HMI. It was only in 1989 that a seven-authority pilot was established to share the thoughts and practice of these two strands of quality assurance.

Basic common sense would indicate that it is essential that these two groups should have some shared basis of operation regarding criteria and methods. As a pilot authority, we in Dudley and our HMI colleagues gained from the exercise. Unfortunately, it was an exercise that is now completed, although the working partnerships established continue to operate informally.

I would argue that unless those directly involved with quality assurance can establish a shared and valid philosophy and process for their operations, there is a real danger that they will be imposed from outside. The evidence outlined above does not inspire confidence that the act will be 'got together.' Never-theless, we owe it to our professionally accountable consciousness at least to make the effort. The values and beliefs associated with the introductory section would seem to deserve a better fate. The partnership between all concerned with quality in Dudley is committed to this course and has produced a valid way forward.

To summarize our position based upon the views outlined previously, we would argue that quality is more likely to be identified, understood and improved if the quality assurance system reflects the following criteria:

1 The system must be founded upon partnership, positive attitudes and the creation of shared values.

2 It must focus on a planned and systematic approach to the management of development.

3 Associated objectives must be clear, based on agreed criteria and integrated into operations at all levels.

4 These objectives must balance the qualitative as well as the quantitative aspects.

5 They should provide for both rigour and challenge yet accept that failure can be an important aid to learning.

6 It should utilize both self-review and external review, using a communications network to ensure a shared perception of an agreed reality on which to base future action.

7 Most importantly, these attributes must be contained within a framework that facilitates the planning, resourcing and implementation of the quality improvement process.

In Dudley, such a framework, called the Development Network, was created during the 1980s and is at the heart of the authority's quality improvement process. It provides the opportunity to use individual strengths through partnership, it has created a positive climate that motivates participants and it has improved quality, as will be shown.

THE NETWORKING OF QUALITY

The network was developed over a five-year period and incorporated existing structures within a range of new initiatives that owed much to the resources made available to the LEA through TRIST, GRIST, etc. The structure is set out diagrammatically in Figure 14.1 and consists of a policy, planning and implementation thrust supported by various stimuli to development and a resource infrastructure which, through the network, can be integrated into a development planning process, implemented in specific schools and across the whole authority. The monitoring and review are carried out by the Advisory Service and its management involves a team working in partnership through the Development Committee. The Chief Adviser provides the function of the 'managing director', working through the Chief Education Officer to the Education Committee.

The overall guidelines for the operation of the network are provided by three key policies for: curriculum and learning; staff development; and review, incorporating school (inspection) and individual (appraisal) strands. The planning dialogue centred on the Development Committee (see Figure 14.2) establishes through task teams and authority-wide surveys what should be the main strands of the authority development plan and manages its implementation at authority level. The Advisory Service, in addition to working as full partners in the authority plan, also has its own complementary strategy and clearly individual schools plan for development in the context of the wider objectives.

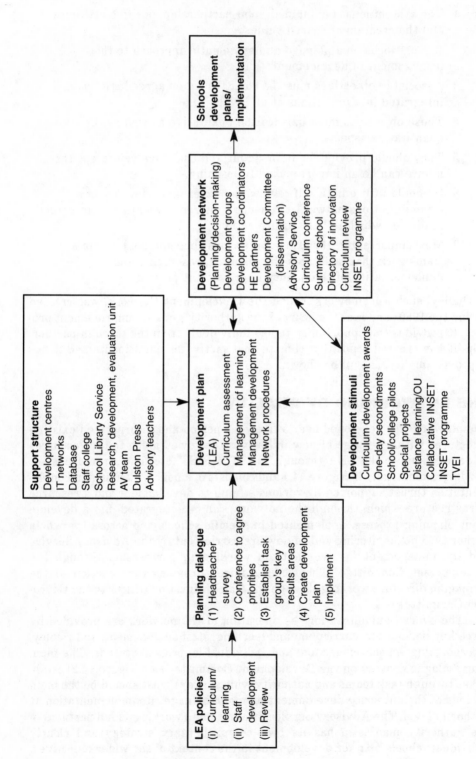

Figure 14.1 *The Dudley LEA framework for development*

Support structure
Development centres
IT networks
Database
Staff college
School Library Service
Research, development, evaluation unit
AV team
Dulston Press
Advisory teachers

Development plan
(LEA)
Curriculum assessment
Management of learning
Management development
Network procedures

Development network
(Planning/decision-making)
Development groups
Development co-ordinators
HE partners
Development Committee
(dissemination)
Advisory Service
Curriculum conference
Summer school
Directory of innovation
Curriculum review
INSET programme

Schools development plans/ implementation

Development stimuli
Curriculum development awards
One-day secondments
School/college pilots
Special projects
Distance learning/OU
Collaborative INSET
INSET programme
TVEI

Planning dialogue
(1) Headteacher survey
(2) Conference to agree priorities
(3) Establish task group's key results areas
(4) Create development plan
(5) Implement

LEA policies
(i) Curriculum/ learning
(ii) Staff development
(iii) Review

Purpose
To provide a forum in which representatives from the development groups can work in partnership with the Advisory Service to plan, implement and review the authority's development plan.

Focus areas
The major focus of the Committee will be to ensure that the authority development plan both supports and is informed by those being developed in the schools.

To facilitate this, a number of key functions will be undertaken.

(a) The assessment/identification of development needs.

(b) Maintaining an overview of the resources available for development and monitoring their effective deployment.

(c) Facilitating the provision of whole authority INSET appropriate to identified development needs.

(d) Encouraging and supporting collaborative INSET in general and development group INSET in particular.

(e) Providing a clearing house for the accreditation of school based/development centre INSET within the authority.

(f) Ensuring that the authority information base for development contains material relevant to the needs of teachers and schools.

(g) The dissemination of good practice.

(h) Contributing to the planning of professional development programmes for headteachers.

(i) Actively supporting the monitoring and evaluation of development activities in collaboration with the RDE.

(j) Through the standing conference, ensuring that the authority's headteachers, advisers and the officers are kept aware of development issues.

Composition of the DGC
Ten headteachers representing the development groups. (These would provide a balanced membership representing the educational phases.)

The management team of the Advisory Service, which includes the development centre leaders.

Representatives of the authority's major HE partners.

Figure 14.2 *The Development Committee*

The authority is able to utilize its infrastructure and the resources that are available to support the LEA, Advisory Service or school development plans. These include a team of over forty advisory teachers, including thirty permanent members of a core support team based on two development centres, IT and database networks, the Regional Staff College, which was a Dudley led initiative, a Research and Evaluation Unit to organize objective evaluation external to the authority and an audiovisual team and publishing unit to produce resource materials in collaboration with the School Library Service.

A range of financial resource stimuli for development are also available. These include: Development Awards ranging from £250 units to those of £500 and £1000, which have to be bid for on a competitive basis; a number of action research one-day secondments throughout the year linked to accreditation;

specific pilot projects in schools; collaborative INSET awards to groups of schools and a whole range of INSET opportunities for individual teachers.

Development planning can clearly, therefore, tap both structural and financial resources for support, as indeed can the review system as it identifies needs in particular schools or colleges. There is a constant and healthy dialogue sparking new ideas across the authority network, which assists in the creation of positive attitudes and a commitment to development.

The network itself is founded upon ten Development Groups, which consist of two or three secondary schools, their contributing primary schools and the special schools in the area. Each secondary school and its partner primary schools has its own adviser and the headteacher and advisers meet regularly to share ideas and plan development.

For TVEI purposes a consortium consists of two development groups, which means that every paired group has a specialist primary adviser, a general secondary adviser with a whole-school brief, e.g. flexible learning and two or three subject specialists. This grouping provides a powerful resource in its own right for the schools. Each school also has a development co-ordinator, whose major role is to identify staff development needs and to work with the headteacher as part of an INSET/development team.

One headteacher from every development group and two elected development co-ordinators are members of the Development Committee. Here they are joined by a group of advisers and teacher association representatives on the major decision-making body for school development. Colleagues from partner HE institutions are also members of the Committee.

Through a Directory of Innovation, the Committee is able to disseminate good and interesting practice and there is a curriculum review journal to publish research and developments. Vehicles such as the curriculum conference and summer school can be used to reinforce major development thrusts.

The authority therefore has a powerful partnership structure available to it, which helps to create a shared purpose that forms a basis for collaborative action and for critical self-review but that can also power the identification and dissemination of improvement. The external review programme of the Advisory Service is therefore based upon partnership and a critical friendship with a shared commitment to improvement.

DEVELOPMENT REVIEW: THE CONCEPT AND THE PRACTICE

The purpose of the inspection and the development review process is the same, basically 'to improve the quality of learning'. But whereas inspection is founded on the belief that the system should be monitored, development review is focused on its improvement. The Dudley review strategy was developed on the premise that the most important means of ensuring quality in education was through an effective advisory service. An effective advisory service not only promotes high standards and good practice but also ensures their dissemination. It is also, perhaps, the most important component for the creation of a healthy climate in an education service and thereby facilitates the achievement of a high morale and a powerful sense of purpose among its staff.

A systematic programme of inspection is clearly at the heart of such a service. Needs must be identified and assessed, information filtered and inter-preted, all (importantly) in the context of a knowledge and understanding of schools and colleges acquired over time. It thereby enables a consensus view of the curriculum and entitlement to evolve and be stated. This can then be translated into development plans at every level of participation.

It is, therefore, absolutely essential that the inspection function should not be divorced from the advisory and the developmental. The new Education Act reinforces the need to have an even closer working relationship between the local authority and its partners, headteachers, principals, governors, parents, teachers and lecturers. This will ensure that agreed authority policies, them-selves incorporating the requirements of the Act, will provide effective guid-ance for schools and colleges in delivering effective teaching and learning for their pupils and students.

Legally, the LEA has a responsibility to ensure that young people are being educated to a satisfactory standard. The fact that the educational needs of pupils and students are continually changing means that there is a need for responsive development. The traditional idea of the inspection, held at frequency levels that could be a decade or more, does not, in our view, adequately meet today's needs. Inspection is, we believe, an integral part of continued development and must, to be really effective, be complemented by advice and the deployment of a managed service of support to bring about the desired change. The concept of development review is, therefore, a richer and more effective agent of quality improvement. It integrates the identification of need, with advice based upon wide experience and a range of resources to bring about the desired improve-ment. The concept is consistent and applies equally well to individual appraisal, turning it from a monitoring into a staff development strategy based on planned development.

The education service is, of necessity, complex and requires an inspection system embedded in the wider context of the development review approach. This approach itself must encompass a capacity for controlled observation, reflection based upon understanding, shared values, a capacity for flexible response and a commitment to partnership robust enough to cope with criticism.

The review process is also seen as dynamic rather than passive, in that the reporting stage is only seen as the first step in a cycle of development. This cycle clearly has a direct value to the organization but increasingly the material acquired from review is contributing to the wider authority's development. For example:

1 The Education Committee is informed of the effectiveness of its policies but also has access to information that will enable new policies to be formulated.

2 The annual report to the Education Committee is a good example of the proactive use of review. Not only does the report look back at

performance, it also looks forward and makes recommendations for action related to quality improvement.

3 Increasingly, the market forces approach to the management of the education service nationally requires that submissions for development funding must be related to evidence. A review strategy founded upon school improvement provides a natural source of such management information for development.

4 The review programme, by identifying good practice, provides a natural basis for an authority-wide dissemination strategy.

5 The partnership inherent in the approach provides for a complementary internal review system. Integrating these two elements not only provides for a more consistant view of 'reality' but also ensures that subsequent action has the commitment necessary for maximum benefit.

6 Development review, therefore, provides a baseline for the creation of both the school and the authority development plan.

7 The partnership model also reinforces networking and team action and helps to contain the fragmentary forces increasingly seen in the current market driven education strategy.

Development review, therefore, is action focused, forms a basis for coherent action, facilitates a shared understanding and provides a process for quality improvement.

The review programme is based upon a cycle of four years in the case of secondary schools and six years (now to be four years) for primary and special schools. In both cases, the appraisal cycle for the headteacher is built into the programme so that it takes place in the context of the organization revealed by the review. In secondary schools a series of curriculum area visits to all 'subject' areas is an integral part of the cycle in year 3, thereby providing a look back at progress since the review and look forward to potential developments at the next review. The cycle in primary and special schools includes a 'paired visit' in years 3 and 5 in which the pastoral adviser and a specialist colleague carry out a monitoring review.

The pastoral adviser plays a key role in the whole process, which begins with the negotiation of the review agenda. The adviser represents the authority's views regarding focus areas and the senior management team represents the school's perception of needs and desired outcomes. The agreed agenda is then built into the programme, which takes place over three days (secondary) (four days from 1992) or two days (primary/special) (three days from 1992), with eight advisers for a secondary review and four for an average sized primary school. Pre-visit documentation from school and authority is collated and brought to a pre-meeting for the review team where the programme is agreed. Performance indicators for the identified focus areas are established and shared with the school.

The review utilizes interviews with key staff, classroom observation, pupil tracking, surveys of pupils' work and an unstructured amount of planned free time for individual advisers to follow a particular line of interest. At the conclusion of the review verbal feedback is given to the headteacher and the senior management team. This is followed by a written draft report within a month. When this is finally drafted it is taken to the governing body in their next cycle of meetings. Copies of the report go to the CEO and on to the authority database from where it is used to inform the annual report to the Education Committee.

The report contains a description of where the school is now in relation to the agreed focus areas but the most important element is that of recommendations for future development. It is these recommendations that assist in the creation or modification of the school's development plan and form the basis for a development contract. The contract agrees the level of need and the resources necessary to achieve the desired improvement. These are provided from the school's own resources and from within the authority's development network, which includes the deployment of advisory teachers. The review process, therefore, both informs the authority's development plan and helps to monitor its effectiveness.

In post-16 institutions reviews are related to the needs of both individual colleges and the wider authority, with each college participating in one institutional and one cross-authority review annually. Areas for review are decided in consultation with the Further Education Executive in relation to the priorities for development established through the mechanism of the FE development plan. The post-16 review programme is therefore, like the main 3 to 16 programme, development focused, reflecting current situations and containing recommendations for the development of curriculum, staff and the organization. The whole process informs the authority's development planning priorities and feeds into the subsequent responsive action.

The role of the authority's advisers is crucial to the success of the strategy and the investment in its human resource capital has been a central feature of the authority's development during the 1980s. The authority has achieved the best adviser to school or college ratio in the country and in the 1989-90 school year was the highest spending metropolitan authority on the professional development of teachers. The leading role played by the authority in major educational initiatives, such as the GRASP Project, the Regional Staff College, the National Flexible Learning Data Base, the CD-ROM Project, the IT in the Management of Learning initiative and the national HMI/LAI collaborative project, all testify to the effectiveness of the advisory service and its capacity to sustain a development strategy.

The development network is facilitated, innovation stimulated, good practice disseminated and the implementation of the development plans of schools and colleges and the authority guided and supported by the advisory team.

At the heart of quality improvement, I believe, lies the quality of relationships based on partnership between all those involved with the service. As a consequence of the development review approach, information flows and access have been improved. There is a greater sense of shared purpose and self-confidence has grown with a sense of identity and pride in being part of the Dudley network. Institutions have become more responsive and educational quality has been improved in both quantitative and qualitative ways.

THE IMPROVEMENT PROCESS

Overall, we believe that there is a coherent, purposeful and consistent approach to 'review' in the authority. Increasingly found at the heart of review is the process known as GRASP (getting results and solving problems) as the dissemination of this major initiative is carried across all the authority's schools. We believe that the learning partnership upon which GRASP is founded integrates both individual and organizational learning (see Figure 14.3). Effective development and quality improvement are founded upon effective learning. The creation of the learning organization, which in the case of schools involves parents, governors, teachers and headteachers, as well as pupils, is therefore our major purpose.

The GRASP process, which is intrinsically simple, can be used to good effect and its basics learned rapidly by anyone. It creates a learning partnership and focuses on progressive improvement. In our experience, it provides the foundation for quality because it continually challenges where we are now and what we have achieved as a precursor to looking forward and planning to get better next time. This commitment is not forced but emerges as a natural part of the process.

This is achieved by, first, clarifying with all participants (partners) what our purpose is — what we are trying to learn, described in terms of learning outcomes. This may sound simple yet in visits to classrooms anywhere it is usually rare to find all the pupils and teachers sharing an agreed purpose couched in terms of learning expectations. If, therefore, learners do not know what is expected, how can they learn effectively or how indeed can they be assessed? Those involved in the GRASP process together describe the criteria required for successful achievement of the task, thereby reinforcing and clarifying the purpose and providing the basis for review.

The process requires learners to generate a variety of ways in which the purpose might be achieved, from which the most promising is chosen and implemented. Regular progress reviews help to ensure that the way chosen is effective. Such reviews may result in a change of plan and through the final review potential or real failure becomes a learning experience. Even when the purpose is successfully achieved against the agreed criteria, the final review always asks, 'Could we have done this better?'

The same process can be applied with equal effect in any learning situation or to facilitate the achievement of any purpose. It therefore integrates well into the management and decision-making process of schools and other organizations. Indeed it was the process that facilitated the growth and success of Dexion International, whose founder Demetrius Comino developed the concept. When used in the area of school review or management it provides for a shared understanding and makes joint planning and subsequent implementation more effective.

The GRASP approach, now being used in half the schools in Dudley, is providing a most powerful agent for quality improvement. As its dissemination increasingly influences the whole authority network, the improvement in educational performance will continue. Gradually, all the contributing factors that have influenced quality improvement in Dudley should be drawn together into

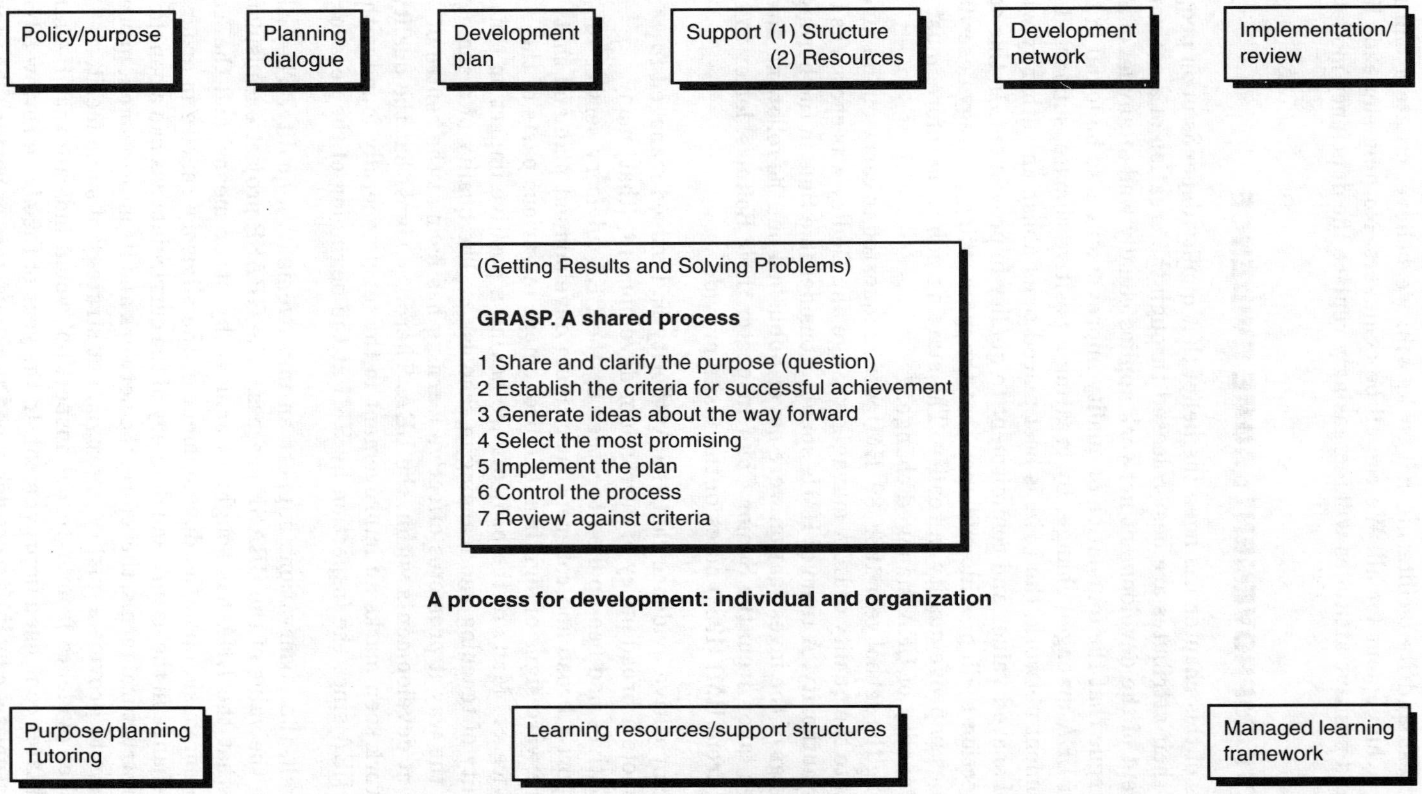

Policy/purpose

Planning dialogue

Development plan

Support (1) Structure
(2) Resources

Development network

Implementation/ review

Purpose/planning Tutoring

Learning resources/support structures

Managed learning framework

(Getting Results and Solving Problems)

GRASP. A shared process

1 Share and clarify the purpose (question)
2 Establish the criteria for successful achievement
3 Generate ideas about the way forward
4 Select the most promising
5 Implement the plan
6 Control the process
7 Review against criteria

A process for development: individual and organization

Figure 14.3 A framework for development: organization and individual

181

even more effective action. There remains much to be done but partnership, shared purpose and commitment, continually reinforced through the development process and its facilitating network, will, we believe, create a culture based on achievement for all. We can all be achievers. Nothing succeeds like success and positive attitudes will increasingly replace the deficiency model of the past.

QUALITY IMPROVEMENT: SOME EVIDENCE

The focus of this chapter has been the belief that quality depends upon people and that their attributes are best released through the creation of a network. The concept of the development network applies equally well at any level and I would argue that the foundation of quality improvement is to be found in the quality of LEA managed change. By creating a positive climate, supported by a development network, the LEA is best placed to establish an authority-wide system of shared values and commitment to quality improvement. In this concluding section I will provide evidence that the networking strategy described earlier does improve quality in reality. The starting point, therefore, must be with the quality of LEA managed change.

During the school year 1988-89, HMI were requested to carry out an investigation into the quality of LEA managed change and Dudley was chosen as the exemplar authority. A team of HMIs spent a considerable time in the borough. The findings of the investigation were never published but the following direct references taken from the Senior Chief Inspector, Eric Bolton's, letter to the CEO and from HMI (1989) notes of the visits provide

> much positive evidence that the Authority had indeed managed to promote a broad policy of curriculum development, [that] many initiatives had been pulled together by the LEA advisory service to support a broad and coherent curriculum development plan and that there were signs of significant improvement in various parts of the service.... Many of the projects are having a positive impact on the quality of teaching and learning in schools.... The quality of teaching and the way it promotes effective learning has been at the centre of recent developments within the LEA. There are signs that the quality of work seen marks an improvement in the level generally found within the LEA since the inspection by HMI at the beginning of the decade.

Overall, the observations support an improvement in quality. They also recognize the value of the GRASP process. 'The GRASP project encapsulates most of what the LEA has sought to achieve by other means' and the 'considerable emphasis upon the development of the advisory service in order to promote change in the nature and delivery of the curriculum has had a beneficial effect'. In structural terms, therefore, the network and its improvement process would seem to provide a quality improvement strategy of some merit.

Further evidence from external 'inspection' would indicate that the strategy facilitates continued improvement. In the year of the above review 80 per cent of lessons seen by HMI were described as satisfactory or better. The report by HMI for the following year had 85 per cent of lessons in this category with 40 per cent classed in category 1, while an individual school inspection report for 1991 indicates virtually 50 per cent of lessons in category 1. Less than satisfactory lessons in all reports were identified as about 15 per cent against a regional and national average of 30 per cent.

An inspection report by a Central TVEI team led by Malcolm Deare during this same period also provides evidence of another important contribution to quality, teacher morale. 'Across the Authority teachers indicated that they felt the LEA had done so much for them that they wanted to give something back.' Similar observations can also be found in the GRASP project evaluation report carried out by Janet Jones (1990) under the auspices of the RSA. This report identified headteachers who 'feel that they are better managers' and teachers who showed 'improved teamwork, better morale, more purposeful planning/ delivery, more awareness of pupils as learners, sharing learning objectives with pupils, positive attitudes towards managed classrooms'.

The same report states that pupils 'were generally more creative, planned their own work, were more reponsible, habitually reviewed their own achievements and were constructively self-critical'. More direct evidence of improved pupil performance can be seen in the steady improvement in examination results. For example, the figures for five or more GCSE A to C passes in 1989-91 show a steady improvement from 24 to 27 and 30 per cent. In the last of those years maths A to C passes rose by 4.2 per cent to over 30 per cent.

It would therefore seem reasonable to conclude that a range of positive approaches, facilitated by a network which itself facilitates partnership and provides support as part of an 'enterprising strategy' has had 'considerable beneficial effects on the range of curriculum development in response to local and national need and on the quality of teaching and learning in Dudley schools'.

This observed quality of teaching and learning is not static but the result of an ongoing commitment to improvement by a significant number of participants in the operation of the authority's Education Service. The achievement of such a critical mass is, we believe, the key to quality. Quality, we believe, thrives on shared challenges met through collaborative working and cannot be provided by simplistic audit type models. The development network should be greater than the sum of its individual parts. It should never be complacent but continually challenging itself to move from the tolerable to the good and from the good to the better. Through the network will come, we believe, proof that 'learning pays', in the words of Sir Christopher Ball's report (1991) and this, in the end, will create the learning society where quality is endemic.

REFERENCES

Association of Metropolitan Authorities (1987) Education Committee report, item 11, 9 July.

Audit Commission (1989) *Assuring Quality in Education: The Role of the Local Education Authority Inspectors and Advisers*. London: HMSO.

Bainbridge, B. (1990) 'Inputs, outcomes and quality', *Times Educational Supplement*, 23 March.

Ball, Sir Christopher (1991) *Learning Pays: The Role of Post-compulsory Education and Training*. London: RSA.

Chartered Institute of Public Finance and Accountancy (1986) *A Statement on Performance Indicators in the Education Service*. London: CIPFA.

Coopers & Lybrand (1988) *Local Management of Schools: A Report to the Department of Education and Science*. London: DES.

Esp, D. (1988) 'Week by week', *Education*, 17 June.

HMI (1989) *The Quality of LEA Managed Change: Observations from the Inspection Work in Dudley LEA*. London: HMI.

Jones, J. (1990) *Evaluation of Dudley GRASP Project, Final Report*. London: Janet Jones Associates Ltd.

Nubesnuick, D. (1991) *Promoting Quality in Schools and Colleges*. London: Education Management Information Exchange.

Society of Chief Inspectors and Advisers (1989) *LEA Advisory Services and the Education Reform Act, 1988: A Discussion Document*. London: SCIA.

Stillman, A. and Grant, M. (1989) *The LEA Adviser: A Changing Role*. Windsor: NFER-Nelson.

Wilcox, B. (1989) 'Monitoring for survival', *Education*, 24 March.

Chapter 15

Collaborating for Quality

Jo Stephens

'The Issue Is Quality' was an apt title for the 1991 series of seminars that led to this book. The programme was spot on in saying that 'whoever wins the next election *quality* will be a key theme in education in the 1990s.' My prediction was that 1992 would be the year in which the national spotlight turned to the processes of teaching and the ways of organizing schools and classrooms. There were already signs that what we know about children's learning and teacher professional development may not be taken into account in that debate. If that is so then the quality of education will be threatened by actions that, ironically, are presented as a means to improve it.

That could happen if the processes used for assessing standards, such as certain ways of testing achievement or over-heavy inspection and public reporting, are known to have side-effects that slow down the very learning by pupils and teachers which leads to sound pupil progress.

WHAT ARE WE AIMING FOR IN THE EDUCATION SERVICE?

I will begin by spelling out the underlying principles that inform our practice in Oxfordshire. There is nothing so practical as a good theory in trying to deal with turbulence! Given fundamental principles we can separate out what doesn't matter too much for our prime purposes, such as the structure or distribution of local authorities or whether children should sit in rows facing the teacher. Then we can concentrate our energy on changes that really matter for reaching even higher standards.

Our version of back-to-basics is given in our current LEA curriculum statement. Our product is learning. This learning includes

- skills (processes);
- knowledge (facts);
- concepts (principles);
- attitudes (values).

Our aim is even more effective learning.

But what do I mean by effective learning? It is *learning that lasts* rather than here today and gone tomorrow learning. It is *learning that is fit for its purpose*:

- by being a match to known needs of both the individual and society;
- by being adaptable so that the learner can apply it to different situations now and in the future;
- by providing the learner with the means for further learning.

PROVING AND IMPROVING QUALITY

In this chapter I shall not be writing about how to tell how far you have achieved that quality of learning. That is a fascinating and important task. Indeed it is one of the two great debates in education and is as old as the societies that have educated their young. It is the debate about *proving quality*, once you think you know what quality is. The other crucial debate is about *improving quality*, assuming you have agreed not only what it is but also how to measure it. My message in this chapter is a contribution to the debate about processes for improving quality in education.

No doubt like me you find that chance events suddenly throw up a framework that kicks into place a whole host of disconnected ideas and experiences and provide a foundation for new work or new understandings. By chance a few years ago I saw an Open University programme about quality control and quality assurance methods in a production industry. Have you ever noticed how often a new context illuminates principles that have lain unnoticed within your own familiar field?

In this particular industrial context *quality control* was described as an end-of-line inspection process, sometimes including samples tested to destruction (a sort of terminal test?). *Quality assurance*, in contrast, was seen as a process-based concept in which every individual stage in the manufacture of the product was identified and tuned up to the highest possible quality level. Quality process was thought to lead to quality product; hence the term 'quality assurance'. That well describes the methods we use for quality assurance in education, to improve learning by analysing and improving all aspects of teaching, of the teaching and learning environment and of the support services for both teachers and learners.

It is this process approach that underpins British Standard 5750 for *total quality management* (TQM). To quote from the Department of Trade and Industry booklet:

> BS 5750 sets out how you can establish, document and maintain an effective quality system. . . . Your procedures will be more soundly based and more efficient . . . because you will have built in quality at every stage.

LEARNING TO SEE

My earliest professional memory of what I would now see as part of the quality process approach is of some years spent as an inspector of mathematics. I soon realized that I could more than double the use of the same amount of time spent in a primary school by taking the head along as a partner and engaging in a running commentary on what I thought I was seeing in classrooms. Thus developed a purposeful leaving-my-eyes-behind-me strategy. It led me to state criteria at the beginning of inspection reports and then state evidence of observations related to those criteria. The ILEA 'Checkpoints for primary mathematics', a programme of criteria for achievement and individual diagnostic tasks, was underpinned by that same principle. On a broader canvas the ILEA self-evaluation booklet, 'Keeping the school under review', was an attempt by inspectors to pass on their craft. This was to become a seminal document in other school evaluation and improvement schemes, such as the scheme in Oxfordshire introduced over ten years ago and still in place.

HMI have been needlessly coy about their criteria for inspecting teaching and ought not to have been. Those of us who have over the years managed to get a glimpse of some of their inspection schedules and their useful five-point scale descriptions for quality course provision or classroom performance know how powerful a tool for self-administered inspection and improvement programmes they would have been. The proposed commercial inspection plan, working to common schedules produced by HMI, unwittingly contributes to improved learning by making such useful frameworks widely available for do-it-yourself inspection. Recent DES sponsored publications on school development planning issues have been useful in this context.

The school self-evaluation programme that Oxfordshire LEA began in 1979-80 is now in its third cycle, having been adapted as a result of learning within the Education Service and changing national conditions. The first five-year cycle was a pioneering venture, with experiential learning and some rudimentary external researcher interest. We had no packaged in-service training modules to guide our learning. Introspection was the norm; only a few schools sought external evidence or support and only a few were offered it by LEA staff following the HMI comment in 1979 that self-evaluation should be just that. With hindsight I know that acting on this comment in fact slowed the learning process within the service as a whole.

Tracing the development of the school self-evaluation programme would take a chapter of its own. Suffice it to say that the learning of the first cycle was far from systematic but was put to good use in the second cycle. There emerged a need, expressed by schools, for consultancy style adviser support in the process. Capacity for stating objectives, evaluating the achievement of them and engaging in forward planning developed more strongly. Thus the groundwork for producing whole-school development plans in the third cycle has been done.

STUDENT ACHIEVEMENT

The development of Records of Achievement for secondary school pupils was a major part of the work of many local education authorities throughout the 1980s. In Oxfordshire we collaborated with three other LEAs, Coventry, Somerset and Leicestershire, and with the University of Oxford through the Oxford Delegacy of Local Examinations and the Department of Educational Studies, on the Oxford Certificate of Educational Achievement (OCEA).[1] The fundamental principles developed for continuous formative assessment and recording of achievement at 16 plus leading to a summative record (the Certificate) are

- student self-review and assessment as a fundamental component;
- clearly stated curriculum goals and assessment criteria;
- external help in assessing progress, especially help from teachers and parents.

Thus attention to assessing the quality of learning throughout the course assures the quality of the learning described in the certification portfolio. Similar methods emerged elsewhere and secondary school Records of Achievement are now well established at the end of the compulsory years of schooling and spreading to other age groups.

STAFF APPRAISAL

Funnily enough it took the emergence of thinking about *teacher* appraisal to trigger a powerful connection between aspects of the evaluation of school performance, the assessment of student performance and the appraisal of staff performance. The industrial management literature on staff appraisal is heavily weighted towards the involvement of staff in self-appraisal and target-setting in conference with their manager. Suddenly it becomes clear that one set of processes — self-review of progress against stated criteria, external consultancy in that review and clear target setting for the next phase — applies to all three assessment contexts, and who knows what others. Not surprisingly, therefore, the Oxfordshire Education Service framework for staff appraisal rests on these conditions as we move into the first cycle and apply our now well established principles to the appraisal process.

COLLABORATIVE EVALUATION

The three assessment contexts I have described all rely on relationships between the school, the student or the member of staff and 'critical friends', be they advisers, teachers or managers. What really excites me now, and is the first example I offer under my title 'Collaborating for quality', is that some schools have begun to work together in an *evaluative* way; not only in the more familiar curriculum development and in-service training fields but also in questions of the quality of their current practice, thrown open to each other through critical 'intervisitation'.

Do not underestimate the leap forward that this represents. It is of course in its infancy. A secondary headteacher writing to me about it described the work with the visiting team (a governor, an LEA adviser, the head of a secondary school, the principal of the local college of further education) with whom the quality assurance collaboration is being developed. Staff of the host school identified some quality of learning issues for monitoring and analysis. The visiting team worked out with them a programme for the visits. There was follow-up discussion and analysis, and feedback to staff, governors and parents. He wrote:

It is quite clear that even this programme, which is four people $\times$ $1\frac{1}{2}$ days equivalent can only touch on the issues which we have already identified. The confidence and trust should lead to honesty and self-criticism. Will it? I remain concerned that we are often nice to each other, sparring gently and avoiding the meaty issues, but I understand how difficult it is for a visitor to know when he/she is seeing the truth.

I know it will take time to reap the benefits in quality improvement terms, but benefit is much more assured with this method of inspection, which is a sought and shared part of a programme for analysis and improvement, than with the quick-and-easy formal inspection of a here today and gone tomorrow team, from whatever source.

School intervisitation between some Oxfordshire primary and secondary teachers and staff from a primary/secondary partnership group in Liverpool is now reaching a crucial phase as a method of improving the quality of work in both groups. The one-off visits popular ten years ago are not enough. Where environments differ significantly, where stereotyped views of Liverpool or Oxfordshire have to be seen off by observation and analysis of teachers and children at work, the 'critical friend' consultancy comes slowly. In writing to one of our advisers following a recent visit to Liverpool, various Oxfordshire teachers said:

> I found it far more worthwhile this year as I had got over the shocks of last year. In the school where I was we were able to get down to the nitty-gritty of cross-phase continuity.

> It was useful to make a second visit to enable comparisons in both the schools I'd visited before. I find courses which give an experience by far the best for learning. It was interesting to hear other colleagues say they also had taken a long time to assimilate last year's experience — a tribute to the quality/depth of the learning.

> In addition to 'being together' and 'being daft' we came away with much to think about and act upon. I felt that there was such a lot in what we saw that has real implications for personal and corporate strategies.

In this collaborative series of intervisitations we are seeing the clear signs of growth beyond the 'cosy chat, nice to see you, feel a lot better' level into genuine looking together and the asking and answering of challenging questions that lead to improvements. In fact our first experience of this powerful 'intervisitation' method of providing external consultancy came from the accreditation method used by the OCEA Records of Achievement consortium. As part of this process teams drawn from the consortium members visit each LEA periodically to enable the home LEA to account for its progress in supporting its schools in their Records of Achievement work. They discuss that support, ask questions and provide feedback as a result of gathering evidence from sample schools, and assist in setting targets for future work.

Why do we believe that such processes between institutions have potential for improving the quality of learning? Surely the principles for assessment and development can be applied without the expense of meeting. What value is added by collaboration through intervisitation? I have three answers and they are sufficiently powerful to be applied to evaluation of the work of an institution, of a student or of a professional worker.

- Learning is usually enhanced by interaction with other learners.
- Collective statements can, and do, shape attitudes and policies beyond the group.
- The need to prepare thoughts and materials for collaborative activities helps to make objectives and progress explicit and so helps learning.

CONCLUSION

The collaborative consultancy method, based on observation and mutual questioning, underpins the activities I have described. Its power is recognized in the 'Leadership and Quality Management' guide first published by the Department of Trade and Industry over ten years ago.

> If you go for external assistance, it is important to choose a consultant who will act as a catalyst, helping your managers to develop their own skills, rather than selling you a report which tells you what has to be done, then leaving you to do it. No one can make the breakthrough for you.

I believe passionately in the principles for assessment and the collaborative practices for quality improvement that I have described.

The message I want to give is very simple. Looking *at* and doing *to* is not enough. Looking and doing *with* is what leads to quality in the processes of teaching and learning, and so brings us nearer to our shared goal of quality learning for all our young people.

NOTE

1 Since 1991 National Records of Achievement have been introduced and OCEA is now the acronym for the Oxford Consortium for Educational Achievement.

Chapter 16

Promoting Improvement in Schools: Aspects of Quality in Birmingham

Elizabeth Burridge and Peter Ribbins

INTRODUCTION

In 1993 we face the eighteenth Education Act in fourteen years. For some the changes proposed 'aim at continuing the developments started by the 1988 Education Act' (Greenfield, 1993). The White Paper, *Choice and Diversity*, on which the latest Act is based, claims to set out 'an evolutionary framework' designed to 'complete the transformation of the education system of England and Wales begun in the 1980s' (DFE, 1992, p. 1). This claim has been challenged. Ranson (1993) argues that, 'under the mask of continuing the changes begun in 1988', what is being proposed is 'a decisive turn . . . a final break with the post war values of universalism in favour of an earlier tradition of private and selective education'. This break amounts to a 'quiet revolution' in policy in which ' "progression", "entitlement" and "local management" is substituted by [*sic*] a new [or renewed] emphasis on "specialization", "selection", "autonomy" and "standards".'

It may be that in its continuing search for better schools and higher levels of pupil achievement, the 'quiet revolution' that the Government is currently sponsoring can be seen as a shift from an approach stressing the merits of *quality development* to one that emphasizes the need for *quality control* (Ranson, 1993). In this chapter we seek to explore what such a shift might entail, with an examination of the sometimes competing claims of ideas drawn *inter alia* from the literatures of school effectiveness and school improvement and an account of the efforts of the local education authority and schools in Birmingham to develop a holistic approach to the promotion of quality.

SCHOOL EFFECTIVENESS AND SCHOOL IMPROVEMENT

Chapters in this book by David Hopkins, David Reynolds and Pamela Sammons examine aspects of what we know about school effectiveness and school improvement, and possible relationships between the two. They emphasize the strengths and limitations of each approach and stress the need for a productive linkage between the two. As Reynolds acknowledges, this may not be easy given their very different histories and core beliefs and assumptions. Rather than replicate this analysis, the main tenets of which we largely accept, we shall restrict our discussion at this point to the close linkage that, we claim, tends to exist between notions of school effectiveness and ideas about quality control on the one hand and school improvement and quality development on the other. As a prelude to this, it is necessary to clarify in a preliminary way what we mean by such key terms as 'quality assurance', 'quality control' and 'quality development'.

We begin with quality development. Since much of the rest of our chapter deals with this concept, our treatment of it here will be brief. As used in Birmingham, quality development refers to a set of activities centring on monitoring and evaluation. It is about any aspect of school life where 'quality gaps' have been identified by working through a sequence of actions. The essential purpose of such a process is to use it to enable development, for improving what is happening.

Walsh (1991) defines quality assurance as 'all those planned and systematic actions that are necessary to provide adequate confidence that a product or service will satisfy given requirements for quality'. In an educational context, quality assurance can be seen as all those planned and recognizable procedures and working practices that are designed to ensure that the service meets the needs of students in the context of national and local criteria and priorities. As such, quality assurance is about making sure that quality can be delivered — in this sense it entails a 'before the event' guarantee of effectiveness.

Quality control may be described as all those planned and recognizable procedures for checking on whether and to what extent outcomes are achieved that meet specified standards. Such checking can take place by measuring pupil outcomes, such as levels of attainment or levels of attendance, and by inspecting the quality of provision against more or less predefined criteria of effectiveness. Such an approach offers an essentially 'after the fact' account of how the school has worked. The Government's commitment to this approach to quality is evident. In the foreword to the White Paper, the Prime Minister asserts that 'the drive for higher standards in schools has been the hallmark of the government over the last decade' (DFE, 1992, p. iii). To achieve this the Government 'is absolutely committed to testing. Assessment and testing are the keys to monitoring and raising standards in our schools' (p. 9). It also believes that 'critical to the working and the improvement of school education ... will be the role of the new schools' Inspectorate, regularly investigating how schools are getting on, and making the results of that investigation freely, regularly and easily available to parents and the local community' (p. 8). As a consequence of these reforms, the Government claims that 'the results achieved by pupils and their schools are now subject to much greater scrutiny, and will inform action necessary to secure improvements in individual schools' (p. 16).

The connection between this approach and the ideas of the school effectiveness paradigm are clear. Indeed it can be argued that given the specifications of the National Curriculum and the contents of the *Handbook for Inspection* currently being used in the training of the new Inspectorate, what the government expects of schools and how it defines effectiveness have rarely been so fully set out (OFSTED, 1992). It is easy to exaggerate such claims and some have taken a very different view. Greenfield (1993), for example, claims that the

White Paper is 'somewhat coy on stating exactly what sort of schools the government seeks to create to ensure that they are "successful", and that they will "raise standards". However, because of repeated references to "damning" evidence readers can deduce what the government considers are ... "failing" schools.' Furthermore, it is by no means clear what sort of National Curriculum the Government has sought to create since 1987 nor, for that matter, is it easy to predict what it will look like in 1997 (Sweetman, 1991, 1992; Chitty, 1992; Ribbins, 1992).

We share these concerns but emphasize different reasons for doubting if the Government's quality control approach will succeed in raising standards significantly. First, it assumes a linkage between school effectiveness and school improvement whose existence has been increasingly challenged. Second, it is based upon a touching faith in the powers of external inspection, a faith which has, of late, become less fashionable in industry, commerce and even in other government departments. Thus, for example, a recent paper from the Department of Trade and Industry claims that 'to believe that traditional quality control techniques, and the way that they have always been used, will result in quality is wrong. Employing more inspectors, tightening up standards ... does not promise quality.' What is needed is to change 'the focus of control from outside the individual to within; the objective being to make everybody accountable for their own performance, and to get them committed to attaining quality in a highly motivated fashion' (DTI, 1991).

Similar assumptions inform the approach to quality that Birmingham has been trying to implement within its schools and colleges over the past seven years. The approach is developmental in character and draws upon a number of sources, including the literature on school improvement. It entails an approach to quality development that seeks to locate a high level of responsibility for quality with individual teachers and groups of teachers and in doing so to embed a commitment to continuous improvement as a normal 'way of working' within each school. As those involved in this initiative became more experienced it became increasingly clear that while quality development must be at the heart of any effective approach to school improvement, on its own it was not enough — it needed to be supported by quality assurance and quality control. It also became increasingly obvious that for a comprehensive quality strategy to work, it required that all three elements were in place and that they were structurally interrelated in appropriate ways. What this means and how it is being attempted within the education service in Birmingham is the subject of much of the rest of the chapter.

TOWARDS A STRATEGY FOR QUALITY IN BIRMINGHAM: A HISTORICAL PREFACE

For over eight years, the local education authority in Birmingham has been engaged in the evolution of an ambitious approach to quality development in its schools and colleges. This began in 1984 with the appointment of a Co-ordinator for Monitoring and Evaluation, who was initially given the task of evaluating the YTS programme within the city. With members of the Continuing Education

Division and with key staff from each of the eight City Technology Colleges she began to develop an approach to monitoring and evaluation which, in retrospect, has come to be known as *supported self-evaluation* (Whale and Ribbins, 1990; Ribbins and Whale, 1992). So successful was this initiative that in September 1989 the approach was adopted as city policy for monitoring and evaluation within further education as a whole.

The year 1989 was also notable because it was in this year that supported self-evaluation first began to make an impact in schools, initially through the evaluation of TVE and Compact. In June 1990 the Education (Policy and Finance) Committee resolved to implement this approach to quality development within all the city's schools. Prudently, it also decided that the approach 'be piloted initially in a limited number of schools and evaluated fully before more extensive implementation'. Following training of key teaching and advisory staff from each of a representative sample of nineteen schools (one sixth-form college, eight secondary schools, eight primary schools, one nursery school, one special school) in autumn 1990, the pilot took place between January and December 1991. It was evaluated by a team from the Centre for Educational Management and Policy Studies, the University of Birmingham. In February 1992 the team published its findings in a major report entitled *Proving, Improving and Learning in Schools: Towards Enabling a Strategic Approach to Quality* (Ribbins *et al.*, 1992). The evaluation reported positively upon the pilot and recommended that the approach be extended to all the city's schools wishing to be included within a three-year programme.

The findings of the evaluation were welcomed by the Education Committee and a decision was made to accept, insofar as possible and practicable, its main recommendations. To progress this, the Chief Education Officer was asked to produce a detailed extension plan. Translation of this decision in principle into a practical extension plan was retarded, *inter alia*, by the general and local elections of 1992, the 1992 Education Act, the 1992 White Paper and growing uncertainties over the future financial position of the local authority. However, the Strategy and Policy Report to the Education Committee of June 1992 included a statement from the chairman which confirms the Committee's commitment to 'press ahead with the implementation of our Quality Development Initiative in all Birmingham schools'. So far over 150 schools are involved at various stages in implementing quality development, and over the next three years it is hoped that all schools will wish to join the initiative. To enable this an extension plan has been produced. The following sections will outline the ideas and proposals contained in this plan and in doing so will draw upon, as appropriate, evidence drawn from pilot and post-pilot evaluations.

THE QUALITY DEVELOPMENT INITIATIVE AND ITS EXTENSION

A statement of mission

The stated mission of the quality development initiative is to enable the LEA to work in partnership with schools to develop the quality of education for all pupils by establishing monitoring and evaluation procedures that enable the achievement of *three key purposes*:

1 To support the development of schools and the LEA as learning communities in which professionals can learn together, with and from each other, and with and from pupils, parents, governors, elected members, employers and the wider community — *learning*.

2 To improve teaching and learning — *improving*.

3 To permit schools, governing bodies and the LEA to respond proactively to accountability demands — *proving*.

Quality development as process and strategy

Within the Birmingham approach, quality development is seen as a *process* and a *strategy*. It is a 'way of working' that facilitates change and supports improvement. It makes a difference to learning and teaching by providing the stimulus and practical support for colleagues to build monitoring and evaluation into their day-to-day work, so that they can increasingly achieve the three purposes identified above and the principles and working practices described below.

A set of principles for quality development

Over time ten key *principles* for effective quality development have been identified.

1 Its impact on *learning* and *teaching* should be as direct as possible.

2 It should be built on actual school needs and built into its processes of *development planning*.

3 It should involve a *collaborative* and *participative* way of working on *monitoring* and *evaluation*.

4 It should be based on *school responsibility* and *school ownership*.

5 Its effective introduction into a school entails *appropriate training*.

6 It flourishes best in a *responsive organizational structure* with an *open management style* and a *whole-school commitment*.

7 It requires the allocation of *roles* and *responsibilities* which are both clearly designated and carefully articulated.

8 It must be *appropriately resourced* — particularly with respect to the allocation of time to undertake monitoring and evaluation.

9 It should involve as wide a range of *stakeholders* as possible.

10 Its *methodology* should be agreed and understood and should include:

- building both formative and summative review mechanisms into development planning;
- consulting widely on the selection and use of techniques of data gathering and methods of establishing criteria;

- negotiating access to information;
- generating both qualitative and quantitative information;
- substantiating judgements made about worth or effectiveness by collecting evidence and setting this against open, agreed criteria;
- interpreting evidence in context;
- ensuring that the findings of monitoring and evaluation are used, that they inform decision-making and lead to action;
- documenting the systems and procedures developed for monitoring and evaluation and subjecting them to internal review and external moderation and validation.

These principles should not be regarded as parts of a self-service package from which it is possible to mix and match to taste. They are not likely to be effective if applied piecemeal. Furthermore, the evidence suggests (Ribbins *et al.*, 1992) that a *top-down/bottom-up* approach to gaining support for them usually works best and that it is worth spending time and effort on explaining what each principle might mean for those involved in terms of its practical implications in a wide variety of specific circumstances.

A set and system of working practices

Quality development is a strategic approach to improvement which is intended to guide and support the process of development planning rather than to be a form of 'surveillance'. It is at its most effective when it both enables the identification of a 'quality gap' (the gap between 'where we are now' and 'where we want to get to') and informs the development of measures that will help to close such gaps and by doing so reduce shortfalls in desired levels of performance.

Development planning has been found to be an effective starting point for quality development and a key vehicle for enabling learning, proving and improving to happen. Experience suggests that development planning for quality and the working practices it entails are relevant to the needs of every school and can be applied in all educational settings — including whole-school, classroom and individual learning and teaching experiences (Ribbins *et al.*, 1992, Chapter 3). In its advanced form it involves a wide range of stakeholders (e.g. teachers, managers, pupils, parents, advisers and governors) working together to a common and shared set of purposes and principles. At its best, as those in the pilot schools stressed, quality development is an empowering mechanism — a different way of doing things and not just another thing to do.

Constructing a *quality development action plan* has been found to be an effective and workable means of structuring and integrating monitoring and evaluation activity into school development planning. For each development priority, at whatever level, a cycle of planning and practical work is needed. There are various ways of depicting such cycles (Hargreaves and Hopkins, 1991) but the quality development initiative has been most influenced by the work of Peter Holly (1990). In any case the approach suggests the sequence of activity outlined in Figure 16.1.

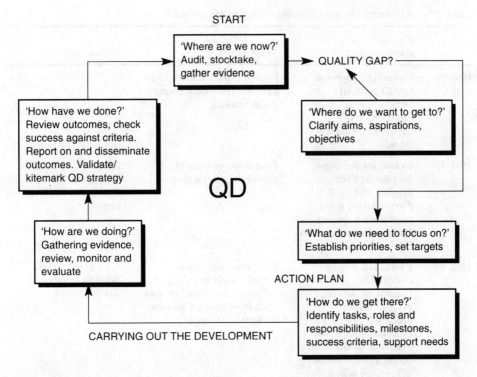

START

'Where are we now?'
Audit, stocktake,
gather evidence

→ QUALITY GAP?

'How have we done?'
Review outcomes, check
success against criteria.
Report on and disseminate
outcomes. Validate/
kitemark QD strategy

'Where do we want to get to?'
Clarify aims, aspirations,
objectives

QD

'How are we doing?'
Gathering evidence,
review, monitor and
evaluate

'What do we need to focus on?'
Establish priorities, set targets

ACTION PLAN

CARRYING OUT THE DEVELOPMENT

'How do we get there?'
Identify tasks, roles and
responsibilities, milestones,
success criteria, support needs

Figure 16.1   *The cycle of development planning for quality*

At each stage, colleagues work collaboratively, supporting one another to reflect critically and systematically on the process of development and always using real evidence and clear criteria to back up decisions. But it must be stressed that quality development in practice is rarely as tidy as Figure 16.1 suggests. As the pilot demonstrated, there will be problems and failures along the way as ideas and practices are 'chewed over' and challenged. Even so, as a whole, the development cycle and the approach that underpins it must be characterized by a commitment to the concepts of *professional discourse* and *community involvement* and as such entails:

- taking collective responsibility for the task(s) in hand;
- engaging in a continuous process of reflection and analysis;
- being constructively critical of practice and performance;
- being optimistic about the potential for improvement;
- involving pupils, parents, governors, etc. wherever possible.

Implementing the ideas described above in the LEA and within schools is a demanding task, made no easier, as we have argued earlier, by developments taking place nationally. Strenuous efforts have been made to consider how this might be achieved. What are proposed are three-year development cycles for the initiative as a whole and for the implementation of the approach within

Table 16.1 *Extending the quality initative across the service*

	Planning and preparation	Training	Implementation
1990-91	Committee approval for QD pilot. QD working group established. QD advisory committee set up.	Nineteen pilot schools and advisers from both teams begin training.	
1991-92	Evaluation strategy for pilot devised. Briefing and dissemination takes place across the city. Progress is reported to Education Committee.	Four more cohorts of schools begin training.	Pilot schools begin to implement QD. Evaluation of Pilot begins.
1992-93	Evaluation findings reported to Committee. QD extension plan prepared. Education Committee approves extension of QD to all Birmingham schools. QD related school inspection piloted.	Four more cohorts of schools begin training. Advisers, headteachers and staff from support services undertake training.	Schools of 1991-92 begin to implement QD.
1993-94	QD working group prepares resource material for schools, advisers and governors. QD related school inspection introduced. Validation of QD in schools introduced. Progress reported to Committee.	150 more schools begin training. Training for LEA officers begins and continues for more support services staff. Training for governors introduced.	Schools of 1992-93 begin to implement QD. Support services begin to implement QD.
1994-95	QD working group prepares evaluation strategy for whole QD Initiative. Progress reported to Committee.	150 more schools begin training. Training for school governors, LEA officers and other support services continues.	Schools of 1993-94 begin to implement QD. LEA and support services implement QD. Comprehensive quality strategy in place across the Education Service.

individual schools. In the next sections we shall consider each of these and discuss the strategic objectives set out in the *extension plan*.

Developing the quality initiative across the service as a whole

In 'A strategy for quality development in Birmingham', submitted to the Education Committee in June 1990 as a background paper to the report recommending the setting up of the pilot project, a three-year programme of implementation was proposed. It was envisaged that 150 schools a year would become involved between 1992 and 1995, until all schools wishing to be involved had done so. The purpose of the pilot was to learn from the experience in order to make recommendations for widescale implementation.

In September 1991 the *Quality Development Advisory Committee* (the group set up to oversee the project) agreed an implementation process. This proposed a two-phase approach, with schools undertaking a year's preparation training before committing themselves to implementing quality development more fully. By the end of 1992, 171 schools had undertaken preparation training and are now preparing quality development extension plans.

It is helpful to classify the development activity related to the extension of the Quality Development Initiative across the service as a whole under the headings of *planning and preparation*, *training* and *implementation*. Table 16.1 sets out the sequence of activity year by year.

This programme is predicated on the general assumption that over a five-year period all schools who wish will have had the opportunity to become involved in quality development. It is also envisaged that during that time quality development will be implemented within the policy and praxis of the authority and its support services.

The initiative will continue to be managed at an operational level by the *quality development working group*. Membership of the group includes officers, advisers, headteachers and quality development co-ordinators with support from the School of Education, University of Birmingham. Membership of the working group is reviewed annually, with a significant turn-over from year to year. The group is chaired by the Policy Adviser: Monitoring and Evaluation. At a strategic level, the initiative has been steered by the *quality development advisory committee*. This is chaired by the Assistant Director: Quality Development and Review and the committee includes representation from each of the three directorates of the LEA (Policy and Finance, Services, Individual and Community Support), from the main teachers' associations, from schools and governing bodies and from the School of Education, University of Birmingham. As the initiative proceeds the role, functions and membership of the advisory committee will be adjusted to meet the strategic demands of the work involved.

Developing the quality initiative within individual schools

It takes time for the purposes, principles and working practices of quality development to acquire real meaning and status within the competing demands

Table 16.2 *Implementing quality development in schools: a three-phase model*

Year 1

1   Awareness raising — school gets to know about QD and consults with staff about possible involvement.
2   Preparation training — school nominates a QD co-ordinator who undertakes the QD ACE training programme.
3   Action research — QD co-ordinator focuses on an agreed priority for development to try out the theory and methodology of QD.
4   Transition via dissemination — the findings from the action research and the processes of QD are disseminated across the whole school. A QD extension plan in produced.

Year 2

5   Embedding — the processes of QD are embedded into development planning and the school begins to formulate a QD policy.
6   Policy-making — the school's QD policy is agreed and made public.

Year 3

7   Implementation across whole school — QD processes and procedures are built into the routine working practices of all staff; the school becomes a 'self-evaluating institution'.
8   Maintenance — QD is subjected to review internally (within school) and externally (for purpose of validation/accreditation) and to 'renewal' activity to help sustain the momentum and commitment.

of contemporary school life. The ultimate aim is for each school to become a self-evaluating institution, in which rigorous and systematic processes of monitoring and evaluation are built into the routine working practices of the staff and the wider school community.

Some schools might achieve this on their own and quite quickly but many will need extensive support and take a good deal of time to do so. Table 16.2 and Figure 16.2 chart the stages through which schools will need to go and point out their likely support needs. It should be stressed that such an approach is heuristic. No single blueprint, let alone one with a detailed and prescriptive timetable attached, will offer a blueprint that is equally relevant to all schools. Each school will have to find its own path towards becoming self-evaluating. Some will take longer, others shorter, some will require more, others less support.

Promoting quality: nine strategic objectives

To implement the mission statement, a range of support mechanisms will be required. These have been identified from the findings of the pilot and the city's experience of promoting quality to date, and are listed in Figure 16.2. In the extension plan these mechanisms are defined as nine strategic objectives. In line with the approach as a whole, for each objective development priorities are identified (where do we want to get to?). Each development priority is accompanied by a review statement on progress so far (where are we now?) and a detailed action plan (how shall we get there?). A comprehensive account of these proposals will be beyond the scope of this chapter but we will seek to illustrate what is involved.

STAGE OF DEVELOPMENT   SUPPORT NEEDS

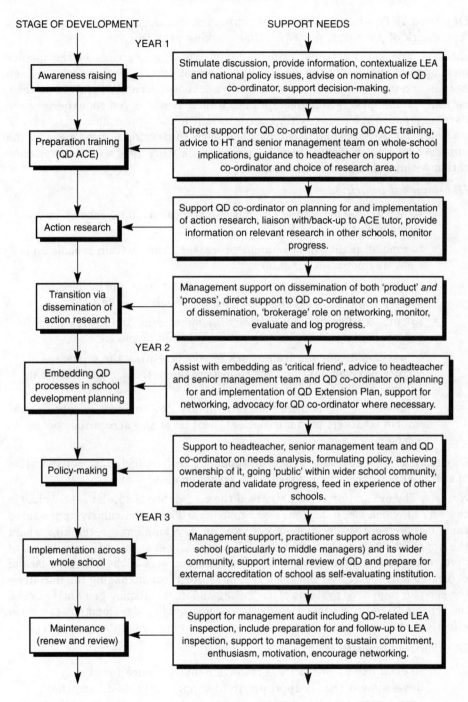

YEAR 1

Awareness raising ◄── Stimulate discussion, provide information, contextualize LEA and national policy issues, advise on nomination of QD co-ordinator, support decision-making.

Preparation training (QD ACE) ◄── Direct support for QD co-ordinator during QD ACE training, advice to HT and senior management team on whole-school implications, guidance to headteacher on support to co-ordinator and choice of research area.

Action research ◄── Support QD co-ordinator on planning for and implementation of action research, liaison with/back-up to ACE tutor, provide information on relevant research in other schools, monitor progress.

Transition via dissemination of action research ◄── Management support on dissemination of both 'product' and 'process', direct support to QD co-ordinator on management of dissemination, 'brokerage' role on networking, monitor, evaluate and log progress.

YEAR 2

Embedding QD processes in school development planning ◄── Assist with embedding as 'critical friend', advice to headteacher and senior management team and QD co-ordinator on planning for and implementation of QD Extension Plan, support for networking, advocacy for QD co-ordinator where necessary.

Policy-making ◄── Support to headteacher, senior management team and QD co-ordinator on needs analysis, formulating policy, achieving ownership of it, going 'public' within wider school community, moderate and validate progress, feed in experience of other schools.

YEAR 3

Implementation across whole school ◄── Management support, practitioner support across whole school (particularly to middle managers) and its wider community, support internal review of QD and prepare for external accreditation of school as self-evaluating institution.

Maintenance (renew and review) ◄── Support for management audit including QD-related LEA inspection, include preparation for and follow-up to LEA inspection, support to management to sustain commitment, enthusiasm, motivation, encourage networking.

N.B. At any stage during the development of QD, support may be required in preparation for, or as a follow-up to, an OFSTED inspection conducted by a registered team.

Figure 16.2 *Support for the implementation of quality development in schools*

Objective 1: To provide a range of support mechanisms, including a common framework of purposes, principles and working practices.

Review: The key purposes, principles and working practices of the quality development approach have evolved over several years. The approach has been readily accepted within the pilot and other schools currently involved as theoretically sound, practical and adaptable to their needs. Even so, experience to date suggests that it takes time to internalize the approach and to realize its potential. A particular challenge has been to develop commitment to the approach beyond those who have been most closely involved with its implementation within schools and the LEA.

Development priorities:

- to achieve ownership of the mission statement in all schools in the city and within the LEA;
- to embed quality development processes firmly within schools and LEA development planning;
- to establish a common set of relevant and realistic principles to underpin quality development both in schools and the LEA;
- to embed a flexible methodology for monitoring and evaluation into the routine working practices of schools and of the LEA;
- to develop a common framework for documenting the processes of quality development and for reporting the outcomes and impact in schools and in the LEA;
- to develop a mechanism whereby quality development in schools can inform strategic planning both at local level and across the service as a whole.

Objective 2: To provide a range of support services including collaborative operational and strategic management arrangements.

Review: The evaluation report stressed the confidence that pilot schools had in the way in which the pilot phase was managed. They particularly appreciated their involvement in decision-making and in developments in thinking about the approach. Among the weaknesses identified were: the different levels of involvement and commitment of the three Directorates of the LEA; the lack of dedicated administrative and clerical support for those managing the initiative; the need for improved systems of budgeting and financial management; the need for schools to be given more guidance on how quality development can most effectively be managed; and the need for continuing consultancy support.

Development priorities:

- to establish an operational management structure for quality development that is appropriate to support schools during the three-year extension period;
- to establish an appropriate level of effective and efficient clerical and administrative support for quality development;
- to develop a system enabling budget profiling and financial

management that is efficient, responsive to the needs of schools and flexible enough to meet the needs of the whole initiative;

- to establish a commitment to quality development throughout the LEA so that the department as a whole contributes to its successful implementation within the working practices of the LEA and schools;

- to sustain an advisory/consultative management function for quality development that is representative of all the major stakeholders and interest groups;

- to set up a suitable structure for the strategic management of quality development that ensures an integrated approach to the issue of quality across the LEA in terms of both policy-making and the support services.

Objective 3: To provide a range of support mechanisms, including training and development opportunities for all interest groups.

Review: Drawing upon the lessons of the limitations of earlier attempts to introduce self-evaluation within schools, from the outset the provision of appropriate training and development opportunities has been seen as a necessary condition for the introduction of effective quality development in Birmingham. A model of preparation training has been developed, which provides the route for schools into the quality development initiative. A tailored modular Advanced Certificate course in monitoring and evaluation has been designed and delivered by the School of Education of the University of Birmingham in collaboration with officers, advisers and teachers of the authority. The course is constructed to introduce participants to theoretical aspects of evaluation in educational contexts and to the role that such evaluation might play in facilitating effective development planning at every level of the school. It is designed to equip teachers and advisers with the skills they require and to give them an opportunity to try out their skills in practice. To facilitate this the ACE is in two parts. A lead taught module in term one is followed by two terms of project-based work taking an action research approach. The course has been well received and provides an effective means of preparing colleagues for initiating monitoring and evaluation activity in their schools.

There have, however, been a number of concerns, many identified within the pilot evaluation report. For the most part these focus on the restricted character and limited availability of training. The report develops ideas for a more wide-ranging and flexible package of training. In doing so it discusses the needs of *nine groups* — training of trainers, LEA officers and advisers, support services, heads and other senior staff, all teaching staff, governors and other stakeholders, including parents — and considers *four main forms* of training: intensive, facilitating, awareness raising and briefing.

Development priorities:

- to continue to provide access to the quality development initiative via the ACE programme for all schools wishing to become involved;

- to structure the training so that 150 schools a year can participate;

- to offer further training opportunities to heads and advisers;
- to prepare schools for participation in the ACE programme via awareness raising, structured support and briefing opportunities;
- to continue to support 'follow-up' development opportunities in schools so that a whole-school approach to evaluation can be developed (LEAP 4 will assist in this);
- to establish a 'training the trainers' course to increase the number of colleagues able to lead quality development training;
- to ensure that the quality development approach is built into training related to other quality initiatives, such as appraisal, management development and assessment;
- to provide quality development training for colleagues working in the LEA's support services;
- to investigate the possibility of offering an appropriate form of quality development training for pupils, parents and others;
- to develop a resource pack capable of use in a wide variety of the forms of training described above.

Objective 4: To provide a range of support mechanisms, including external consultancy support, to schools through advisers, colleagues in other support services, from schools, or elsewhere.

Review: The need for an external support role for schools engaged in implementing a quality development approach was recognized in the pre-pilot phase of the initiative. Advisers (both policy and services) have therefore played a key role during the pilot and subsequently in all aspects of the project in terms of its management, training provision and support to schools engaged in introducing quality development. The evaluation report listed the *roles* an adviser acting as a *quality development consultant* might be called upon to play. These included: advising a school on when and how to join the initiative; helping a school to shape the quality development approach to its own needs and circumstances; networking the school with other schools; raising and maintaining the profile of the initiative within the school; assisting in the dissemination of the approach to all aspects of the school and throughout the school community; supporting the quality development co-ordinator; advising the head and senior staff; and validating the system and procedures of quality development implemented by the school.

The *characteristics of the effective quality development consultant* were also identified. These included: credibility with headteachers, senior management teams and co-ordinators; training in quality development theory and methodology; ability to work with staff at all levels and with the governing body; sensitivity to the needs of the school according to its stage of development; ability to monitor, moderate, evaluate and validate a school's monitoring and evaluation systems and procedures; ability to stimulate and provide support for networking and dissemination within a school and across groups of schools; understanding of and commitment to the quality development approach; and ability to handle the tensions inherent in consultancy between support and judgement.

It was clear from the pilot evaluation that in many of the schools advisers as consultants had played an important, even crucial, role in enabling the successful introduction of quality development. The range, complexity and demanding character of what can be involved is illustrated in the following by no means untypical account:

> In many ways the role of a school adviser at [. . .] is marginal; it has excellent teachers, highly motivated staff . . . [My] work as [a consultant] adviser for the quality development project changed dramatically: in the spring term I seemed to be driving it forward but this changed hugely in the summer term. The headteacher and staff tend to lack confidence and the validating, celebrating role is as important as the status giving role. Being a critical friend and a comparer were also roles which were important at the school during this period. I was able to make specific technical suggestions which could loosely be described as a facilitator's role; enskilling roles seemed critical when it came to action plans, aims, criteria for success and the structuring of meetings. By the end of the summer term there was real evidence . . . in the quality of debate which was then turned into action plans, of improving. There was substantial evidence of proving making use of detailed and documented observation and there was evidence of learning by the quality of debate turned into action plans, by the revision of action plans, by avoiding drift and by meeting agreed deadlines. The role of the adviser changed so dramatically during the summer term because they were improving and they were learning and because they could prove this to me.

Although school advisers constitute the group who seem best placed to provide the range of external support outlined above, recent developments related to the Government's proposals for a national system of external inspection and its funding implications may mean that it will be necessary to seek supplementary ways of delivering such support. In any case, it may well be that other colleagues could meet the support needs of schools. It is consistent with the principles of quality development that schools should be able to elicit support from whomsoever they may consider to be appropriate. It follows that it would be beneficial if a wider range of colleagues were trained and prepared to undertake an external consultancy support role. In any case, it is envisaged that eventually schools will have to seek consultancy support for quality development on a consultancy basis. In doing so they will probably wish to negotiate a package that meets their particular needs and circumstances.

Development priorities:

- to ensure that the schools' need for external consultancy support for quality development is clearly identified and recognized;

- to work with schools to identify the forms of external consultancy support required;
- to establish support for quality development in schools as a core task for schools advisers;
- to identify other support staff in the LEA, in schools or elsewhere in whom schools would have confidence for the provision of external consultancy support;
- to prepare and train staff taking a quality development consultant role for their support work;
- to provide support for those undertaking the quality development consultancy role, including a system for documenting the progress of schools;
- to incorporate into the quality development framework support for schools at the preparation and follow-up stages of the programme of national inspection.

Objective 5: To provide a range of support mechanisms, which include a programme of networking and dissemination activities.

Review: Early in the pilot, the quality development working group identified support for networking and dissemination as a priority. In the evaluation report, nine key tasks for networking are listed:

1 Stimulating the sharing of development experiences.
2 Informing practice in the development of strategies for monitoring and evaluation.
3 Giving status to other developing networks.
4 Enabling colleagues to tap into existing and create new networks.
5 Sharing in bringing good practice to the forefront.
6 Encouraging the overlaying of quality development principles and practices on to existing forums and networks.
7 Sustaining enthusiasm among and supporting key staff.
8 Celebrating and publicizing achievement.
9 Acting as a sounding board for schools, the QDWG and the LEA.

This dimension of the initiative has been highly valued by schools. At first the lead was taken by the QDWG but as time has passed first advisers and then teachers and schools have played an increasing role in ensuring that appropriate networking and dissemination takes place. This will need to be sustained in the future.

Development priorities:

- to recognize and promote networking as a critical success factor in support of quality development and develop a flexible, structured approach from which all schools can benefit;

- to develop a clear purposeful framework programme of networking activity, which includes networking during and as a follow-up to training, area based networks and networks built around particular action research interests and issues;
- to maintain and develop mechanisms for the dissemination of quality development methodology and action research locally and nationally;
- to generate a commitment to documenting Birmingham's collective experience of quality development through a series of regular bulletins, articles, local workshops, seminars, conferences, etc.;
- to develop further the quality development database and establish a resource pack of completed projects;
- to sustain the link with local and national HE institutions and other 'experts' in the field;
- to develop a marketing function;
- to establish mutually supportive relationships with both local (e.g. CSS) and national (e.g. OCEA) support services.

Objective 6: To provide a range of support mechanisms, including a series of user-friendly resource packs.

Review: As schools have begun to implement quality development they have identified a need for a collection of resource material that they could use to support the process. A similar need has been expressed by various other associated groups, including advisers and governors. Similarly, a need for resource packs to support the training and mainstreaming process has been widely acknowledged. Some progress has been made to meet these needs but more remains to be done.

Development priorities:

- to develop a resource pack for use in schools to support the embedding of evaluation into all planning and development;
- to develop a resource pack for advisers/consultants to support and guide them in their role as 'critical friend' to schools;
- to develop a resource pack for governing bodies to support their contribution to quality development;
- to develop a resource pack for training in quality development that can be used in a variety of settings;
- to develop a resource pack for use by LEA officers (and others) seeking to implement quality development within their work.

Objective 7: To provide a range of support mechanisms, including a monitoring and evaluation strategy.

Review: Monitoring and evaluation are central to the quality development initiative. They have been achieved by building mechanisms for systematic reflection, review and critical analysis into the operational management activities of the working group and the strategic policy functions of elected members, officers and the advisory committee. Schools too have been involved and they have been generous in feeding back evidence on their activities. In addition a team from the University of Birmingham has undertaken an evaluation of the pilot, which was formative and summative in character. This evaluation is described in the development plan designed to extend the initiative as 'rigorous, very detailed and informative.... It provides an excellent model of how to conduct evaluation in such a way that it supports evaluation. To add to its credibility and value it has demonstrated the purposes and principles of quality development in practice'. The possibilities of extending this evaluation are being explored but even if this cannot be achieved, there is a need to ensure that the findings of the pilot evaluation are disseminated fully across the city and beyond.

However, it is not appropriate to assume that such external evaluation can be a permanent feature of quality development. A strategy must be developed which ensures that quality development continues to be evaluated but which is accommodated within the routine working practices of the authority and its schools. The LEA can play a significant role in this by working with schools to develop a user-friendly monitoring system and a moderation and validation service. With regard to the latter various possibilities have been explored (see Ribbins et al., 1992, pp. 156-8), including, most recently, a careful examination of the potential of the 'investors in people' approach as a means of accrediting quality development systems and procedures in schools (Burridge, 1992).

From the outset, the principles underpinning quality development have included a commitment to external validation. Schools are increasingly aware of the value of a nationally respected 'kitemark' serving as a quality assurance signal of real currency. Schools would welcome an opportunity to work towards a quality award that acknowledges improved performance in terms of *process* (e.g. development planning, monitoring and evaluation) and *product* (e.g. pupil achievement, professional development) and that focuses upon three *fundamental areas of investment*; (a) the pupil population; (b) the workforce; (c) the wider community.

Investors in People (IIP) is a national quality award that can be used for this purpose. It advocates a range of good practice, includes adherence to the four key principles of *making the commitment* ('from the top to develop all employees to achieve its ... objectives'), *target setting* ('regularly review the training and development needs of employees'), *action planning* ('to train and develop individuals on recruitment and throughout their employment') and *monitoring and evaluating* ('the investment in training and development to assess achievement and improve future effectiveness').

In applying these ideas to education it would be necessary to link the IIP accreditation process to LEA inspection in order to create the required kitemark for Birmingham schools. For each of the three fundamental areas of investment the school development plan would need to identify its overall mission and key objectives. Quality development methodology would drive the process of transforming the objectives into measurable outcomes, which provide the evidence of continuous improvement. In the same way that supported self-evaluation backed up by external moderation and validation forms the building

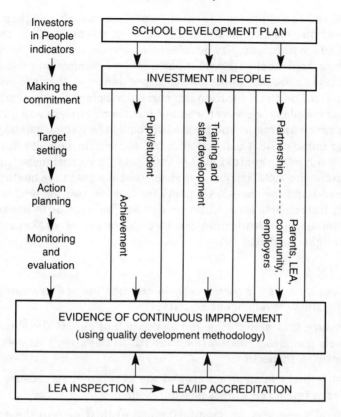

Figure 16.3   *Quality assurance — the accreditation of the QDI in schools*

blocks of the quality development initiative, supported self-assessment backed up by external review and accreditation underpins IIP. These two strategies could be brought together into the kind of single quality assurance mechanism set out in Figure 16.3.

For each area of involvement, a school would set targets for improvement, devise action plans, agree monitoring and evaluation procedures, provide evidence and report on progress. The school's development plan would bring them together into a single framework of priorities and provide the driving force for the school's efforts to raise quality and achieve the IIP kitemark. TEC licensed assessors and LEA accredited advisers would work together on reviewing each school's portfolio of evidence and deciding with the school when it is ready to submit its work for accreditation to the IIP recognition panel of the TEC Board and nominees of the Education Committee. Preliminary discussions have been taking place between the LEA and TEC in Birmingham and an agreement has been reached to consider how a feasibility study with a small number of schools might be launched. At the time of writing, discussion is taking place on a draft action plan, which, if implemented, would enable the service to introduce a general scheme towards the end of 1993.

The relationship between the external moderation and validation of quality development and the approach to school inspection that Birmingham has been trying to develop recently also requires further attention. This approach is located explicitly within a quality development framework and is being trialled in some of the schools that took part in the quality development pilot. While the authority is trying to make sense of the inspection and other proposals of the 1992 Schools Act and the Education Bill currently before Parliament, it is hard to make concrete plans. However, elected members, officers and advisers are examining a range of options and possibilities, including the feasibility of a continuing programme of LEA inspection conducted within a quality development framework. Even in the context of the 'hard nosed' external inspection system proposed within the 1992 Schools Act there is still a place for quality development in general and for the LEA's plans for local inspection within a quality development framework. Both will provide tools for schools to use to prepare themselves for national inspection and to tackle areas of weakness that such inspections might identify.

Development priorities:

- to develop a way in which schools can monitor and evaluate their own quality development activity;
- to ensure that monitoring and evaluation of quality development in schools includes a moderation/validation dimension that relates directly to inspection;
- to sustain the momentum around the evaluation and ensure that the findings reach the widest possible audience;
- to build a strategy for monitoring and evaluation into the quality development initiative so that the findings inform decision-making on both policy and service delivery.

Objective 8: To provide a range of support mechanisms, including the integration of quality development into all quality-related initiatives at the level of the school and the LEA.

Review: As we have argued earlier in this chapter, quality development is essentially a *process*, a way of working that facilitates change and progress. As such its purposes, principles and practices can be applied across a range of innovations. Over the past few years, many quality-related initiatives have been pursued in Birmingham. There is a danger in their being seen as separate and put into practice on the basis of a variety of more or less compatible approaches. Quality development offers a means of bringing such potentially disparate initiatives together into an integrated and coherent whole. The final chapter of the evaluation report highlights such issues and advocates the kind of integrated and unified approach discussed above (Ribbins *et al.*, 1992, Chapter 10). It locates the need for consistency across the range of such initiatives within a broader debate, which acknowledges the merits of a holistic quality strategy that includes quality development at its heart but that recognizes the need for quality assurance and quality control as well. The last strategic objective addresses this need.

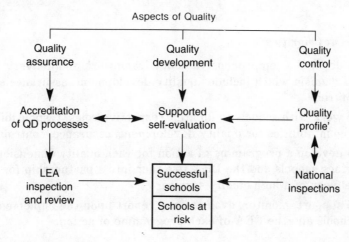

Figure 16.4 *Towards an integrated approach to promoting quality*

Development priorities:

- to work collaboratively with schools and across the LEA to clarify the links between quality development and other quality initiatives that are statutory responsibilities or strategic objectives of the Education Committee or LEA development priorities;
- to build into all the above the relevant components of quality development, e.g. its purposes, principles and working practices;
- to develop a unified policy, implementation strategy, documentation and support to assist schools to put into practice an integrated approach to all quality-related initiatives.

Objective 9: To provide a range of support mechanisms, including locating quality development within a comprehensive quality strategy, which includes quality assurance and quality control.

Review: If Birmingham has made its most important advances in the area of quality development, this is unsurprising given the effort it has lavished on this topic over the past eight years. More recently it has given greater attention to developments in its thinking and practice on the control and assurance of quality. For example, under the quality control heading, work on such things as pupil assessment, both in schools and within the LEA, is growing apace, particularly in response to recent legislation. Similar progress has been made in quality assurance. A team of advisers from the Policy and Finance Directorate has devised a framework for quality assurance that integrates a series of audits (information gathering strategies) with a group of policy areas (priorities for development). For each audit an action plan has been drawn up, which specifies the tasks to be tackled over the next three years. At this point, what requires urgent attention is *bringing together* these dimensions of work on quality. Some helpful thinking has been achieved on this (see Whale, 1991; Ribbins *et al.*, 1992, pp. 285-303) but much has still to be done. To date, Birmingham's hopes of producing an integrated approach to the promotion of quality might best be represented diagrammatically as in Figure 16.4.

Development priorities:

- to develop a comprehensive policy framework and delivery mechanism which includes quality development, assurance and control;
- to work with schools to identify respective roles, responsibilities and accountabilities for quality development, assurance, control;
- to develop a programme of action for each quality dimension that brings schools and the LEA together into a partnership for the delivery of a high-quality service;
- to support, monitor, evaluate and report upon the implementation by schools and the LEA of each programme of action.

The quality development initiative: looking back and looking forward

In much of this chapter we have tried to describe what is involved in quality development in Birmingham, how the authority and its schools have tried to implement the purposes, principles and practices it entails, and what the LEA proposes, if it is allowed the opportunity, to attempt in the future. In attempting a final statement we feel that it might be helpful to locate this within a context which focuses on the origins of quality development as theory and practice.

WHERE DOES QUALITY DEVELOPMENT COME FROM?

The aim of this final section is to say something about the theoretical and practical roots of quality development within the education service in Birmingham. A fuller statement is beyond the scope of this chapter and, in any case, is available elsewhere (Burridge, 1992).

Quality development is not new. Each of its purposes, principles and practices is derived from a long tradition of conceptualizing and engaging in the demanding work of striving to improve. This hard work is part of the natural history of education — a characteristic of generations of dedicated professionals determined to do a good job and to find ways of doing an even better one. It follows that those who have worked for the introduction of this approach to improvement in Birmingham do not assume any lack of quality within the schools of the city. On the contrary, it is based upon a set of ideas that has at its heart a conviction about the difference that teachers can make to quality when they are empowered to do so.

The *four main strands* from which Birmingham's ideas on quality development are derived are theories about educational evaluation, the traditions of teacher and classroom based action research, concepts to do with the pursuit of quality in industry and commerce, and ideas about and research into school effectiveness and school improvement. All four sources have a long and rich history and each deserves fuller treatment than we can possibly give it here. For each source only a few key ideas, values, practices and people are outlined, along with an attempt to make their links with quality development explicit.

Educational evaluation

There were two basic traditions within the early examples of educational evaluation and they related closely to the dominant models of research at the time. The first was within the logical positivist tradition. This was based upon an epistemology that saw social reality in objective terms and as essentially unproblematic. Accordingly, evaluation studies were designed in that light. Characteristically, such studies within this tradition were set up like experiments with a group that was the object of the experiment and a control group running alongside. The difference between the two groups was then 'measured' and the worth of the intervention was evaluated according to how it had affected those in the experimental group.

In contrast, interpretive evaluators saw such interventions as fundamentally problematic and held that they could not be 'tested' as objective phenomena that existed independently of those who constructed them. Evaluators within this tradition sought to understand or interpret the complexities of aspects of education in subjective terms and in doing so focused on the meanings, motives, intentions and actions of those involved. Their key assumption was that the social world is socially constructed. A key text within this tradition was Parlett and Hamilton's *Evaluation as Illumination* (1972).

The relevance of all this to quality development is that early in its evolution decisions had to be made about which approach to evaluation was likely to be the most productive and relevant to education in Birmingham. A search of the literature led to the conviction that the positivistic model was flawed when applied to the complexities of schools and classrooms. In contrast, the work on evaluation associated with the Schools Council's national curriculum projects of the mid-1970s and the idea of 'insider evaluation', which achieved prominence half a decade later, seemed to have more to say that had relevance to the untidy day-to-day reality of schools and colleges and those who work within them. Such studies stressed the need to encourage teachers to engage in their own evaluation and emphasized the idea that properly understood evaluation had an intrinsic and educative value in its own right. From these ideas the purposes of improving and learning were derived. Proving, the third key purpose in the lexicon of quality development, came from the work of Simons (1987) and Holly (1986).

Teacher and classroom based action research

The need for preparation training and the role of action research as a key aspect of quality development have been understood in Birmingham since the outset. They provide an ideal framework for teachers to study aspects of their work and a manageable means of trying out quality development in practice. In the very early days of quality development's evolution within further education, it was presented to teachers in colleges as an alternative to inspection.

As a movement, action research grew out of a growing concern among educationalists about what they came to view as a form of academic imperialism — that is, professional researchers in higher education and elsewhere claiming a monopoly of expertise and understanding of the curriculum and its enactment in practice. In contrast, those who advocated the merits of the teacher as researcher and the idea of action research argued that the teaching profession was quite capable of improving the quality of provision through a direct involvement in reflective pedagogic practice. In a sense action research can be conceptualized as entailing the same qualities and skills that make teachers good at teaching.

The father of action research is commonly thought to be Kurt Lewin. What was distinctive about his approach was a concern for prompting improvement in practice and improvement in understanding simultaneously by carefully structuring opportunities for groups of people to organize the conditions under which they can learn from the own experience. More recently, John Elliott, Lawrence Stenhouse and Stephen Kemmis have all made a major contribution to the development of educational action research and method. The central feature of the model they propose is the idea of action research as a spiral of steps involving planning, action and evaluation of the action. A core assumption of their approach is that as an action researcher managing change you do not wait until the end of the development process to undertake evaluation. Rather, the implementation of action is carefully monitored as it takes place for unintended and intended effects, and modified accordingly. In addition, a number of key elements have been identified, which describe action research as situational, top-down and bottom-up, participative, collaborative, self-evaluative, empirical and involving triangulation. Both the processes and the key elements identified above have directly influenced quality development and continue to form an integral aspect of how it is currently enacted.

Lessons on quality from industry and commerce

There is a huge and varied literature on improving quality within industry and commerce. In recent times the ideas of *total quality management* (TQM) have experienced something of an ascendence. Certainly the views of those who have come to be known as the quality gurus (e.g. Lawrence Deming, John Oakland and Tom Peters) are widely acknowledged. The key values of such approaches are a delight in meeting the needs of the customer and a stress upon the need to 'get things right' and to do so first time. Along with this, there are ideas about how and how not to improve. Quality will not be achieved through inspection; rather it is achieved through people. People want to achieve and more often than not they are prevented from doing so by failures of the organization and its senior managers. Deming argues that 90 per cent of quality problems are caused by managers and the first step towards improvement is to dismantle the barriers preventing employees from doing a good job. To achieve this requires commitment from the top of organizations along with high levels of involvement of the workforce. It entails better communication between the various levels of an organization, encouraging people to be open, to take risks, to be individually accountable, to work in harmony. In short, TQM is user driven — it assumes that organizations are best improved from the inside, that improvement needs to be continuous and that the way to achieve improvement is to enable the workforce to be smarter rather than to exhort them to work harder.

It can be argued that such ideas may be best expressed in terms of the Japanese concept of quality, or KAIZEN. As Smith (1990) puts it 'The idea at the heart of KAIZEN is that poor quality arises from bad systems rather than bad people. The product is defective not because the worker is lazy or stupid but because he or she is inadequately trained, has poor tools, or has insufficient time to do the job — or because of a myriad of possible system defects.' To improve quality, 'You start by charting the steps of your process and then measure those steps. You identify where the biggest improvements can be made and begin there on a process of measuring, trying an improvement, measuring again and so on forever. . . . The aim is to shift the whole process towards greater quality.'

Those responsible for taking quality development forward in Birmingham have adopted many of these ideas. They have done so at a time when the DFE, if not the DTI, has been increasingly wedded to ideas that dominated thinking about quality in an earlier generation within industry and commerce. As such, there is a certain irony in the claims the Government makes that it is drawing upon best practice in industry and commerce in shaping its ideas and in its suggestions that others in education should do so as well.

Research into school effectiveness and school improvement

To an extent, ideas about school effectiveness and school improvement were addressed in part at the beginning of the chapter. At this point we would wish to stress only that these areas of work have contributed significantly if rather less clearly than the previous three to thinking about quality development in Birmingham. They form a kind of 'backdrop' against which thinking about quality development has taken place. In a sense, the history of quality development in Birmingham and its schools can be seen as a large scale, wide-ranging, eight-year attempt to resolve the dialectic between what we know about school effectiveness and school improvement. If we have arrived at one general conclusion it is that the more schools and teachers know about themselves, particularly in terms of the outcomes they are generating across the whole spectrum of academic, social and moral achievement and for all groupings of pupils, the more they are likely to want to improve and to succeed in doing so.

A final thought: postscript or epitaph?

For those of us who have been involved in promoting quality in Birmingham and its schools, the past eight years have sometimes seemed like an unending struggle to make sense of the ways in which we and others have experienced it. This is not to complain that it has often been difficult. Of course, it has often been difficult. As Thomas Greenfield (Greenfield and Ribbins, 1993) reminds us, drawing upon the words of William Blake:

> What is the price of experience, do men buy it with a song?
> Or wisdom for a dance in the street? No, it is bought with the price
> Of all a man hath, his house, his wife, his children.

Those of us who have been involved in promoting quality in Birmingham have come to realize that the price of improvement is high and the path to it difficult. But the price is worth paying and the path has been shown to be passable. Sadly, these are lessons the national government has yet to learn.

REFERENCES

Burridge, E. (1992) 'Accrediting the quality development initiative in schools — a discussion paper', unpublished.

Burridge, E. (1993) 'Where does quality development come from?', unpublished paper.

Chitty, C. (1992) 'What future for subjects?', in P. Ribbins (ed.), *Delivering the National Curriculum*. London: Longman.

DFE (1992) *Choice and Diversity: A New Framework for Schools*. London: HMSO.

DTI (1991) *Total Quality Management: A Practical Approach*. London: DTI.

Greenfield, C. (1993) 'Will the 1992 Education Bill lead to better schools?', *Educational Management and Administration*, 21(2), 101-7.

Greenfield, T. and Ribbins, P. (eds) (1993) *Greenfield on Educational Administration: Towards a Humane Science*. London: Routledge.

Hargreaves, D. and Hopkins, D. (1991) *The Empowered School: The Management and Practice of Development Planning*. London: Cassell.

Holly, P. (1986) 'Developing a professional evaluation', *Cambridge Journal of Education*, 6(2).

Holly, P. (1990) *School-based Development in Action*. London: IMTEC.

OFSTED (1992) *The Handbook for the Inspection of Schools*. London: OFSTED.

Parlett, M. and Hamilton, D. (1972) *Evaluation as Illumination*. Edinburgh: Edinburgh University Press.

Ranson, S. (1993) 'Public education and local democracy', in H. Tomlinson (ed.), *Education and Training 14-19: Continuity and Diversity in the Curriculum*. London: Longman.

Ribbins, P. (ed.) (1992) *Delivering the National Curriculum*. London: Longman.

Ribbins, P. and Burridge, E. (1992) 'Improving schools: an approach to quality in Birmingham', in H. Tomlinson (ed.), *The Search for Standards*. London: Longman.

Ribbins, P. et al. (1992) *Improving, Proving and Learning in Schools: Evaluation of a Pilot Initiative in Quality Development*. Birmingham: University of Birmingham.

Ribbins, P. and Thomas, H. (1993) 'School reform in England and Wales', in S. Jacobson (ed.), *Educational Perestroika: A Decade of School Reform*. New York: Corwin.

Ribbins, P. and Whale, E. (1992) 'Supported self-evaluation in schools and colleges', *Management in Education*, 6(1), 8-11.

Simons, H. (1987) *Getting to Know Schools in a Democracy: The Politics and Process of Evaluation*. Lewes: Falmer.

Smith, R. (1990) 'KAIZEN', *British Medical Journal*, 3 October.

Sweetman, J. (1991) *The Complete Guide to the National Curriculum: Curriculum Confidential Two*. Leamington Spa: Bracken Press.

Sweetman, J. (1992) *The Complete Guide to the National Curriculum: Curriculum Confidential Three*. Leamington Spa: Bracken Press.

Walsh, K. (1991) *Going for Quality*. Luton: Local Government Training Board.

Whale, E. (1991) 'Quality development: an LEA case study', paper delivered to the BEMAS National Conference in Leeds University, September.

Whale, E. and Ribbins, P. (1990) 'Quality development in education', *Educational Review*, 42(2), 167-81.

Name Index

Subject Index